ESSAYS
ON THE
POLITICAL
ECONOMY OF
ALBERTA

Edited by

David Leadbeater

ESSAYS ON
THE POLITICAL
ECONOMY OF ALBERTA

Edited by
David Leadbeater

NEW HOGTOWN PRESS
TORONTO

Canadian Cataloguing in Publication Data

Main entry under title:
Essays on the political economy of Alberta

ISBN 0-919940-19-6

1. Alberta – Economic conditions – 1945–   *
2. Alberta – Politics and government.
3. Alberta – Economic policy. I. Leadbeater, David, 1947–

HC117.A4E87 1984   330.97123'03   C84-098432-4

Special thanks to New Hogtown Press volunteers John Crossley, Marta Danylewycz, Alison Prentice, and Pat Staton, who would like to dedicate their work on this book to the memory of our friend and colleague Pat Schulz.

New Hogtown Press would like to acknowledge the support of the Students' Administrative Council of the University of Toronto.

Printed in Canada by union labour.

Contributors

Jim Anderson has done graduate studies in Political Science at the University of Alberta and has co-authored (with Jack Masson) the book *Emerging Party Politics in Urban Canada* (1972). He now lives in Regina where he works for the Government of Saskatchewan.

Warren Caragata is a journalist now working for Canadian Press in Ottawa. He wrote *Alberta Labour: A Heritage Untold* (1979) while working as public relations director of the Alberta Federation of Labour.

Tony Fisher is a professor and former acting chairman of the Department of Anthropology at the University of Alberta. He has written and taught in the fields of North American Indians and anthropology and education, including co-editing (with Roger Owen and James Deetz) *The North American Indians* (1967).

David Leadbeater has studied at the University of Alberta and Oxford University. Although he has lived most of his life in Alberta and B.C., at the present time he is working on his doctorate from the Department of Economics at the University of Toronto.

Larry Pratt is a professor of Political Science at the University of Alberta. He is the author of several books, including *Prairie Capitalism: Power and Influence in the New West* (1979), which he co-authored with John Richards, and *The Tar Sands: Syncrude and the Politics of Oil* (1976).

Ed Shaffer is a professor of Economics at the University of Alberta. He specializes in energy economics and has recently written *Canada's Oil and the American Empire* (1983).

Contents

Tables

Figures

Preface

Eppur si muove.*

Galileo

The following set of articles is decidedly critical of conservative orthodoxy about Alberta. There are a variety of topics and views, but each in its own way punctures some of the establishment mythology on Alberta perpetuated both inside and outside the province, and tries to produce a more realistic and adequate treatment of certain important aspects of Alberta's economic and social development.

These articles appear at a time of deepening crisis and heightened concern about the future of Canada. A burgeoning lineup of problems—from chronic unemployment and inflation, to escalating foreign ownership, to regional disparities, to unresolved questions of self-determination in French Canada and among the Native peoples, to the "energy crisis," to the deteriorating urban environment, etc.—have compelled increasing numbers of Canadians, including Albertans, to question, to criticize, and to act. Since the late 1960s, some of this has been expressed in the re-emergence of Political Economy in Canadian social science.[1]

Spurred by the growth of anti-imperialist and anti-American currents during the war in Vietnam, what became the most visible element in this trend, the "New Political Economy," was closely associated with the so-called "New Left." During the 1970s, the New Political Economy coalesced in some loose organizational structures,[2] whose early basis was generally Anglophone and centred in Ontario. While there was a considerable heterogeneity in theoretical approach, the early and primary focus of the New Political Economy was on Canadian-US economic and political relationships, in particular, the "Canadian independence" issue. Later, with the growth of movements for self-determination in French

---

*Nevertheless, it moves.

Canada and among the Native peoples, the focus broadened. As well, concerns with questions relating to "regional disparities," urban development, and the working class movement intensified. As the range of interests and involvement in the New Political Economy has widened significantly, there has also been a growing consciousness of the diversity of its participants. At the present time, the predominant theoretical influence appears to be Marxism, broadly understood; however, several other influences, notably the staple theory of the Canadian economic historian, Harold A. Innis (1894-1952), also play a strong role.

These articles will probably be seen by some to fall into the ambit of this new trend in Canadian social science and, to a degree, this is correct. However, there are also other 'roots' here that, like the New Political Economy itself, go much deeper. For instance, the appearance of these articles also converges with the proliferation of material on 'western Canada' and Alberta during the last decade.[3]

However, by comparison with eastern Canada, there has been a much weaker development of writing on and within Alberta, especially of material from a critical political economy perspective.[4] This is a debilitating legacy of the generally lower level and subordinate character of economic, scientific, and cultural development in Alberta. As illustration, Alberta had only one university centre (in Edmonton) from 1908 until a branch was established in Calgary in 1945. The social sciences were slow to develop. While a Department of History was formed in 1909 and a Department of Political Economy in 1920, the staffs were tiny, and research was limited.[5] It was not until the 1950s and the post-Sputnik upsurge in educational funding that the 'social sciences' in Alberta mushroomed. In rapid succession, departments of Psychology (1960), Political Science (1963),. Economics (1964), Anthropology (1967), and Sociology (1967) were established; also, a related expansion took place in such areas as Education and Business Administration.[6] During this 'boom' period, Alberta like many provinces was flooded with US-trained social science teachers and practitioners, to the extent that some university departments became little more than ideological branch plants of US imperialism. During the late 1960s, an increasing differentiation appeared in social science fields as certain progressive currents began to surface[7] and the stranglehold of conservative US-oriented social science weakened.

Of course, the development of patterns of domination of conservative social science ideology, including their origin, adaptation, maintenance, and diffusion in Alberta, existed long before the Cold War era, and far beyond post-secondary education and research.[8] Moreover, this important problem remains virtually an open field for research, and is a key to understanding the particular ideological brakes put on Alberta's social and cultural development.[9] What appears obvious is that most serious material published about Alberta was done either in conjunction with government royal commissions, inquiries,[10] reports, and data collection, or through the support of a few outside institutions, such as in the case of the important nine-volume *Canadian Frontiers of Settlement Series*, which received assistance from the American Social Science Research Council[11] and was published during the 1930s by the Macmillan Company out of Toronto. It is significant that, aside from the provincial King's Printer, Alberta had not a single substantial book publisher until the 1960s.

The very name of the province exemplifies the weight of a colonial past. As the leading English Canadian encyclopaedia relates:

> The province takes its name from the much smaller District of Alberta, created by federal Order in Council in 1882. The name honoured a daughter of Queen Victoria, Princess Louise Caroline Alberta, who was the wife of the Marquess of Lorne, Governor General from 1878 to 1883, had visited the prairies in 1881.[12]

While Manitoba and Saskatchewan have names bearing some relation to the people of their provinces—in particular, the Native peoples[13]—"Alberta," not unlike "Rhodesia" (now Zimbabwe) 'honours' a colonial history of which many vestiges remain, not the least being the appalling 'tradition' of racism accorded the Native (Indian and Métis) peoples.

Among the many conceptual obstacles holding back the development of critical political economy in Alberta, and in the prairies generally, two of the most prevalent have been the tendencies to view the province, often patronizingly, as a 'curiosity' or aberration, or to be side-tracked by the mythology of frontier romanticism and parochial "boosterism." Today, the boosterist and romantic literature has lost much of its appeal, and things do not appear so curious or exceptional. Increasingly, connections are being drawn with the patterns of development in other regions and countries, and common phenomena and causes are being studied. Consequently, certain politico-economic concepts of analysis (colonialism, imperialism, racism, the state, class structure, etc.) are becoming important—and necessary—to provide adequate explanations of Alberta's development as one related part of world development as a whole.

In this respect, there is a considerable weakness with standpoints that do not recognize both what is general as well as what is particular in the process of development in Alberta in relation to the rest of the world. A one-sided view in either direction has its difficulties. In the latter case, concepts of regional 'uniqueness,' 'particularism,' or even regional 'exceptionalism' can lead to narrow and parochial approaches, as well as the dangers of 'exclusiveness' or regional chauvinism—and isolation. On the other hand, concepts that do not identify or appreciate particular features of development tend to dogmatism by absolutizing general historical observations, and risk the dangers of cutting off fruitful avenues for study, of failure to recognize new phenomena, and generally of producing a superficial rather than a full understanding of development.

The essays contained in this volume express a variety of approaches and emphases, yet there are certain general themes that can be drawn out. Four of them deserve special mention.

First, there is the question of the role of big business (or 'monopoly capital') in dominating development in Alberta. These articles are united in their explicit treatment of corporate groupings as not only a major determining force, but also *the* dominant politico-economic power in Alberta's development. Such an 'anti-monopoly' theme is not new in the history of Alberta nor in current times; however, it has not yet moved from its more 'popular' base into a central position in established writing about Alberta. As Larry Pratt comments on the traditional perspective of academic economics:

...while comparative advantage remains an important arbiter of the success of regional development strategies, too much emphasis can be given to orthodox location economics. In the real, as opposed to the neo-classical academic, world, political and economic power tend to be as important as the principles of location theory in determining the regional distribution of wealth, industry and jobs.[14]

Ed Shaffer also raises important issues about the explanatory power of certain theories of development in Alberta when he considers the appropriateness of H.A. Innis's staple theory, J. Levin's theory of foreign factors, and V.I. Lenin's theory of imperialism for analyzing oil development in the province.

Second, there is the question of the role of the state in development, particularly its relationship with business interests. Under Canada's federal system, the analysis of the state role is made more complex by the varying degrees of conflict and cooperation existing in its internal relations (such as among the federal, provincial, and municipal levels, or among national, regional, or local areas, or among certain departmental, agency, or corporate units, etc.) and external relations (especially among competing sections of capital). These articles discuss various aspects of the role of the state in Alberta and its relationship with business interests, but they each underscore the function of the state as an instrument of business to maintain its dominant position and advance its particular interests. Several significant analyses are provided concerning the use of sections of the state by particular parts of the business class—at times competing, at times collaborating.

The essays by Larry Pratt and Ed Shaffer consider the role of the provincial administrations, including relations with the federal government, in the development of petroleum resources, with an emphasis on the period since World War II. Tony Fisher focuses sharply on an important period in federal government relations with the Native Peoples. Jim Anderson's study of the so-called "municipal reform movement" in early municipal development in Alberta also reveals the business domination of this important but neglected section of the state.[15]

Third, there is the problem of determining the historical relationships of Canadian and foreign (especially British and US) capital to Alberta capital, and the effect of their evolving alignments on the character and direction of development in Alberta. This necessarily involves an analysis of colonization and other features of development under the National Policy, which are treated by Tony Fisher and in the introductory article. The introductory article, together with the articles by Larry Pratt and Ed Shaffer, also consider the more recent decades.

While this third theme might appear to be of more 'local' interest, it does have something important to contribute to the study of the development of capitalism in Canada generally. In particular, considerable debate has taken place on the nature of Canada's transition from a colonial to advanced capitalist economy and the characterization of Canada's relationship with the US: roughly, whether Canada must be considered to have remained or become essentially 'semi-colonial' and dependent (viewed analogously to a 'Third World' country), or to have entered the ranks of the world's imperialist countries, like the US and Britain.[16] The material here adds weight to the view that Canadian capital, based primarily in central Canada, did reach a stage of development where it engaged actively in various rivalries involving the control of markets, capital export, and territorial expansion. Although weaker in degree and somewhat lagged in evolution, there have evidently been patterns of development in Canada similar to those of the older, more powerful imperialist countries.

Fourth, there is the question of the growing role of the working class in Alberta. Much writing on Alberta has tended to focus on farmer and small business sections of the population, especially their political parties and movements of protest.[17] By contrast, relatively little has been written on Alberta's wage earners, including the development of their political parties and other forms of political expression, and the rise of the labour movement. However, the history of the working class in Alberta and its impact on relations between labour and capital, as well as other, intermediate sections of the population is fundamental to understanding the major determinants of development. While the few general histories of the labour movement in Canada usually recognize in some degree the part played by Alberta labour (especially the miners), it is significant that, at least until recent years,[18] the question was virtually ignored if not suppressed in established writing on Alberta. The introductory essay (which treats various aspects of the above three themes) outlines some of the key structural changes occurring in the rise of the working class in Alberta. As well, to give a clearer background to the growth of working class organization, Warren Caragata has narrated a brief history of the labour movement in Alberta.

There is little doubt that certain views, as these presented here, which recognize the predatory character of Alberta's development and do not brush it aside as 'merely accidental' or incidental, may prove controversial, for they run counter to the ideological status quo. Whatever the reaction from these quarters, serious criticism of the character of capitalist development in Alberta is needed as much now as it ever was—and in both theoretical and practical ways. The approaches in this volume help explain some of the particular and legitimate concerns of prairie people about their position in the Canadian economy and state, and also raise larger questions about the general nature of development in Canada as a whole. However, they do so without falling prey to narrow and, indeed, reactionary regionalism, which has been used more than once to divide working people in Canada. The characteristically self-serving regionalism promoted among the Alberta 'establishment' has contributed to the balkanizing tendencies prevalent in English Canada, and thus helped to clear the way for further multinational corporate control of both the province and Canada as a whole. Correspondingly, isolationism and 'go it alone' attitudes have been encouraged, especially where they have appeal among backward sections of the popular organizations, such as labour, farmer, and student groups, who have been traditional sources of progressive protest in the province.[19]

Alberta's working people, including the Native peoples, are justified in having a genuine pride not only for their achievements on the prairies but also for what they have contributed to Canada as a whole. And, lest it be said that the picture of Alberta's development presented here is 'unduly negative,' what is truly significant, and what follows from the present analyses, is how much has been achieved by Alberta's working people *in spite of* their provincial and federal corporate politicians.

For many years, the kind of provincial leaderships suffered in Alberta have wrought their primary damage to working people in Alberta. However, since World War II, particularly with the "energy crises" of the 1970s and Alberta's higher profile in the rest of Canada, it has become increasingly apparent that the impact of Alberta's provincial corporate-government power has extended far beyond the borders of Alberta. This is not a new phenomenon in the history of Canada, but it accentuates the fact that Canadians—and Albertans—are perceiving something much deeper than a so-called 'regional problem.'

Many Canadians, including Albertans, have viewed Alberta as a conservative political backwater in Canada—the "Texas of Canada." This is one-sided, for it ignores deep progressive traditions in Alberta's history and the underlying socio-economic structure of the province. Despite a superficial political torpor, many rapid and important changes have been occurring in the economy and society of the Alberta region. Perhaps, in seeking future directions, these articles can help advance debate.

* * *

In the production of this volume, there have been several persons who have been involved either directly or indirectly, in typing, proofreading, transporting, criticizing, duplicating, providing information, or otherwise aiding and abetting the project.

Special mention must be made of my parents, Betsy and Thomas Leadbeater, who helped me in innumerable ways. Mrs. Evelyn Munro and Mrs. Barbara Jacobson did the largest amount of the manuscript typing. Prof. Dennis

B. Johnson of the Department of Geography of the University of Alberta assisted with maps. New Hogtown Press came through at a stage when their support was most needed and saw things to completion. In particular, I would like to mention the contribution of John Crossley who was manuscript supervisor for New Hogtown Press and Edith Klein who did the final copy editing. The work of these and others along the way is greatly appreciated. However, as is the standard caveat, any errors or shortcomings in the book are the responsibility of the authors alone. Finally, it may be of some consolation to purchasers of this book to know that the royalties, as limited as they are, will be contributed (once the *faux frais* of production are covered) to a fund for supporting projects similar to this one.

Notes

1 See, for example, the "Preface" and "Rediscovering Canadian Political Economy" in Wallace Clement and Daniel Drache, *A Practical Guide to Canadian Political Economy* (Toronto, 1978); the "Editor's Preface" in Leo Panitch, ed., *The Canadian State: Political Economy and Political Power* (Toronto, 1977); and Mel Watkins, "The Legacy of Harold Innis," *This Magazine*, 12, no. 1 (March 1978), 26-27.

2 These include the Political Economy section of the Canadian Political Science Association, the Political Economy Network Newsletter, SPEC (Studies in the Political Economy of Canada), conferences of the Canadian Left in Britain, and, recently, the journal *Studies in Political Economy: A Socialist Review*.

3 See, for example, Richard Allen, ed., *A Region of the Mind: Interpreting the Western Canadian Plains*, Canadian Plains Studies 1 (Regina, 1973), especially L.G. Thomas, "Historiography of the Fur Trade Era," 73-85, and T.D. Regehr, "Historiography of the Canadian Plains After 1870," 87-101; Alan F. Artibise, *Western Canada 1870: A Select Bibliography and Guide* (Vancouver, 1978); A.F. Artibise and Gilbert A. Stelter, *Canada's Urban Past: A Bibliography and Guide* (Vancouver, 1981); Hartwell Bowsfield, "The West," in J.L. Granatstein and Paul Stevens, eds., *Canada since 1867: A Bibliographical Guide* (Toronto, 1977; 1st ed., 1974), 101-123; Bruce Peel, *A Bibliography of the Prairie Provinces to 1953 with Bibliographical Index* (Toronto, 1973; 1st ed., 1956); Dorothy E. Ryder, *The Canadian West and the North: A Bibliographical Overview* (Edmonton, 1978).

4 A significant exception (perhaps the kind that proves the rule) was C.B. Macpherson's *Democracy in Alberta: Social Credit and the Party System* (Toronto, 1962; 1st ed., 1953), a book that has been a major influence in much writing on the political economy of Alberta. For some recent criticisms of Macpherson's theory see Larry Pratt and John Richards, *Prairie Capitalism: Power and Influence in the New West* (Toronto, 1979), chapter 7.

5 For example, the first MA thesis written in Alberta (in 1911), was in history, but it was the only history thesis written in Alberta in the 1910s. Only two others were written in the 1920s, 7 in the 1930s, and 5 in the 1940s, but 27 in the 1950s, and 49 in the 1960s

(including 5 PhD theses). The first history PhD thesis was not written until 1964. In political economy, the first MA thesis was not written until as late as 1928. Possibly one other was written during that decade. A total of only 7 were written in the 1930s, 9 in the 1940s, and 19 in the 1950s. The first PhD thesis in economics was not written until 1965 and in political science until 1968. The first sociology MA thesis (1961) and PhD thesis (1968) and the first Anthropology MA thesis (1968) and PhD thesis (1972) were not written until significantly later. Of course, the subject matter and content of the theses raised even deeper questions about the development of education in Alberta.

6 An autonomous Faculty of Commerce was formed in 1960 and broadened into the Faculty of Business Administration and Commerce in 1965.

7 One can note, for example, some 'democratization' of educational institutions, a broadening of the social composition of academic staff and students, a heightened concern for 'Canadian content,' and even some explicit efforts to criticize established social science ideology and make academic study more 'relevant' to societal 'problems.'

8 See, for example, Patricia Elaine Oviatt, "The Educational Contribution of H.C. Newlands," MEd thesis (University of Alberta, 1970), with regard to the development of "Enterprize education" in Alberta; also, Robert Steven Patterson, "The Establishment of Progressive Education in Alberta," PhD thesis (University of Michigan, 1968).

9 One of the few treatments of a cultural aspect is found in David C. Carpenter, "Alberta in Fiction," PhD thesis (University of Alberta, 1973). For the prairies as a whole see also Edward McCourt, *The Canadian West in Fiction* (Toronto, 1949), and Dick Harrison, *Unnamed Country: The Struggle for a Canadian Prairie Fiction* (Edmonton, 1977).

10 See Christine E. Backhaus, *Royal Commissions and Commissions of Enquiry in Alberta, 1905-1976* (Edmonton, 1977).

11 Regehr, "Historiography of the Canadian Plains," 90-91.

12 *Encyclopedia Canadiana* (Toronto, 1968), I, 105.

13 The *Encyclopedia Canadiana* writes that the most likely derivation of the name Manitoba is probably that "it came from 'Manito-bau,' the strait of the Manitu, being the narrows of Lake Manitoba. Another possibility is that it derived from 'Minne' ('water' in Assiniboine) and 'Toba' ('prairie' in Sioux). Certainly the Lake of the Prairies was an early name given to Lake Manitoba." *Encyclopedia Canadiana*, VI, 337. As for Saskatchewan, the name is derived from "the Cree Indian word for 'swift-flowing,' used to describe the great river of the Canadian prairies. The name appeared first in fur trade literature, cited as 'Keistatchewan' by Henday (1754) and as 'Saskatchewoine' by Henry (1775), forms of 'Kisiskatchewan,' believed to be the aboriginal form." *Encyclopedia Canadiana*, IX, 213.

14 See chapter VI of this volume.

15 For further useful research on this second theme, see David Nock, "The Intimate Connection: Links Between the Political and Economic Systems in Canadian Federal Politics," PhD thesis (University of Alberta, 1976), and, by the same author, "Intersecting Political and Business Careers Among Alberta Federal Politicians," unpublished paper; Pat Murphy, "Analyzing Elites: Canada and Edmonton," unpublished paper; Larrie Taylor, "Small Town Alberta," unpublished paper.

[16] This problem has generated a major literature of its own, due largely to its direct relation with political strategy on the Canadian 'independence' issue. The problem has been a central question, if not the principal preoccupation, of the New Political Economy, but the question is not new. In fact, its history among progressive Canadians goes back to Canada's colonial period. Among some of the many writings of the post-World War II period are, for example, Irving Martin Abella, *Nationalism, Communism and Canadian Labour* (Toronto, 1973); Tim Buck, *Canada: The Communist Viewpoint* (Toronto, 1948), and *Lenin and Canada* (Toronto, 1970); Wallace Clement, *The Canadian Corporate Elite* (Toronto, 1975) and *Continental Corporate Power* (Toronto, 1977); George Grant, *Lament for a Nation: The Defeat of Canadian Nationalism* (Toronto, 1965); Craig Heron, ed., *Imperialism, Nationalism, and Canada* (Toronto, 1977); Robert M. Laxer, *(Canada) Ltd.: The Political Economy of Dependency* (Toronto, 1973); Kari Levitt, *Silent Surrender: The Multinational Corporation in Canada* (Toronto, 1970); Charles Lipton, *The Trade Union Movement of Canada, 1827-1959* (Toronto, 1973; 1st ed., 1967); Ian Lumsden, ed., *Close the 49th Parallel, Etc.: The Americanization of Canada* (Toronto, 1970); Steve Moore and Debi Wells, *Imperialism and the National Question in Canada* (Toronto, 1975); Gustavus Myers, *A History of Canadian Wealth* (Toronto, 1972, 1st ed., 1914); Tom Naylor, *The History of Canadian Business, 1867-1914* (Toronto, 1975), 2 vols.; Panitch, ed., *The Canadian State*; Libbie and Frank Park, *Anatomy of Big Business* (Toronto, 1973; 1st ed., 1962); Philip Resnick, *The Land of Cain: Class and Nationalism in English Canada, 1945-1975* (Vancouver, 1977); Stanley B. Ryerson, *Unequal Union: Confederation and the Roots of Conflict in the Canadas, 1815-1873* (Toronto, 1968); Gary Teeple, ed., *Capitalism and the National Question in Canada* (Toronto, 1972); and various issues of *This Magazine*. At the very least, as a Soviet writer, A. Borodayevsky, has suggested, "The example of Canada makes it possible to trace how imperialism originates and develops in new territories" (*Modern Capitalism: Its Nature and National Features* [Moscow, n.d.], 141).

[17] Notably, the ten-volume series *Social Credit in Alberta: Its Background and Development*, published by the University of Toronto Press in the 1950s.

[18] For instance, an important step forward was taken by the Alberta Federation of Labour, who initiated and supported financially the publication of the first general history of the organized labour movement in Alberta: Warren Caragata, *Alberta Labour: A Heritage Untold* (Toronto, 1979).

[19] Within the last few years, for example, several right-wing efforts at decertification, disaffiliation, and non-association, etc., have played opportunistically upon the theme of 'western alienation' in order to weaken or break the ties of Alberta workers and students with their counterparts in other areas of Canada.

An Outline of Capitalist Development in Alberta

David Leadbeater

This land of such dear souls, this dear dear land,
Dear for her reputation through the world,
Is now leased out...
Like to a tenement or pelting farm.

William Shakespeare

For the people who have lived and laboured there, Alberta has had a reality far different from the glittering images associated with the 'petro-gold' currently overflowing its corporate and provincial government coffers. Yet these images and the immediate preoccupation with the 'Alberta problem' in energy and constitutional negotiations do reflect an important event of recent history: Alberta has become a major factor in the crises of capitalist economy and political federalism now confronting Canada. The following outline of the economic history of Alberta emphasizes the main contours of the province's development: the structural features, driving forces, and critical turning points. The introduction suggests a general periodization of the history and begins the story in Alberta's pre-capitalist era; of necessity the commentary is brief. The next section analyzes the years of 'internal colonization' in the North-West Territories (1870-1905). During these formative years a subordinated capitalist economy was established and gave rise to pressures for provincehood. Section three considers the movement for autonomy, specifically its economic causes and the special status reflected in the autonomy arrangements of 1905.

The main phases and structural features of the Alberta economy since 1905 are surveyed in Section four and the subsequent sections. The formation and growth of the provincial state has been of special significance, both in revealing and in determining the general direction of development. The fifth section treats the state's emerging role in the provincial economy, with particular attention to the politico-economic composition and policy orientation of government leadership. Also of special significance, and treated in the sixth section, has been the powerful role of US capital, as exemplified in the oil industry. The final section summarizes and considers certain aspects of the changing alignment of politico-economic forces in Alberta, including the growing importance of the working class.

1. Introduction

At the most general level, the economic history of Alberta and the western interior of Canada can be divided into three major periods. The first period begins with the earliest presence of the Native or aboriginal peoples in the area, about 17,000 to 7,000 years ago,[1] and continues until the penetration of European merchant capital, in the form of the fur trade, during the second half of the eighteenth century. The second period covers the time from the establishing of the fur trade to the ending of its leading position in the 1870s and 1880s. The third period opens in the 1870s and 1880s with the process of internal colonization under the direction of the newly formed Canadian state and extends to the present.

In the earliest period, development was dominated by Native bands living at a subsistence level in a 'natural' economy based generally on nomadic hunting and gathering—sometimes referred to as a "primitive communal mode of production."[2] The areas of the Alberta region used by the many bands varied greatly over time in relation to a multiplicity of factors such as climate, hunting conditions, terrain, technique of travel, and power relations existing among the different bands. By about 1725, towards the time of the first European and Canadian probes into the area, there were in and near Alberta four main groupings of Native peoples, defined linguistically: sections of the Athapascan, including the Beaver, Chipewyan, Sarcee, Sekani, and Slave, in the areas north of the North Saskatchewan River, which typically were covered by forests; the Algonkian, including the Blackfoot, Blood, Cree, Gros Ventre, and Piegan, generally in the areas south of the North Saskatchewan, which were primarily prairie and parkland; the Siouan, including in Alberta only the Assiniboine (some of whom are today known as Stonies), also in the southern part of Alberta, but to the east; and the Kootenayan, principally the Upper Kootenay, again in southern Alberta, but along the eastern side of the Rockies.[3]

The second period, while still dominated by the primitive communal mode of production, was a transitional stage leading to the dominance of the capitalist mode in the third period. Merchant capital, with its concomitant class of merchants and their agents, established itself as the leading economic force in strategic areas of the region. The process was exemplified in the history of the Hudson's Bay Company, one of the state-chartered trading monopolies of English mercantilism.

The Hudson's Bay Company (HBC), chartered in 1670, made its first appearance in Alberta in 1754, when Anthony Henday, an agent of the Company and perhaps the first white man to arrive in Alberta, reconnoitred the trade potential in parts of central Alberta as far west as Rocky Mountain House. However, it was not until the 1790s and 1800s that a permanent and direct trading presence was established. In their fierce struggle for control of the fur trade, the Hudson's Bay Company and the Montreal based North West Company (NWC) advanced a network of posts and depots further west. Connecticut born Peter Pond of the NWC reached the Athabasca River in 1778 and the Company built Fort Chipewyan by Lake Athabasca, making it probably the earliest post in Alberta. Inevitably, the main line of rival posts, which followed the Saskatchewan River system, reached Alberta. In 1792, Fort George (NWC) and Buckingham House (HBC) were established. These were followed in 1794 and 1795, respectively, by Fort Augustus (NWC) and Edmonton House (HBC), both about 20 miles (32 km) east of present day Edmonton. The next major westward jump was made in 1799 with the beginning of Rocky Mountain House (NWC) and Acton House (HBC), about 200 miles (320 km) further upstream.

After years of intense competition, including piracy and sabotage, it became evident that the Hudson's Bay Company's powerful financial position—enhanced by its shorter and efficient transportation system using the Hudson Bay route and its direct access to English markets and manufacturers—was sustaining it against the overextended North West Company. A merger was forced on the latter in 1821. Thereafter, until 1870, the Hudson's Bay Company enjoyed a virtual monopoly of commerce in Alberta, particularly in central and northern areas. Increased challenges arose from independent "free traders," especially after the 1840s, and a substantial US rival, the Montana based I.G. Baker and Company, moved into southern Alberta in the late 1860s; however, these pressures did little to alter the Bay's effective dominance.

While the fur trade advanced, merchant capital remained dependent upon the Indians' traditional hunting and gathering form of production to provide the furs and some of the provisions for the fur trade. Certain functions, particularly in transportation, were performed directly by the Hudson's Bay Company, but the labour of Native producers—in hunting, trapping, fur preparation, and freighting—remained throughout the foundation upon which the entire trade was erected. The HBC itself maintained a longstanding strategy of opposition to settlement and industrialization in the prairies—the alleged "hostility of beaver and plow." In fact, the commanding force for capitalist development came neither from merchant capital, nor from the prairies itself, but from the outside: principally, from industrial and banking interests centred in Montreal, Toronto, and London, England.

The drive for westward expansion, which had been rising during the 1850s, especially in Canada West (Ontario),[4] led in the 1860s to the takeover of the Hudson's Bay Company by industrial and banking interests. A key figure in this move was Edward Watkin, President of the London based Grand Trunk Railway and noted proponent of the building of a transcontinental railway. He was assisted by the firm of Baring and Glyn, also of London, England, who were bankers to the Grand Trunk and the Canadian colonial government. The takeover put the Company under the ultimate control of forces who supported confederation and westward capitalist expansion, and it strengthened British imperial interests by counteracting the drift towards annexation of the North-West by the United States. The next major change in the 'old' Hudson's Bay Company came in 1869 and 1870 when the Company's monopoly charter was purchased by the new Canadian government, through the Imperial government, for a cash payment of £300,000 plus one-twentieth of the land in each township established in Rupert's Land[5] and a substantial parcel of land surrounding each of the Company's trading posts.

Although the hunting and gathering form of production of the Native peoples was dominant throughout the second period, the original mode was seriously eroded. The introduction of commodity production into the natural economy, the rise of widespread exchange and permanent trade centres, the limited growth of wage labour and small-scale production utilizing handicraft skills and simple cooperation, and the advance of transportation combined to provide a basis for future capitalist development. By the 1860s a major portion of the pre-capitalist economy was subordinated to alien merchant capital accumulation. The decisive change occurred in 1870 when the Canadian state took over ownership of Rupert's Land from the Hudson's Bay Company. The pressures in eastern Canada and Britain for unbridled capitalist expansion were unleashed. By the 1880s, a new leading capitalist force—and a new form of development—had arrived.

2. The Process of Internal Colonization
The era of internal colonization began in the early 1870s, with the first efforts of the Canadian state to establish its presence in the North-West, and concluded with the achievement of provincial autonomy in 1905. However, certain aspects of colonialism continued much later, most notably Dominion control of public lands in the province, which continued until 1930. The process itself had six essential features: establishment of Canadian state power, removal and subjugation of the Native population, major railway development, rapid settlement by whites, exploitation of natural resources, and expansion of markets for central Canadian business.

(a) Establishing Canadian State Power. The first phase of internal colonization, the establishing of Canadian state power and central authority, was completed by 1885, with the defeat of the North-West Uprising and the completion of the Canadian Pacific Railway (CPR). Before 1870, various "free traders" had been attempting to break into the Hudson's Bay Company monopoly; after the American Civil War a more organized effort appeared in southern Alberta, manifested in the notorious whiskey trade with the Native population. A group of 'whiskey posts' were opened; beginning with Fort Whoop-Up (near Lethbridge) in 1869, followed by Forts Spitzee, Slideout, and Standoff. The traders, notably the large I.G. Baker and Company, operated primarily out of Fort Benton, Montana (on the Missouri), and a few managed to trade as far north as the vicinity of Edmonton. The advance of the US trade in the North-West confirmed the expansionist policy of leading circles in the United States—including the "Manifest Destiny" theme—as did the purchase of Alaska in 1867 and American initiatives with Louis Riel during the Red River Uprising of 1869-70.

The 'wide open' whiskey trade declined with the coming of the North-West Mounted Police (NWMP), but US business activity continued and expanded. By the time the CPR construction reached Alberta in late 1882, a trade divide had developed in the region. In the central and northern parts of Alberta, where Edmonton was the principal trading centre, goods supplied were mainly Canadian or British and were carried along the Saskatchewan River. In the southern part of Alberta, goods were more often American and were supplied through the Missouri River system and overland from Montana.

Although administrative arrangements for territorial government were made shortly before the 1870 transfer of territory, the Canadian state, in effect, marched west with the NWMP.[6] The NWMP was formed in 1873 as a paramilitary force patterned after the Royal Irish Constabulary and British colonial experience in India. The leading officers tended to be graduates of the Royal Military College at Kingston, and the officers as a group "were almost invariably upper-class, well educated, and well connected in Eastern Canadian society and politics."[7] The first NWMP contingent of 300 entered Alberta in 1874 and established a series of police posts beginning at Fort Macleod (1874), followed by Fort Saskatchewan (1875) and Fort Calgary (1875).

NWMP activities served to facilitate and defend the colonization process and to normalize private property relations. Their earliest operations focused on controlling the Native population and suppressing the United States based whiskey trade. As the leading institution of the Canadian state in the Territories, the NWMP also functioned as postal, quarantine, and customs officials, and patrolled the Canada-United States border. NWMP efforts in minimizing and defining crime and illegal behaviour closely reflected changing patterns in socio-economic development. The problem of horse-stealing and rustling grew as the ranching industry emerged and overran Native lands and usurped Native hunting rights. In the 1880s, NWMP work was broadened to include assisting the CPR in controlling the approximately 4,000 workers building the railroad, including by strikebreaking.

Organized in part as a reaction to the Red River Uprising of 1869-70, "the Force" had as one of its enduring tasks the carrying out of Canadian state policy towards the Native peoples. The NWMP was a primary instrument used in 'pacifying,' removing to reserves, and eventually subjugating the Native population. And, notably, the NWMP was active, together with an "expeditionary force" of Canadian Militia, in putting down the North-West uprising. The 1885 Uprising was the last major act of Native resistance against Anglo-Canadian colonialism in the nineteenth century. The defeat of the uprising changed the balance of politico-military forces on the prairies and assured the supremacy of the Canadian state throughout the region.

(b) The Native Population. The second element in the process of internal colonization was the removal of the Native population from developable lands, including 'pacification,' to achieve military security. Within a month of the official Canadian takeover on 15 July 1870, the Lieutenant-Governor of the

North-West Territories was requested to report on "the course you may think the most advisable to pursue, whether by treaty or otherwise, for the removal of any obstructions that might be presented to the flow of population into the fertile lands that lie between Manitoba and the Rocky Mountains."[8]

The course chosen by the Canadian state was a reserve system established on the 'legal' basis of treaties, which would lead to the "extinguishing" of Indian title—and presence—on lands necessary for the Pacific railway and white settlement and agriculture. The first of the "numbered treaties," Treaties 1 and 2, were obtained in 1871 and covered land in southern Manitoba. Treaty 3 (1873) dealt with western Ontario and a south-eastern part of Manitoba. Treaty 4 (1874) surrendered southern Saskatchewan and Treaty 5 (1875) surrendered central and western Manitoba. The next three treaties directly affected Alberta.[9] First came Treaty 6 in 1876, which surrendered central Alberta (and most of central Saskatchewan); this included the strategic Edmonton area. Next, in 1877, came Treaty 7 which surrendered most of southern Alberta. Clearly, treaties followed from development pressures moving westward, particularly for the railway, farm land (Treaty 6), and ranching land (Treaty 7). Pressures for Treaty 8 came after 1896 when the Yukon gold rush brought hundreds of prospectors and mining companies through the Athabasca-Mackenzie district. The Treaty, obtained in 1899, dealt with northern Alberta to the southern shore of Great Slave Lake. With the discovery of oil at Fort Norman in 1920, the area north of Treaty 8 was covered in 1921 under Treaty 11.

The "reserves" system instituted by the Canadian state was typical of European colonialism, comparable, for example, to the *reduccion* and *congregacion* of Mexico, the Bantustans of southern Africa, the reservations of the US, or the reserves of Australia. The motivations underlying these institutions were "aboriginal removal, creation of labour pools, concentration for more efficient acculturation,"[10] if not the genocide of peoples who had lost their usefulness to merchant capital. The decline of the fur trade, destruction of the buffalo herds, and the disruption of the natural economy had created further pressures on the Natives towards retreat into transitional settlements[11] and reserves. Significantly, the reserve system was prevented from becoming a base for economic or political power. Economic development on reserves was curtailed and sabotaged by successive Indian Affairs administrations, especially if it threatened white settler enterprises. Politically, the reserve population ("treaty Indians") was denied so much as Canadian citizenship and the right to vote (until 1960), unless treaty rights were forgone—the policy of "forced assimilation."

The onslaught of capitalist development brought about a fundamental change in relations between the Native and white settler populations. Marked by the passage in 1876 of the first Indian Act, and by the Indian Acts of 1880 and 1884, the Native population became, in effect, oppressed peoples. The colonist "foreigners," fearful for their privileged position, generally supported state policy and practice towards the Native peoples. Racist concepts necessary to legitimize the new social order—an implanted white settler society—permeated the white population, particularly the top levels of territorial society which were overwhelmingly Anglo-Saxon and the standard-bearers of Anglo-Canadian imperialist interests and ideology.

(c) Railway Development. The third element in the process of internal colonization was the building of a transportation and communication infrastructure based on a Canadian transcontinental railway to the Pacific. For Alberta, and for modern capitalist development, railways have had a special significance:

Railways combine within themselves the basic capitalist industries: coal, iron and steel; and they are the most striking index of the development of international trade and bourgeois-democratic civilization.... the railways are linked up with large-scale industry, with monopolies, syndicates, cartels, trusts, banks and the financial oligarchy. The uneven distribution of the railways, their uneven development—sums up, as it were, modern world monopolist capitalism.[12]

Leading the capitalist juggernaut into Alberta was the CPR. In the 1870s, the Montreal based Canadian Pacific syndicate defeated the London based Grand Trunk in the rivalry to build the first transcontinental railway. The Canadian Pacific syndicate was tightly tied to the Bank of Montreal through George Stephen, President of the Bank, and Richard R. Angus, General Manager of the Bank. Also among the CPR syndicate was Donald Smith, later "Lord Strathcona," whose presence reflected the shift in the locus of politico-economic power in the North-West towards central Canadian capital. The main momentum for capital accumulation was passing from the HBC to the CPR. Smith, who became the single largest shareholder of the HBC and its land commissioner (after 1874), reoriented the HBC towards land dealing. By 1887, Smith captured stock control of the Bank of Montreal, then one of the largest banks in North America, and became its president for 27 years.

The building of the Pacific Railway was promoted by successive Canadian governments as virtually a matter of "national emergency" in their rivalry with US interests. In 1870, Prime Minister Macdonald expressed this major fear of leading Anglo-Canadian circles:

It is quite evident to me...that the United States Government are resolved to do all they can, short of war, to get possession of the western territory, and we must take immediate steps to counteract them. One of our first things to be done is to show unmistakeably our resolve to build the Pacific Railway.[13]

Macdonald's approach to the Pacific Railway was that it "must be taken up by a body of capitalists, and not constructed by the government directly," but that "Canada can promise most liberal grants of land in alternative blocks and may perhaps...induce Parliament to add a small pecuniary subsidy."[14] The initial state support lavished by the Conservative government under the 1881 contract included: $25 million cash; 25 million acres of land; over 709 miles (1141 km) of government-owned line completed under the Liberal government of Alexander Mackenzie for a cost of $38 million; tax exemption for 26 years for CPR land and perpetually for the entire capital stock; and a "monopoly clause" prohibiting competition against the CPR south of the main line to the United States border. As for the impact on the Territories, the Minister of Railways bluntly expressed the Cabinet view: "Are the interests of Manitoba and the North-West to be sacrificed to the interests of Canada? I say, if it is necessary, yes."[15]

The construction of the CPR began in June 1881. By the end of 1882 the track had reached the vicinity of Medicine Hat, and in August 1883 it arrived in Calgary. Among the hordes of speculators and promoters who closely followed the CPR's routing plans and construction were some who made their first 'primitive' accumulations, establishing themselves as leading local businessmen.[16] The completion of the CPR mainline was followed by the extension of "colonization railways." The first of the colonization lines, a coal line belonging to Galt's North-Western Coal and Navigation Company, was to the US border completed from Dunmore to Lethbridge (105 miles or 169 km) in 1885. This line together with a southern extension to the U.S. border at Coutts (1890) brought their owners 1.1 million acres of Dominion land grants. The second main colonization line, the CPR-associated Calgary and Edmonton Railway, built a line from Calgary to Strathcona (South Edmonton) by 1891, and south to Macleod by 1892, a total distance of about 295 miles (475 km). In the process, a Dominion land grant of 1.9 million acres was obtained.

At the turn of the century, during the world-wide escalation of interimperialist rivalry leading to World War I, the CPR pressed through the Crow's Nest Pass extension from Lethbridge to Nelson in the mineral-rich Kootenay area of British Columbia, and two new, rival transcontinental lines, the Canadian Northern and the Grand Trunk Pacific (GTP), were initiated. The latter was a subsidiary of the old Grand Trunk Railway. The former was a promotion of two Canadians, William Mackenzie and Donald Mann, who had made their first big accumulations as contractors for the CPR. From its inception, the CPR was closely identified with the Conservative Party while the Liberal Party became identified as anti-CPR and a political voice for the Grand Trunk interests. During the 1904 Dominion election, which "pitted the Grand-Trunk-Liberal Party nexus against the CPR-Tory machine,"[17] the Liberal leader, Wilfrid Laurier, campaigned with the slogan "Canada Cannot Wait." Once reelected, the Liberals proceeded with massive aid to the GTP and Canadian Northern, although as much of the best land had already been given away, the Laurier Liberals (and the succeeding Borden Tories) relied mainly on cash grants and government guarantees of railway debt, usually floated in the London money market.

The Canadian Northern mainline (1903) reached Edmonton from Grand-view, Manitoba, by 1905, but the entire British Columbia section to Vancouver was not completed until 1915. The Grand Trunk Pacific (1903) reached Edmonton by 1909, but its British Columbia section to Prince Rupert was not completed until 1914. The wasteful duplication and overcapacity generated by this railway rivalry was prodigious. For example, between Edmonton and the Yellowhead Pass both the Canadian Northern and the GTP followed virtually the same route. The pitiful standard of construction, which caused high maintenance costs, became another contributing factor to the financial collapse of the two companies during World War I. Between 1917 and 1923 the Dominion Government took over and amalgamated these and other non-CPR lines into the Canadian National Railways (CNR) system.

By 1917, the railway explosion generated during the heights of interimperialist rivalry had reached a turning point. Railway crises led to massive state intervention, attempts at rationalization, and a lessening of competition and expansion. By 1930, the early era of extensive development had come to an end, as indicated in the following figures for net operating miles of trackage in Canada.[18]

Year	Total Miles	Increase	Year	Total Miles	Increase	Year	Total Miles	Increase
1840	30	30	1890	14,090	7,166	1930	44,745	4,051
1850	80	50	1900	19,017	4,927	1940	44,713	−32
			(1905	22,385)				
1860	2,495	2,415	1910	27,541	8,524	1950	44,547	−166
			(1915	39,243)				
1870	3,121	626	1920	40,694	13,153	1960	45,598	1,051
1880	6,924	3,803				1970	45,655	57

The history of the railways during internal colonization exemplified the evolution of state relations with big business. In terms of land alone, the Dominion government made nearly 31.8 million acres of railway land grants in the prairie region. Over 13 million (41 percent) were selected in Alberta and virtually all of this Alberta land went to the CPR.[19] By 1916, state-monopoly capitalist collaboration had reached the extent that public investment—but not public ownership—accounted for at least 43.0 percent of the total investment of the CPR, 59.5 percent of the GTP, and 60.3 percent of the Canadian Northern.[20]

(d) White Settlement. The fourth element in the process of internal colonization was the rapid and extensive settlement associated primarily with agricultural development. Between 1880 and 1890, the population of Alberta, estimated for its present boundaries, grew from 18,075 to 26,593. However, in the late 1890s a torrent of settlement hit the prairies. Alberta's population

jumped to 73,022 in 1900, 185,412 in 1905, 375,295 in 1910, and 496,525 in 1915. The pre-World War I immigration channelled to Alberta was not only the first but the largest wave in Alberta's history: prior to 1905 there were nearly 100,000 immigrants to Alberta, and in the subsequent decade, over 346,000. Migration into Alberta (from other parts of Canada) was also greatest during this period; in the first decade of the century about 184,900 Canadians settled in Alberta and Saskatchewan.

Thus, by the 1906 census, only about 20.8 percent of the population were Alberta born, while about 26.1 percent were born in other parts of Canada. Of the majority immigrant section of the population, the largest group in 1906 was from the United States (23.3 percent of the population), and the second largest was from Britain (12.8 percent). Despite the rampant Anglo-Saxon chauvinism of the time, reflected in alleged fears of the "British element" being swamped by "less desirable elements," eastern Europeans, who were a typical target, constituted less than 10 percent of the population. It was not until the 1941 census that native born Albertans made up over half the Province's population.

Soon after HBC control of prairie lands was transferred to Canada, the Macdonald government formulated policy and administration of these new "Dominion Lands." Orders-in-council approved during April and May 1871, followed by the important Dominion Lands Act of April 1872, initiated Dominion policy governing railways and settlement grants, and the leasing of lands for grazing, mining, water rights, timber, and school purposes. The central control of prairie lands "for purposes of the Dominion" under the Dominion Minister of the Interior was coupled with the promotion of immigration under the Dominion Minister of Agriculture and private companies. Against the position of placing control of the lands in a prairie province, the Dominion government maintained, in Macdonald's words, that:

It would be injudicious...to have a large province which would have control over lands and might interfere with the general policy of the Government in opening up communications to the Pacific, besides the land regulations might be obstructive to immigration. All that vast territory should be for purposes of settlement under one control, and that the Dominion legislature.[21]

The main attraction to agricultural settlement was the 1882 "free homestead" provisions of Dominion Lands policy. Settlers could obtain entry on one quarter section (160 acres) by paying a $10.00 registration fee. Title to the land could be obtained in three years after meeting a minimal residence requirement. Available data on homestead entries begin in 1887 with 271 entries, but a major jump appears in 1898 (1,049 entries), rising to a peak in 1910 (17,187 entries). However, cancellations were also high. Martin estimated that between 1870 and 1927, over 41 percent of the original entries did not obtain title.[22] This "silent but deadly attrition going on upon the frontier" was a result of a variety of forces:

insufficient capital and, related to it, onerous debt burdens and credit difficulties; storage and transportation problems, including high freight rates and tariffs; weather and soil conditions; inexperience in the western prairie environment; the personal hardships of farm living; and speculation in farm land. The Dominion pressure for settlement even opened lands that were poor for farming, such as in southern Alberta, a policy that later cost huge sums in irrigation and resettlement. This prompted the provincial government to comment (generously) in 1938 that "if less attention had been given to the speed of settlement and more attention to the ultimate success of the settler on the land, large parts of this area would not have been thrown open under a homestead policy."[23]

In conjunction with "free homesteading" was the private sale of lands owned by the CPR, the HBC, and the Dominion Government. In Alberta, as in the prairies as a whole, there was actually more land disposed of through corporate grants and individual purchase (at least 23 million acres) than through free homesteading (19.1 million acres).[24] By January 1928, those lands alienated by the Dominion Government "by sale or for sale" included 3.8 million acres of school lands, 2.1 million acres under pre-emptions, 970,000 acres for irrigation, 755,000 acres under sales, and 306,000 acres under purchased homesteads, while the CPR was granted over 13.0 million acres and the HBC over 2.4 million acres. The Dominion Government had also leased 3.0 million acres under grazing leases and 2.1 million under timber births. Indian reserves covered an area of 1.4 million acres; parks and forest reserves covered 17 million acres.

The CPR strongly supported free homesteading, since under the system of having railway and homesteading sections located adjacent to each other in belts on either side of the rail lines, the encouragement of free homesteads created a transportation market and gave a value to CPR lands.[25] Between 1893 and 1905, just one CPR-related real estate operation, the Calgary and Edmonton Railway Company, sold nearly 1.1 million acres, reaching a peak of 323,500 acres in 1902.

The CPR's massive irrigation schemes in southern Alberta promoted settlement and another form of land development. One of the CPR's irrigation projects, begun in 1903, encompassed 3 million acres adjoining the Bow River in southern Alberta and was promoted as the "largest private enterprise of its kind ever carried out." Indeed, in 1926, the CPR's Department of Colonization and Development claimed that the company had spent "nearly $75,000,000 for colonization, land settlement, irrigation or similar works—an amount exceeding that spent by the Dominion Government in like work in the same period."[26]

As a result of rapid settlement, commercial agriculture predominantly in the form of the small, 'independent farmer' (or simple commodity production) was firmly established by 1905. About 916,000 acres of land were under field crops and 4 million acres were under pasture. The advent of commercial agriculture and with it the growth of a capitalist land market also permanently displaced the hunting and gathering economy of the Native peoples. However, settlement during internal colonization was not exclusively, or even essentially, agricultural. In Alberta, the development of urban centres, particularly the towns and cities, dominated and often preceded rural development. In the growth of markets and transportation, and in the control of investment and credit (both public and private), rural interests were subordinated to more powerful business groups in the towns (one of the factors that accounts for Alberta's long history of town-country conflict and uneven development). Nevertheless, Alberta centres were themselves usually subordinate to outside capital, notably the railways and banks. The many small towns that acted as agricultural service centres were established by the railways about 5 to 15 miles (8 to 24 km) apart as elevator depots. They were especially vulnerable not only to scheduling and freight rates, but to line closures. Some larger centres, such as Lethbridge, grew up as company coal mining towns serving the CPR or later railways. Centres like Calgary—"the CPR town"[27]—were most diversified, but still dependent on key railway-related activities such as cattle marketing. Consequently, urban settlement was also rapid. While the rural population of Alberta in 1905 was 127,320, the urban population was 57,875, of which 30,119 were in cities.

(e) Natural Resource Exploitation. The fifth element in the process of internal colonization was the establishing of a system of primary production based on agriculture and mineral extraction—natural resource exploitation. Central Canadian capital dominated this development either directly through ownership or financing, or indirectly through its control of transportation and markets.

One can distinguish two forms of capital accumulation in Alberta, the first under essentially local ownership and control and the second under essentially external ownership and control, usually in central Canada or England. The first was typified by the simple commodity producer such as the small farmer and the local craftsman or artisan (blacksmith, butcher, gunsmith, etc.); the local 'independent' merchant or real estate agent (in non-productive sectors); and the local capitalist who operated, for example, a contracting business, lumbering enterprise, or ranch. The second was typified by the absentee-owned firm and their agencies, offices, branch plants, or other properties, which was managed by an employee ("residential manager"), minority shareholder, contracted professional, or a combination of these. It was this second form of capital accumulation that dominated the key sectors of industrial capital during internal colonization.

In transportation, the power of the CPR extended into virtually every sphere of production, in part because the CPR controlled the only viable mode of long distance transportation in the landlocked prairies. In determining scheduling, freight rates, and branch line organization, the CPR could indirectly determine production patterns. Generally, the CPR and central Canadian capital as a whole directed prairie production as a source of raw commodities for central Canadian manufacturing and trading interests: "since early development the thrust has been to move raw materials to industrial Canada for refinement and consumption."[28] One of the best known examples of this was the discriminatory freight rates policy contained in the Crow's Nest Pass agreement of 1897.[29]

The Crow's Nest Pass agreement between the Dominion Government and the CPR was the first major effort of the Canadian state to regulate freight rates. The CPR desired to build the Crow's Nest Pass, a rail line from Lethbridge into south-eastern British Columbia. As a concession for a cash and land grant subsidy to aid its construction, and under strong farmer pressure, the CPR agreed, beginning in 1899, to reduce the freight rates on grain and flour carried from the west to Fort William-Port Arthur (Thunder Bay) by three cents to 14 cents per 100 pounds from Winnipeg, 20 cents from Regina, and 26 cents from Calgary. However, the rates on eastward freight in manufacturers were not similarly reduced,while the westward freight rates on some manufactured products of central Canada were reduced (more as a concession to eastern capital than prairie consumers). The freight rate structure that evolved became a long-standing grievance, both among working people and local capitalist interests, for it "permitted the [transportation] system to continue to drain the West of employment and development opportunities."[30]

In agriculture, there were two main specializations, grain farming and ranching. The control of grain production was indirect, since the productive system relied mainly on small proprietary farming on land owned and occupied by the farmer. However, central Canadian capital exercised power through its ownership and control of inputs, such as farm machinery, farm credit, mortgages and homestead land grants, irrigation programmes and transportation.

In ranching, development was dominated by the large-scale capitalist enterprise. Probably the first of the large-scale commercial ranches was Cochrane Ranch Company Limited (1881), owned by the conservative Senator M.H. Cochrane of Quebec. Under Dominion Lands policy, the Dominion cabinet in 1881 approved the granting of leases of up to 100,000 acres for a term of 21 years at one cent per acre per year. The large cattle and horse ranches were capitalized upwards from $100,000 and owned by leading Canadian and English businessmen. By 1884, two-thirds of all stocked land in the south-west was controlled by ten companies; moreover, "four of these companies, the Cochrane Ranch Company, the Walrond Ranch Company, the Oxley Ranch Company, and North West Cattle Company held almost one-half of such lands."[31] The leading ranching interests came to form a "cattle compact" which was clearly visible in such organizations as the Western Stockgrowers' Association and the Ranchmen's Club (in Calgary), and markedly upper class, Anglo-Saxon, and Tory. With the gradual encroachment of agricultural settlement—"sodbusters" and "nesters"—the heyday of the big ranch was over by 1910.

In mining, "coal was King" during internal colonization, although some early interests in gold and later in gas and oil also appeared. The growth of railways was the chief stimulus to coal production. The first and largest coal mining operation, the North-Western Coal and Navigation Company, was established by A.T. Galt in anticipation of the building of the CPR. The company had British financial backing (William Lethbridge, an English capitalist and namesake of the coaltown, was president) and substantial coal, timber,and grazing leases from the Dominion government. On the basis of long-term coal contracts with the CPR, a Dunmore to Lethbridge railway line (106 miles or 171 km) was completed in 1885. High transportation costs and Canadian-US tariff barriers made outside sale of coal uncompetitive east of Winnipeg, west of the Rockies, or in the United States. Consequently, in its early development, Alberta's coal production depended heavily on irregular and slowly growing rail traffic which gave rise to a "limited, fluctuating, regional market."[32]

In several areas of Alberta there were small independent mines—"gopher holes"—supplying local needs, but the main producers were large, heavily capitalized firms owned in central Canada or Britain. Growing outside investment and concentration were particularly evident during the rapid phase of growth that followed the building of the Crow's Nest Pass line of the CPR in 1897, and superseded the slow, irregular growth since the 1880s. Production of Alberta coal (from the Kootenay, Belly River, and Edmonton formations) rose from 43,220 tons (39 209 t) in 1886 to 931,917 tons (845 430 t) in 1905 (or 10.8 percent of Canadian production) to about 4 million tons (3.6 million t) in 1913 (or 26.7 percent of Canadian production).[33]

In manufacturing, enterprises were generally small-scale with production geared to local markets and the demands of the railway or mining industries. The 1891 Census revealed that in the Territorial District of Alberta there were 143 "industrial establishments" (roughly, manufacturing establishments) employing 574 males and 22 females, or about 4.2 employees per establishment. The largest group of these were 14 saw mill operations (202 employees), 35 blacksmithing-forging operations (45 employees), 12 carpentry and joining operations (37 employees), 3 printing and publishing operations (27 employees), 6 harness and saddlery operations (20 employees), 4 sash, door, and blind operations (20 employees), and one meat curing operation (20 employees).

The unmistakeable tendency present in the development of manufacturing was the replacement of local craft or "hand trades" enterprises by the larger-scale capitalist enterprise, although at varying rates in different types of businesses. The former enterprise was typically a sole proprietorship or partnership, in which the proprietor himself worked, perhaps aided by one or two wage earners. The latter enterprise, which came to dominate the key manufacturing areas, was typically a (joint-stock) corporation with a larger capital investment, a clearer separation of labour from ownership, and more often absentee-owned.

By the time of provincial status in 1905, Alberta had 97 establishments with 1,983 employees (or 20.4 employees per establishment), with a capital investment of $5.4 million (or $55,673 per employee) and a gross output valued at nearly $5 million.[34] Large-scale capitalist manufacturing was becoming evident in brewing, electric power generation, lumber milling, flour milling, meat packing, and some textile production. In brewing, for example, there were three breweries with a total of 146 employees, $640,000 capital, and an annual gross output of nearly $407,000. In flour milling, there were 11 mills with a total of 135 employees, $886,000 capital, and an annual gross output of over $1.4 million.[35] However, even the larger-scale enterprises were geared for the local or regional market. Innis suggests that "Success of the flour-milling and pork-packing industry at Calgary and Edmonton were, in large part, a result of Kootenay demands" and also observes that the "dairy industry and, in turn, creameries and cheese factories grew up in relation to mining."[36]

Despite the appearance of manufacturing activity by 1905, its structure and growth vividly reflected Canada's highly uneven regional development. In 1905, the gross value of Alberta's manufacturing activity amounted to about $5 million or only .7 percent of the Canadian total of $718 million, while Alberta's population was 184,412 or 3 percent of the Canadian population of about 6,002,000. The average size of Alberta's manufacturing establishments was relatively low: in terms of labour, only 17.0 employees per establishment compared to Ontario's 23.7, British Columbia's 51.7, and the Canadian average of 24.9; and in terms of capital, only $46,217 per establishment as compared to Ontario's $49,710, British Columbia's $115,516, and the Canadian average of $53,595.[37] Even by 1910, the gross value of Alberta's manufacturing was 1.6 percent of the Canadian total of $1,166 million compared to Ontario's 49.7 percent, while Alberta's population was 5.2 percent of Canada's 7,206,643, compared to Ontario's 35.1 percent.

Alberta's productive system could not reap the advantages of its specialization and natural wealth in a division of labour organized by and directed in the interests of central Canadian and British capital. While Alberta was heavily dependent upon primary production in grain growing, ranching, and coal mining, the terms of trade for primary commodities marketed beyond the region were generally dictated by outside interests through their control of markets and transportation. With grain, for example, major central Canadian and foreign corporate interests allied in such institutions as the Winnipeg Grain and Produce Exchange (formed in 1887, incorporated in 1891) exercised monopoly power in grain buying and elevators. The struggles of farm producers against these 'vested interests' and their political allies became a standard theme in prairie economic and social history. At the same time, some other primary commodities, particularly coal, had a major potential but were uncompetitive in central Canadian markets largely as a result of high transportation costs. About half of Canada's consumption of coal was imported more cheaply from the United States, where some Canadian companies had interests in Pennsylvania mines. The fact that Dominion tariff and freight rate policies were not exercised to integrate Alberta coal production into the central Canadian industrial 'heartland' again revealed who were the major beneficiaries of internal colonization and exposed the inconsistent and less than genuinely 'national' character of the National Policy.

Finally, contrary to mythology, there never was an era of "free enterprise" in Alberta, when competition predominated over monopoly. The mantle of monopoly was passed from the HBC to the CPR and permeated most of the economy. Where competition existed, usually among small producers, it was often to the advantage of large firms for it lowered the prices of inputs for large firms and generally weakened the bargaining position of small producers against monopolies. Since central Canadian and foreign interests, together with their local collaborators, were in a stronger position to defend and advance their monopoly positions in Alberta, development was weak and lopsided, and major streams of economic surplus drained eastward to Toronto, Montreal, and London, England, thus constraining capital accumulation in Alberta itself.

(f) Expanding the Internal Market. The sixth element in the process of internal colonization was the development of an expanded internal market under the control of central Canadian industry and banking. This general market can be divided into a large number of particular markets of two kinds: financial markets and commodity markets. The control exercised by central Canadian interests in both sets of markets was based on their predominant ownership of the means of production (both central and "branch" plants), distribution (foremost the railways), and exchange (principally the banks). Especially prominent was their financial power in determining direct investments, the allocation of loan capital, and the granting of credit.

Well before Confederation, it was evident that leading interests in central and eastern Canada foresaw the West as an expansion area for their domestic market. At the Quebec Conference (1864), for instance, the following resolution was passed:

The communications with the North-West Territory, and the improvements required for the development of the Trade of the Great West with the Seaboard, are regarded by this Conference as subjects of the highest importance to the Federated Provinces, and shall be prosecuted at the earliest possible period that the state of the finances will permit.

The end of the American Civil War (1865) and the abrogation in 1866 of the Canada-US Reciprocity Treaty of 1854 intensified the drive for a larger domestic market. The depression in 1866 and the major depression of 1873 further sharpened pressures for westward expansion as a way out of crisis.

There were several mechanisms of control of North-West markets, but chief among them was the control of transportation and tariffs. In 1866, Canadian tariffs had been lowered as an inducement to the Maritime Colonies to enter Confederation; but with the depression of 1873, tariffs were again raised, partly for the protection of central Canadian industry and partly to offset the decline in government revenues. The most prominent boost in the tariffs came in 1879 with the "National Policy tariffs." These tariffs against imports from the United

States, which raised the price of some key commodities needed by prairie settlers, remained much the same throughout internal colonization and became a longstanding prairie grievance, comparable to the freight rates issue.

The "National Policy" had its roots in the emerging class of Canadian businessmen who, by 1867, had gained leading positions in the colonial governments of British North America—in particular, the Canadas, New Brunswick, and Nova Scotia—and was taking charge of the development of a new Canadian state and Canadian economic expansion. This rising "national bourgeoisie" was overwhelmingly English-speaking and centred in central Canada, principally Montreal and Toronto. Its wealth was acquired during a long history of conquest and capital accumulation, notably in the fur and timber trades, banking, land speculation, construction, military provisioning, and some agriculture. During the 1840s and 1850s, its 'coming of age' was hastened by a marked turn towards industrialization (perhaps Canada's own 'mini' industrial revolution), under the primary impetus of early railway development. The chief components of the new leading business class were railway and steamship-line promoters, financial promoters, industrialists, certain church interests, and successors of the old mercantile bourgeoisie.[38] The most powerful grouping among these interests, represented by such figures as John A. Macdonald, Alexander T. Galt, and Georges E. Cartier, was centred in Montreal at the Bank of Montreal and the Grand Trunk Railway, tied strongly to English capital, and tended to support the Conservative Party. A weaker grouping, represented by such figures as George Brown, was centred in Toronto and Hamilton, and tended to support the Liberal Party.

Most of the key political leaders in the Canadian government during the 1850s and 1860s, including the so-called "Fathers of Confederation" themselves, were members of the new Anglo-Canadian business class; a few came from the top section of the subordinate (French) Canadian business class. Succeeding Canadian governments also reflected the overwhelming presence of vested business interests. As Gustavus Myers described a typical post-Confederation parliament:

Politics was, in fact, a business; the Canadian parliament was crowded with men who were there to initiate, extend or conserve class interests; of the 206 members of the Dominion House of Commons, in 1878, there were 56 merchants, 55 lawyers, 12 gentlemen of leisure, and an assortment of manufacturers, insurance company presidents, shipbuilding and lumber capitalists, contractors, and a few journalists, physicians, and farmers.[39]

The politico-economic policy formulated as a clear expression of these interests was the "National Policy." The term came from the Conservative Party's election platform of 1878, but it first appeared as early as 1869 and had limited use in the campaign of 1872. The National Policy has been associated most prominently with the raising of tariffs in 1879; however, as a state programme of "national" development its conception was much broader:

...by 1879, the year in which the National Policy was formulated, the parts of a more or less complete pattern had fallen into place: a transcontinental railway, protective tariffs, land settlement policy, the promotion of immigration. Agricultural development of the west was basic to the whole programme,and wheat was to become the staple to which the transcontinental economy was geared, the means of attracting capital and immigrants and of creating a mass market for the materials and manufactured products of the other regions of the Dominion.[40]

The National Policy was an aggressive extension of key aspects of the 1867 Confederation arrangements. In the Confederation arrangements the rising Canadian business class attempted to create and consolidate a Canadian home market under its control by the formation of a common market in the formerly separated colonies and by the building of the Intercolonial Railway linking the Maritimes to central Canada. However, to solidify the tenuous Pacific and Maritimes connections, to fend off the heightened expansionism of US capital after the American Civil War (1861-65), and to spur business activity out of a serious depression (which began in 1873 and was reaching bottom by 1879) more aggressive state measures were implemented. Thus, for the benefit of central Canadian capital, the 1879 National Policy tariff sharply increased protection against the products of rival American capital, including in western Canada, thereby enlarging the home market under the control of central Canadian capital.

The Dominion government moved early to check the "free trade" with the US existing in southern Alberta during the 1870s. The first customs collection in Alberta was carried out by the NWMP during the fiscal year 1876-77 at Fort Macleod and amounted to $19,115.47.[41] By 1906, the duties collected on imports into Alberta from the US had risen to over $520,000. That same year, imports at $2.8 million dwarfed exports which were less than $330,000.

A wide variety of imports were hit by the National Policy tariffs, which ranged roughly according to the degree of processing, from about 10 percent for commodities with little processing to 30 percent for finished goods. The rates for some commodities, for example, petroleum products and furniture, were even higher. One item of particular significance was agricultural implements, the tariffs on which were raised from 17.5 percent (1874) to 25 percent under the National Policy tariffs of 1879 (and raised again—to 35 percent—in 1883). Prior to the National Policy tariffs, the implement trade in the North-West was centred in Winnipeg (the Chicago of the Canadian prairies[42])and was dominated by US firms operating through St. Paul. After the tariffs, central Canadian based manufacturing operations, led by firms such as Harris (later Massey-Harris and Massey-Ferguson), were able to take major positions in the market.

Among the most powerful of capitalist institutions during the process of internal colonization were the banks. Their control of major accumulations of Canadian capital and intermediary relationships with British and American capital enabled the banks to play a decisive role in determining the general character of development and, in particular, investment priorities. For the banks, prairie expansion meant major opportunities for capital accumulation through new demands for loan capital, credit, bank 'services,' and new deposits. One of the first chartered banks to establish a branch in Alberta was the CPR-associated Bank of Montreal, which opened a branch in Calgary by 1886. A few private banks appeared in the 1880s and 1890s but they were soon overwhelmed by the chartered banks. In 1890 there were only four chartered bank branches in the entire North-West; in 1915 Alberta alone had 256. A branch of the Imperial Bank of Canada was established in Edmonton in 1891. The Canadian Bank of Commerce opened branches in Calgary, Edmonton, and Medicine Hat in 1902, and in Lethbridge in 1905. The Merchants Bank of Halifax (now the Royal Bank) had a branch in the Yukon in 1899, but opened its first Alberta branch in Edmonton in 1906 and in Calgary in 1907. In 1900 there were only three bank clearing houses in western Canada (Winnipeg, Vancouver, and Victoria); however, by 1907, clearing houses were also operating in Calgary and Edmonton.

The rewards—and historical significance—of the westward expansion of Canadian chartered banking were well recognized. In referring to the decade 1901 to 1911, a review article in the leading journal of Canadian banking commented:

This movement of branch extension in the West...also had a very important effect in increasing Canada's banking power. Thanks to the steady and rapid growth of the West's production, and to the large investment of funds in western farms and other property by outsiders, the branches in that part of the country have acquired a rapidly rising volume of deposits; and a number of the banks having extensive branch representation have thus formed the means to rapidly augment their resources.[43]

Some new markets, particularily in land, opened a wide range of opportunities to fleece succeeding groups of newcomers. Several heavily financed central Canadian and British firms acquired large parcels of land, especially urban land, for the much practised purpose of later selling the land to realize capital gains— of course, without making any improvements to the property.[44] The large-scale speculative enterprises were joined by numerous small-scale speculators who exemplified a hit-and-run entrepreneurialism prevalent during boom times like the Klondike rush in the late 1890s and the "great barbecue" following 1905. In major centres the largest single group of businesses typically was real estate agencies. The massive waves of speculative activity did not create any real capital stock and often obstructed and fragmented development; however, they did speed the concentration of some capitals and the dissipation of others, thus accelerating monopoly trends and the general polarization of wealth.

The area of wholesale and retail distribution was at first more open to local 'independent' merchants, although the presence of the HBC continued as the first outside "chain store." Furthermore, local merchants, like the productive sectors, were subject to freight rates and tariffs policy. The CPR, for instance, affected the development of particular communities by its manipulation of freight rates:

Within the West before the Canadian Northern became important, the CP controlled the competition of local merchants by giving them special distributive rates....Calgary merchants in 1902 could ship along the Calgary-Edmonton branch into Edmonton territory while Edmonton merchants could not ship back. The result was to make one centre, in this case Calgary, more attractive to eastern business as a distribution centre, and a large number of wholesale branches of eastern business moved into that town. Complaints over this were rampant throughout the West, for which town got the special distributive (traders') rate was entirely the decision of the company. In addition, the secret rebate system could be used to hide the differential.[45]

Thus, through a constellation of both general and particular politico-economic relationships, central Canadian capital was able to structure development to suit its own drive for accumulation. This meant, in practice, that despite some significant popular resistance there was a virtually complete subordination of the prairie regional economy to the central Canadian capitalist interests and state.

3. Provincial Autonomy and Capital Accumulation

A major outcome of more than three decades of internal colonization was the emergence of a business class and the achievement of provincial state autonomy in the developing settler economy. Autonomy Bills were introduced in the Dominion parliament in February 1905 and passed in July, officially creating the Provinces of Alberta and Saskatchewan on 1 September, 1905.

The governmental and administrative transition from territorial status to provincial status was gradual and deliberate (see Figure I-1). Beginning in 1870, the North-West Territories was administered through the Lieutenant-Governor of Manitoba and a Dominion cabinet-appointed North-West Council based in Winnipeg. The North-West Territories Act of 1875, passed by the Mackenzie Liberal government, established a resident Lieutenant-Governor (in Battleford) with a North-West Council appointed by the Dominion cabinet. The Act also provided for the election of non-Indian males to the Council as the settler population increased. On the question of democracy in the Territories, the Conservatives took more reactionary positions, as was reflected, for example, during the 1875 debates on the North-West Territories Bill when Macdonald commented that the Liberals "should not clog themselves with...introducing the popular element."[46] In 1882, with the building of the CPR, the capital of the

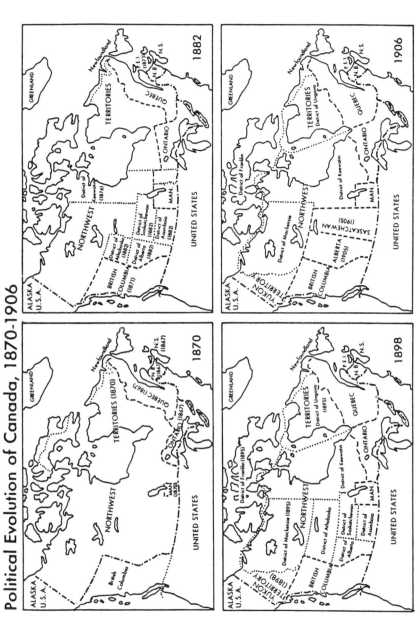

Political Evolution of Canada, 1870-1906

figure 1-1

Territories was moved to Regina and four territorial districts—Alberta, Assiniboia, Athabaska, and Saskatchewan—were created.

By 1884, the North-West Council's elected members outnumbered the appointed. However, it was not until 1897 that the Dominion Government recognized formally the principle of "responsible government" by legislating for an Executive Council which would have majority support of the Assembly. In succeeding years, the territorial state machinery was developed further, on a departmental basis, leading to a relatively smooth administrative transition to provincial autonomy in 1905.

Underlying the movement towards autonomy in the North-West was the advance of settlement and capitalist development. Such development required a state-financed and organized economic infrastructure and certain social programmes: railways and communications; courts and jails; roads, bridges, and other local improvements; public health and education. While successful in the achievement of "responsible government," the Territorial government had not acquired the authority or financial means to support these demands of rapid growth, in particular, the right to borrow money (public debt) and the right to charter railways. Also, Dominion Lands, including timber and mineral rights, remained in the hands of the Dominion government, and compensating Dominion financial grants were relatively low. Above all, since the direction and form of state involvement in the territories directly affected both private capital accumulation in general and the allocation of particular advantages and benefits, the control of the territorial and municipal governments became a matter of profound importance to a wide variety of interests within as well as outside the region.

Municipal development was closely bound up with early capitalist expansion and the rise of local and regional business groupings. Unlike the Territorial government, urban municipalities could issue debentures. Moreover, local municipalities were able to obtain more revenue through their direct taxes on property and incomes than the territorial administration obtained from the Dominion government. By 1903, total municipal tax revenues in the North-West Territories were about $1 million, of which 60 percent was from urban areas. On the other hand, the entire territorial administration received about $1 million from the Dominion and only $120,000 from within the territories (for licences, fees, and fines).[47]

The first Municipal Ordinance of the North-West Territories was passed in 1883. In 1884, Calgary became the first municipality in Alberta to be incorporated as a town. It was followed by Lethbridge (1891), Edmonton (1892), Macleod (1892), Medicine Hat (1899), and Strathcona (1899). With further growth came the drive for city status. Again, in 1894, Calgary became the first town granted a city charter. Edmonton was granted a charter in 1904 (and Strathcona in 1907); Medicine Hat, Lethbridge, and Wetaskiwin were incorporated cities in 1906.

The municipal administrations, like other levels of the state, were seen as an instrument or lever for promoting private capital accumulation, particularly by local business interests. The first organizations of local businessmen, usually independent merchants and small proprietors, tended to be informal, but in due course the local boards of trade (now "chambers of commerce") emerged. The first board of trade in the North-West Territories was established in Edmonton in 1889. In 1890, Calgary saw its first Board of Trade, which had some roots in the Calgary Agricultural Society formed in the early 1880s. Others followed rapidly. By 1900, there were ten boards of trade in the Territories.

A general pattern of municipal development emerged clearly: prominent local business interests, often in the form of a local board of trade, became the leadership behind municipal incorporations and then took control of the town council, treating it as "their own."[48] The formation of boards of trade or other business associations usually predated or at least approximated the incorporation of towns—and sometimes they were initiated for that very purpose. However, the formation of business associations was also stimulated by other goals, such as a rail connection or local improvements. Among business interests in the Territories it was primarily local 'independent' businessmen who were leading promoters of incorporations. Indeed, there is evidence to suggest that outside firms sometimes resisted incorporation, especially if they were large property owners and liable to municipal taxation by a majority they could not control. For example, Elliott Galt, general manager of the North-Western Coal and Navigation Company, by far the largest property holder in Lethbridge, did not permit incorporation as a town until the local Board of Trade agreed to exempt the company's property from taxation.[49]

The jump from town to city status in various municipal areas marked a further step in the growth of settlement and capital accumulation, which was becoming increasingly concentrated and centralized. Correspondingly, boards of trade and municipal councils, particularly in cities, were reflecting a sharpened differentiation between larger and smaller businessmen, and between outside and absentee interests and the local independents. Increasing numbers of corporate professionals, especially lawyers, who had large outside firms as key clients, were also making their appearance. The fierce "bonusing" debates, and the rise of the so-called "reform" movement which attempted to corporatize municipal administration, were indications of these new trends. Further, in the promotion of growth, "boosterism,"[50] and intermunicipal rivalries municipal administrations increasingly geared major capital expenditures towards creating an appealing infrastructure for outside investors. The formation of public utilities, such as Edmonton Power (1902) and Edmonton Telephones (1904), and major capital expenditures in roads, bridges, and public buildings were means of achieving this. The debenture debt of Alberta cities was $1 million in 1906, while the Province had no debenture debt until 1909 and only $206,872 in expenditures on its capital account.[51] By contrast, the municipality of Edmonton alone issued its first debentures in 1893 and had accumulated a debenture debt of over $92,000 by 1901 and $502,000 by 1906.

Some indication of the accelerating pace of local private capital accumulation can be seen in the formation of joint-stock companies (or corporations) and partnerships. Well prior to provincial status, the joint-stock form of firm (with limited liability) typical of modern capitalism had become an established economic institution in Alberta. According to official company records of the North-West Territories, which were initiated with the adoption of the first Companies Ordinance in 1886, the years of most rapid growth in the number and average size of Alberta-situated companies were from about 1899 to 1905 (see Table I-1). The first partnership records date from 1884, though there were earlier partnerships unable or unwilling to register. The number of partnerships also increased rapidly in the late 1890s. By the end of 1905 there were probably around 1,000 partnership registrations in Alberta as compared to about 391 incorporations in Alberta, and about 302 registrations of extra-territorial companies in the North-West Territories.[52]

The earliest anti-colonial struggles for land and self-government in the Territories were led by the Métis and some other sections of the Native population, culminating in 1885 in the North-West uprising, which was essentially a popular democratic resistance to Canadian colonialism. After the crushing of the uprising, the main pressures for autonomy came from the emerging local-regional business groupings in the Territories together with certain central Canadian interests, such as the railways and land companies, who could benefit from having provincial governments with powers to build infrastructures through debt financing, to guarantee private debt, and to bestow grants. The class interests of workers and farmers were generally identified with the shift in control of lands and natural resources and the greater democracy that provincial status was anticipated to bring. However, some fears were expressed among those sections of the population, especially the farmers, that provincial autonomy would lead to increased taxes on their relatively meagre holdings. Further, both worker and farmer sections of the population had not yet broken with the Liberal Party and achieved an independent class based political party organization. Thus, the strength of the emerging working class and farmers was diffused, divided, and often coopted into the Liberal Party. Politically, labour and farm people were a distinctly subordinate force to capital in determining the autonomy arrangement. On the other hand, once there was a sufficiently entrenched and "responsible" settler bourgeoisie, the Dominion government could transfer power without fear of losing control. The limited autonomy concept was an appropriate demand for a class essentially colonialist, racist in its position towards the Native population, and more concerned with advancing particular property interests than with popular democracy.

Some of the early autonomy initiatives in the 1890s, such as the formation of Calgary's "Provincial Autonomy Committee" in 1895, were motivated by

Table I-1

Authorized Capital of Alberta-Situated Companies Incorporated under NWT Companies Ordinances by Size of Capitalization and Year, 1887-1905

Year	Number of firms		Authorized capital ($)		Distribution of capital by size of firm (number of firms)					
	Total	Capital stated	Total	Average (per firm)	Less than $10,000	$10,000-$24,999	$25,000-$49,999	$50,000-$99,999	$100,000-$999,999	$1 million and over
1887	2	2	110,000	55,000			1	1		
1888	—									
1889	4	4	37,000	9,250	1	3				
1890	4	4	33,000	8,250	2	2				
1891	5	5	249,000	49,800	1	3			1	
1892	3	3	57,000	19,000	1	2				
1893	4	4	55,000	13,750		4				
1894	6	6	79,000	13,167	2	3	1			
1895	—									
1896	1	1	3,000	3,000	1					
1897	3	3	45,000	15,000	1	1	1			
1898	4	4	29,000	7,250	3	1				
1899	14	14	1,310,900	93,636	5	4	2	2		1
1900	6	6	69,000	11,500	2	4				
1901	13	12	2,777,000	231,417	1	5	3	2		1
1902	39	24	5,997,000	249,875	3	4	4	5	5	3
1903	43	40	2,755,000	68,875	3	9	8	9	11	
1904	72	65	4,137,000	63,646	3	20	12	19	11	
1905	90	88	7,679,500	87,267	8	24	22	13	18	3
Total	313	285	25,422,400	89,201	36	89	54	52	46	8

Source: Companies records of the Companies Branch of the Government of Alberta and various issues of the *North-West Territories Gazette* and *Alberta Gazette.*

specific business groupings seeking advantage over their rivals. But with the acceleration of settlement and railway construction between about 1897 and 1905, the often rival autonomy pressures were increasingly consolidated and generalized. Moreover, the escalating demands for infrastructural development were overwhelming the Territorial finances. In 1900, for an area of approximately 400,000 square miles and population of 145,000 (plus 75,000 in the "unorganized territories"), the total Territorial revenue was only $467,185, of which $419,000 was from the Dominion government.

As the main forces for autonomy congealed, several points of division had to be overcome. Briefly, they were: the number of provinces, their borders, and their capitals; the control of Dominion lands; the terms of Dominion financial support to the newly autonomous province(s); and the question of whether the provincial educational system(s) should permit separate (Catholic) schools.

Probably no other autonomy issue was more revealing of the internal divisiveness and determining role of vested capitalist interests than the great slice-up of the North-West Territories. The majority view of the North-West Assembly, including the Conservative Premier F.W.G. Haultain, supported the concept of one North-West province. However, the final autonomy arrangements determined by the Dominion government created two provinces, Alberta and Saskatchewan. For its part, the Laurier Liberal government (1896-1911) feared that a single province might become too powerful relative to other provinces. As well, the pressures of central Canadian capital and the intense local rivalries of emerging territorial capitals were being felt.

The most intense pressure for the breaking up of the Territory was centred in southern Alberta, particularly Calgary. Its leading spokesman was the Conservative R.B. Bennett, later Prime Minister of Canada and an English Viscount, whose law firm (with James Lougheed) represented the CPR and the Stockgrower's Association, among numerous other large interests. Prior to Bennett, R.G. Brett and C.A. Magrath were leading Assembly representatives for provincial autonomy. Brett was a surgeon for the CPR and a member of Banff 'society'; Magrath was an executive of the CPR-related North-Western Coal and Navigation Company—and Lethbridge's first mayor.

For the Tory-backed CPR, and the Liberal-backed Grand Trunk Pacific and Canadian Northern, provincial status meant greater opportunities for publicly guaranteed debt financing and grants, as well as more publicly funded infrastructure to facilitate settlement and the growth of markets. The railways, and outside business generally, faced an internally divided prairie West in which provincial (and municipal) governments could be played off against each other. Established ranching interests in southern Alberta, who feared being swamped by the small-holder majority in the Territories, would be stronger in a separate province. For growing capitalist interests in Calgary there was greater likelihood in a divided Territory of dominating the new province. Calgary interests even expected, not unreasonably, that in a divided Territory they could claim the capital for Alberta. However, Edmonton business interests, who also appeared to favour the division of the Territory, had stronger ties with the Liberal Party and won the designation as capital from the Liberal Dominion government over the Tory-dominated Calgary establishment.[53] It is significant that, unlike their opposites in the Calgary Board of Trade, the Calgary Trades and Labour Council supported the one-province concept.

The actual autonomy arrangements were not based on any radical democratic pressures or principles such as gave rise to the Red River uprising and the Province of Manitoba (1870). Rather, the arrangements represented a balance of power between dominant central Canadian capital and a subordinate 'junior partner' developing in the hinterland as both ally and competitor. As ally, it fought to expand capitalist development, including through the encouragement of outside capital; as rival, it sought to gain a leg up on central Canadian capital and to propel itself into top level Canadian—and later, international—business circles.

The 1905 autonomy arrangements did not mean *full* provincial status, in the sense of a status equivalent to that of the older provinces. In particular, Dominion Lands comprising at least 25 million acres for settlement, and additional leasable lands, remained under the control of the Dominion government. The financial terms of the arrangements, which were posed as "compensation" for the loss of Dominion Lands revenues, continued a degree of economic dependency on the Dominion government and did not alter the fact that the use of Dominion Lands—the key means of directing settlement and much economic development—remained outside the control of the province. Nevertheless, the autonomy arrangements did give rise to a provincial state in which regionally based business interests exercised control and rapidly developed a state administrative apparatus and a state-owned economic infrastructure.

Provincial status created opportunities for the acceleration of regionally based capitalist development. But the debilitating legacy of Canadian internal colonization constrained and deformed this development. Even today, when Alberta appears conspicuously as a "have province,"[54] there remain certain so-called "regional disparities," especially in northern parts of the province, which testify to a deeper problem, that is, the uneven development inherent in capitalism wherever it appears.

4. Modern Phases and Features in the Provincial Economy

As a generally subordinate section of the Canadian economy, the Alberta economy suffered from a greater turbulence and vulnerability to external forces. Cyclical crises—'booms and busts'—hit harder, especially prior to the 1950s. Coupled with the major wars, these crises helped to define the five modern phases of Alberta's development.

Rapid economic growth through the formal achievement of provincial autonomy (1905) peaked in late 1912, when the first major depression in the twentieth century hit Alberta. Although World War I began in August 1914, the province was not pulled out of depression until 1915. Thereafter the economy expanded under the added stimulus of war mobilization to a peak in 1917, then continued at a relatively high level of activity until the traumatic post-war collapse of 1919. It is the war and post-war crisis (and, corresponding to it politically, the ejection of the provincial Liberal party from office in 1921) that marks the end of the first phase of provincial development.

The second phase, one of somewhat halting development, covered the 1920s, until the Great Depression beginning in 1929. The third phase of development was the acute crisis of the Depression years, from 1929 until the early 1940s, with World War II and the major penetration of US capital and state (in particular, in the expansion of air traffic and facilities, the construction of the Alaska Highway, and the Canol Project). Corresponding to this at the political level, with some lags, were the demise of the United Farmers of Alberta government and the election of the Social Credit movement in 1935, at the one end, and the demise of the more 'radical' Aberhart Social Credit (1935-43), at the other end. The fourth phase began with the war boom in Alberta and continued into the 1960s, spurred primarily by oil and gas exploitation. Politically, the Social Credit government under Manning shifted sharply to the right and, despite some buffeting in the late 1940s, rode out its difficulties by relying on the Cold War and economic expansion in the 1950s and early 1960s.

With the 1960s, Alberta based capital accumulation advanced to the point of growing restless with the subordinate continentalism and the passive, conservative direction of the economy under Social Credit. In the 1970s, there appeared a more aggressive drive for capitalist development with an increased emphasis on industrialization and a stronger role for the state. Politically, the 1971 election of the Conservative government under Lougheed, following a recession in 1970-71, signalled this change. However, the situation did not change dramatically until the major OPEC oil price increases in 1973, which put a stronger 'provincialist' wind in the Tory sails and opened opportunities for vastly expanded capital accumulation. The fifth phase is thus one of heightened though uneven growth, centred on oil and gas development and led by increasingly powerful provincially based business interests who are committed to aggressive use of the provincial state for accelerating private capital accumulation and achieving their 'place in the sun.'

Throughout these modern phases of development Alberta was transformed from a predominantly agricultural economy with some mineral extraction and manufacturing to an economy predominantly in mineral extraction with some farming and manufacturing (see Table I-2). As well, a substantial construction and utility sector arose. In this fundamental shift in economic structure, the crucial years were in the decade of transformation following World War II, paralleling the significance of the decade preceding World War I. Agricultural production reached its proportionately highest level in 1927, and has been

Table 1-2

Value-Added in Production in Alberta, 1920-1978

Percentage of production in principal sectors

	Total value of production (millions of dollars)	Mines, quarries, and oil wells	Construction	Manu-facturing	Agri-culture	Electric Power	Forestry	Hunting and Trapping	Fishing
1920	264.6	12.4	1.0	12.7	70.9	1.0	1.2	.6	.2
1925	257.0	9.6	1.0	12.6	73.5	1.2	1.3	.8	.2
1930	184.7	15.8	8.4	24.5	44.6	2.4	3.7	.5	.2
1935	147.3	10.9	14.3	16.2	53.9	3.1	.1	.1	
1940	252.7	11.0	11.5	14.9	58.5	2.3	.1	.1	
1945	403.3	10.3	13.1	19.5	52.7	2.0	1.6	.1	*
1950	750.3	16.3	19.7	16.5	44.1	1.9	1.2	*	
1955	1,283.0	23.7	26.4	20.5	25.9	2.3	1.0		
1960	1,857.3	18.8	24.0	18.3	17.7	2.6	1.1		
1965	2,260.9	31.1	20.8	22.1	22.5	3.1	.3		
1970	3,442.9	36.8	23.2	20.8	15.7	3.1	.3		
1975	10,645.9	50.0	19.3	15.4	12.9	1.8	.2		
1978	17,705.2	51.5	24.2	14.4	7.7	2.1	.2	.1	

Source: *Alberta Facts and Figures*, 1950, and Statistics Canada, *Survey of Production*, 1978. (Catalogue 61-202).
NOTE: The series represents in rough magnitudes the total value of commodities produced minus the value of commodities (raw materials) used in the production process, in order to avoid double-counting. The figures are based on current year prices. In the series ending with a * the remaining percentages obtained, unless appearing, were relatively insignificant.

declining in relative significance ever since, to the point that it now ranks third or fourth (to mineral extraction, construction, and possibly manufacturing), depending on how agriculturally-related manufacturing is classified. Quantitatively, between 1945 and 1950, the value of agricultural production dropped to less than half of total production and, by 1960, oil and gas had overtaken agricultural production.

Another major shift in economic proportions was trumpeted by the massive jump in the value of gas and oil production and the consequent tripling of the value of total production. Between 1970 and 1975, the quadrupling of the international price of oil helped to shift Alberta's terms of trade between oil and other commodities, and left the oil companies and provincial government with windfall gains. It also revealed vividly the importance in Alberta's development of the price structure, which largely has been externally determined—and monopoly power.

The enormous expansion of value in Alberta mineral production has little to do with improvements in physical productivity in extracting oil but rather with power in extracting rents. In this respect, much wealth in Alberta rests on a productive basis far less substantial or enduring than indicated by figures based on 'market price' alone. Nevertheless, changes in Alberta's economic position in Canada have been dramatic: while Alberta's share of total Canadian value added was about 6.3 percent in 1935 and 9.3 percent in 1970, in 1978 the share had jumped to 17.1 percent.[55] Although there has been a small increase (from 3.4 to 4.7 percent) in manufacturing production, the main change was in mineral production. In 1970, Alberta accounted for 33.1 percent of Canadian mineral production; in 1978, over 61 percent of all mineral production came from Alberta.

Capital accumulation in Alberta has reflected the general trend towards concentration and centralization underlying all capitalist development. First, there has been a considerable concentration in the scale of production in industry. In manufacturing, for example, the District of Alberta had about 3.6 employees per establishment in 1890, whereas in 1929 this had risen to 16.6 employees per establishment, and in 1972 to 29.8 employees per establishment. The amount of capital invested per worker has also increased dramatically, as has the value of output per worker. Thus, the average value-added per worker in manufacturing was about $1,049 in 1890, while in 1929 it was about $3,014, and in 1972 about $16,339. In the areas of primary industry and utilities the process of concentration has been even more rapid. Moreover, there is a generally higher level of market concentration than in other regions of Canada (see Table I-3), partly since many product markets, such as perishable food product markets, have tended to be smaller and regional rather than country-wide. This lack of integration usually exists because transportation and storage costs and/or market sharing arrangements have reduced prairie-eastern Canada trade.

Table I-3

Comparative Levels of Market Concentration for Selected Industries in 1965

Industry	Total number of enterprises			Percentage of Factory Shipments accounted for by four largest enterprises		
	Alberta	Ontario	Canada	Alberta	Ontario	Canada
Slaughtering and meat-processing	28	131	365	84.6	53.1	58.1
Bakeries	182	738	2,375	50.0	39.0	32.3
Machine shops	75	391	954	55.3	8.4	8.3
Concrete products and ready-mix concrete manufacturers	65	260	738	56.9	33.6	21.3
Soft drink manufacturers	22	121	410	57.5	51.6	40.9
Signs and display industry	40	185	391	53.4	21.1	21.6
Poultry processors	21	55	137	50.6	34.5	24.2
Petroleum refineries	10	14	25	88.4	85.3	80.0
Commercial printing and publishing	471	1,283	3,050	34.3	19.4	13.2

Source: Canada, Department of Consumer and Corporate Affairs, *Concentration in the Manufacturing Industries of Canada* (Ottawa, 1971), Table A-5.

Second, in agriculture, which has seen rapid gains in labour productivity, the trend towards concentration and centralization has been so pronounced that major concerns have long been voiced about the decline of the 'family farm.' The average area per census farm has climbed from 353 acres in 1921 to 790 in 1977, while the number of farms has dropped from 82,954 to 62,702 during the same period. Similarly, the average total capital value for census farms has risen from $11,674 to $46,680 in real dollars. Land ownership, which requires increasingly major sums of capital, has been growing less rapidly than tenancy: in 1921, of the 29.3 million acres in farms, 81 percent were owned and 19 percent were rented; in 1971, of the 49.5 million acres in farms, 64 percent were owned and 36 percent were rented.[56] As well, there is a growth in corporate farming and the penetration of "agribusiness" into farming, particularly in industrial crops. The result has been to give agriculture an increasingly capitalist character by replacing simple commodity production—the so-called 'independent' farmer—by capitalist commodity production.

Third, centralization and concentration in the area of banking and credit have reached massive proportions. With banking, in particular, the number of banks in Canada fell from a peak number of 51 banks (with 230 branches) in 1874, to a twentieth-century high of 38 (with 1,145 branches) in 1904, to 9 (with 5,051 branches) in 1960. For the Alberta economy, this has been of crucial significance to major investment strategies, especially in secondary productive sectors, and in policies governing credit allocation and relief for less established and smaller-scale businesses, farms, and individuals. Historically, the banks have become tightly tied with major industrial interests, forming a 'financial oligarchy.' Perhaps the first such Canadian example was the Bank of Montreal-CPR grouping.[57] The mutual interests of both elements have actually been facilitated by the extension of monopoly power, which can increase security and profitability for both. Several challenges to the central Canadian financial power have occurred, notably in the establishing of the Provincial Government-owned Treasury Branch system in 1938, and in the rise of credit unions in the late 1930s and 1940s.[58] However, the picture of Alberta's industrial capital accumulation and the degree to which it was subject to the interests of outside finance capital did not change dramatically until the 1970s.

In highlighting these development trends, it needs to be emphasized that Alberta never had an era of competitive capitalism, when 'free competition' was not subject to monopoly forces. Right from its capitalist dawn with the Hudson's Bay Company and Canadian Pacific Railway, big business presided over internal colonization and dominated the "commanding heights" of the Alberta economy. Since the 1880s, Alberta witnessed the arrival and growth of large-scale corporate enterprises in railways, ranching, irrigation, coal mining, banking, and land speculation. Indeed, the early appearance of monopoly capitalism in Alberta actually accelerated the transformation of competitive sectors into their opposite—monopoly—and thus also accelerated the concentration and central-ization of capital.

Even the "combination movement," which was a prelude to monopoly capitalism, began in central Canada in the 1880s but was not isolated there. Price fixing and other "restraints on trade" were common in Alberta, both under local and external impetus. One of the better known commercial cartels grew out of the Western Retail Lumberman's Association (1892). Alberta dealers soon formed their own cartel which had price maintenance arrangements with British Columbia lumber and shingle mills and regulated credit conditions. "Farmers in the West bought lumber on credit and paid ten percent on their notes to lumber firms before the due date, twelve percent after, and gave the dealers lien notes on almost all of their property not tied up already by banks, mortgage companies, or implement dealers."[59] The CPR assisted by allowing combine price lists to be posted in its stations.

Of greater significance was the major "merger movement" in the decade preceding World War I. Between 1908 and 1912, Canada witnessed 58 industrial amalgamations including about 275 firms with a total authorized capital of $490 million. Mergers appeared in many industries, including, for example, iron and steel, woollens, canning, cement, flour milling, asbestos, and utilities. Many of these were the promotions of finance capital based in Montreal, but Alberta was soon affected, notably in cement (Exshaw) and electric power (Calgary). Here the role of Max Aitken (Lord Beaverbrook) and R.B. Bennett in establish-ing Calgary Power Company Ltd. (now Calgary Power Ltd.) illustrated a typical method of outside capitalist penetration in Alberta and the involvement of local interests in the process.

The first electric company in Calgary, the Calgary Electric Lighting Company, Ltd., operated in the later 1880s with D.W. Davis, the first member of parliament from Alberta, as President. An American competitor, the Eau Claire and Bow River Lumber Company (of Eau Claire, Wisconsin), was established in 1886 with the public encouragement of the prominent local figure, James Lougheed. The Eau Claire won the charter to operate the city's light plant and later expanded its generating operation to become the Calgary Water Power Company, Ltd. (1902). In the first decade of the century, the Calgary City Council developed their own public power plant (as did Edmonton and other centres), but with the burgeoning growth of Calgary (from 11,967 in 1906 to 43,704 in 1911) the demand for power soon exceeded the plant's capacity. In response to the City Council's initiative to expand the city's own operation, major central Canadian interests entered the field, organized by Aitkin's Royal Securities Corporation through the Toronto-based Calgary Power and Transmission Company (CPTC). The new company, which later took over the Calgary Water Power Company, was Calgary Power Ltd., and included on its first board Max Aitken, R.B. Bennett, C.B. Smith (former president of CPTC), A.E. Cross, and H.S. Holt (head of the Royal Bank, Dominion Textile, Consolidated Paper, Famous Players Corporation, and others). The new company, which completed the Horseshoe Power Plant in 1911, had a major political success in obtaining a contract from the City of Calgary to supply power over and above that generated by the City's own Victoria Park steam plant. From this position and with the assistance of conservatively-led City Councils, Calgary Power was later able to make the next 'logical' move of completely taking over power production from the City's utility. However, another major goal in building the Horseshoe plant was to supply some of the cement operations controlled by Aitken. Calgary Power was committed to sell power to Western Canada Cement and Coal Company Ltd. at Exshaw and Alberta Portland Cement Company Ltd. at Calgary (both of which became part of the Canada Cement Company Ltd.).

The Canadian born Aitken was the main financial power behind Bennett's efforts in Calgary. By World War I, Aitken had amassed holdings from the Maritimes to Alberta to the Caribbean including the Union Bank of Halifax (later part of the Royal Bank), the Canada Power Company, the Western Canadian Power Company, Canada Cement, the Steel Company of Canada, the Montreal Trust and Deposit Company, Robb Engineering Company, Canada Car and Foundry Company, Demerara Electric Company, Camaquay Electric Company, and the Puerto Rico Railway Company. Bennett's early holdings were small by comparison (although he did eventually amass major wealth). Notably, he had interests in some local industry, grain dealing, and finance: the Rocky Mountain Cement Company Ltd. at Blairmore, the Alberta

Pacific Grain Company, and the Security Trust Company Ltd. of Calgary (whose vice-president was Patrick Burns). As well, his law partnership with James Lougheed represented such clients as the CPR, HBC, Bank of Montreal, Bell Telephones, and Great West Life Assurance. The Lougheed-Bennett law firm became, in effect, an organizing centre for the exploitation of Alberta resources and the takeover of provincial markets and firms.

Consequently, the picture of local prairie capitalists battling 'eastern big business' is one-sided at best, especially with respect to the highest levels of the Alberta business class. Local capitalist interests collaborated extensively with outside capital often to the detriment of Alberta based private and public enterprises. The Bennett-Lougheed law practice, business enterprises, and political activities were simply the outstanding examples of an early vanguard of outside big business penetration in Alberta, particularly Calgary.[60] This type of collaborating capitalist or junior partner has emerged in the wake of all major central Canadian and foreign investment promotions and conquests. Most prominent are those with relations to the leading corporations that have dominated Alberta's development, in order, the HBC, and CPR, and Imperial Oil (with the AGTL/Foothills [now Nova] complex rising distantly on the horizon). For example, the Lougheed family has been heavily involved with these corporate forces. The Lougheed-Bennett practice represented the HBC, CPR, and Royalite Oil, which was owned by Imperial Oil. James Lougheed married Belle Hardisty, the niece of Senator Richard Hardisty, the HBC's Chief Factor in Edmonton, and the niece of Donald Smith (of the CPR). One of James Lougheed's grandsons, E. Peter Lougheed, is today Premier of the Province, and another, Don D. Lougheed, has been Senior Vice-President and a director of Imperial Oil.

The specific character of the business class in Alberta and its relations to central Canadian and foreign capital have been determined largely by the main routes of its own accumulations, especially its original or 'primitive' accumulations. In general, local-regional primitive accumulations took place in the interstices of externally based capital and as local partners and agents for it. These were areas with a relatively low fixed investment (in building, machinery, etc.), mainly: land speculation, wholesale and retail trade, small-scale mining and some gas and oil drilling; stock raising, some butchering and meat packing; and construction and contracting. (Very few major local capital accumulations originated in grain farming.) Most of these sectors were geared to local or regional markets, or were directly dependent on contracts with large central Canadian or foreign corporations.

A notable feature of many early accumulations was their source in speculative and non-productive activities. Cashing in on the rapid appreciation in value of capital assets—"unearned increment"—such as in land plays associated with oil and gas discoveries or municipal development, was revered as a means of 'catching up' to those outsiders whose wealth accumulation had been going on for many years. On the other hand, there were only a few substantial pools of industrial capital accumulated directly by Alberta businessmen. Generally, these were in sectors with sizable local markets and a high degree of 'natural' protection. Some exceptional examples of the latter were A.E. Cross, W.H. Cushing, and Patrick Burns. Burns, in particular, by 1914, had control of a system of three packing plants and over 100 retail shops based on a regional market in Alberta and southern British Columbia.

The growth of industrial capital accumulation in Alberta was impeded by several factors already discussed, such as the transportation, freight rate, and tariff structure, and the control of financing in central Canada. Historically, Alberta's major drive for industry in the decade leading to World War I came at a time when the scale of production and capital requirements for competitive industrial development had risen to such a level as to be difficult if not impossible to obtain for those without established wealth. Thus, the principal accumulations were derived disproportionately from non-industrial spheres in a limited number of activities—trading, jobbing, legal services, promotions, royalties, rents—such that development has been adversely affected. Lack of industrial diversification has increased the economy's vulnerability to externally caused crises, particularly in the agriculture and primary industry sectors. The fostering of parasitic forms of wealth accumualtion, such as rentierism, with its attendent social conservatism and lack of innovation and research, has sapped the growth of productive forces and initiatives. As a result of a long history of junior collaborations and minority joint ventures, Alberta capital still remains in a subordinate position to outside capital and with only a few areas staked out in the system of production. To strengthen its weak position Alberta capital has often made use of the provincial state. However, in this area as well, even the more aggressive provincial governments have avoided measures that would endanger its longstanding relations with outside capital or substantially weaken outside private ownership of productive assets in Alberta.

The growth of capital accumulation and its concentration and centralization have been evident in the changing structure of Alberta society, as shown in Table I-4. The concentration of capital necessarily divorces increasing numbers of the population from the ownership of capital, especially productive assets (land, mines, factories, railways, etc.), and compels them to obtain their livelihood through selling their energies and skills for wages or salaries. This process (the separation of labour from capital) has been exceptionally rapid since World War II and in the decade prior to World War I. During the post-World War II decades, the class structure of Alberta was changing towards that of a mature capitalist economy. By 1971, the number of those receiving (although not necessarily dependent upon) some form of labour income had risen to about 83.4 percent of the 'labour force' as compared to 90.0 percent for Canada as a whole, and 91.1 percent for Ontario.[61] Within Alberta's wage and salary earning group, the factory-industrial component—the "industrial proletariat" (or "working

Table I-4

The Growth of the Wage and Salary Earning Population in Alberta, 1885-1981

| | | 1 | 2 | 3 | | | | | |
| | | Economically engaged population[a] | | Wage and salary earners[b] | | | Known full-time and full-year[c] | | |
Census year	Total population	Total	% of (1)	Total	% of (2)	% of (1)		% of (2)	% of (1)
1981	2,237,724	1,195,175	53.4	1,051,855	88.0	47.0			
1971	1,627,875	692,425	42.5	562,985	81.3	34.6	369,470	53.4	22.7
1961	1,331,944	489,511	36.8	362,794	74.1	27.2	238,963	48.8	17.9
1951	939,501	353,497	37.6	226,970	64.2	24.2	166,422	47.1	17.7
1941[d]	796,169	287,831	36.2	141,838	49.3	17.8	90,482	31.4	11.4
1931	731,605	285,740	39.1	142,421	49.8	19.5			
1921	588,454	215,584	36.6	102,730	47.7	17.5			
1911	374,295	160,811	43.0	75,720	47.1	20.2			
1901[e]	65,876	28,656	43.5	3,531	12.3	5.4			
1891	25,277	14,264	56.4	3,040	21.3	12.0			
1885	15,533	10,278	66.2	1,347	13.1	8.7			

Source: *Census of Canada,* various years, and *Census of the North-West Territories,* 1885. The data for total wage and salary earners in Alberta in 1971 and 1981 was provided directly by Statistics Canada.

a) Engaged in remunerative activity (for wages, salaries, profits, rents, interest) in any branch of the economic system. For census years 1951 to 1981, the "labour force" concept was used. Prior to 1951, the "gainfully occupied" concept was used. Data for years 1911 to 1961 are taken from *Census of Canada,* 1961, Vol. III (Part I), Table 1.

b) Includes those receiving piece-rated as well as hourly-rated wages, tips, and commissions. In 1971 and 1981, the figures for total wage and salary earners exclude the self-employed in incorporated companies.

c) At least 35 hours per week and 40 weeks per year.

d) Excludes those on "active service" (in the military forces).

e) From 1885 to 1901, figures are for the Territorial District of Alberta, a somewhat smaller area than the post-1905 Provincial boundaries; in the former, Medicine Hat and environs were excluded. Given the limitations on currently available data, all these figures must be viewed as rough estimates.

class" in its narrow sense)—had risen to approximately 188,345 or about 32.6 percent of the labour force, of which roughly 123,425 or about 17.9 percent were involved directly as production (or "blue collar") workers.

Corresponding to the rise in the proportion of wage and salary earners has been the decline in the proportion of the self-employed and small business people. The process is most pronounced in the agriculture sector, which has the largest element of "self-employed" (in 1971, the Census included both those with and without hired labour). In 1971, for instance, the total number of self-employed was 75,000, of which 43,175 (or 57.5 percent) were in agriculture. As well, off-farm income of farm families has been increasing as a proportion of total income to the extent that off-farm wages and salaries reached 40.7 percent of total farm income in Alberta in 1973. Most dramatic has been the absolute and relative decline in the number of self-employed and their families in agriculture, to 9.5 percent of the labour force in 1971, from nearly half of the labour force in the 1920s and 1930s. Also notable is the increased proportion of wage earners and unpaid family workers in agriculture, respectively, 23.8 percent and 25.8 percent of the agricultural labour force. Of the self-employed, the largest proportion have been those who do not hire labour or whom certain censes have classified as "own-account." This is the so-called "independent commodity producer" analyzed by C.B. Macpherson as the class basis of the Social Credit movement in Alberta.[62]

The rapid growth—and decline—of the major "petit bourgeoisie" described by Macpherson followed from the process of internal colonization. The "free homesteading"of Dominion Lands policy, which made possible low cost land under private ownership, helped establish large numbers of immigrants and migrants as small proprietors. Yet within one to two generations, the inexorable pressures of capitalist development had more than halved the numbers of these small-holders from their peak of over 90,000 between the late 1920s and early 1940s to fewer than 45,000 in the 1970s—despite an overall rise in Alberta's population.

Another major consequence of the growing concentration and centralization of capital was rapid urbanization. The closing of the era of extensive agricultural settlement by the 1930s, the migrations of the Great Depression, and the war boom in the 1940s saw the end of Alberta's predominantly rural settlement structure. The growth of large-scale enterprises and public institutions, the improvement of roads, transport, and communications, and the centralization of markets have propelled the movement towards larger agglomerations of settlement—and urbanization. Between 1911 and 1941 there was a considerable absolute growth in both urban and rural populations, but the general urban-rural (including rural non-farm) proportions did not change. However, during the 1940s and 1950s, there was a radical shift towards urbanization, which corresponded with the burst of capitalist expansion that followed on World War II. During these years, as during the first years following provincial status in 1905, Alberta had the highest rate of urbanization in Canada.

5. Building the Settler State
Since Alberta moved from territorial to provincial status, officially on 1 September 1905, the government has been dominated by varying alignments of politico-economic forces through four political parties and ten administrations (see Table I-5). The successive governments captured parliamentary power with decisive legislative majorities and maintained their positions for relatively extended periods. However, each party came to an end (1921, 1935 and 1971) following a time of sharpened capitalist crisis, under undistinguished and generally conservative leadership, when mass opinion was seeking more popular if not radical changes.

The dominant but often shifting socio-economic forces in the province have been closely reflected in its governments. The Liberal governments represented

Table I-5

Provincial Administrations and General Elections of Alberta, 1905-1981

Parties	Premiers	General Elections
1) Liberal Party (1905-1921)	Alexander C. Rutherford (2 September 1905 - 26 May 1910) Arthur L. Sifton (26 May 1910 - 30 October 1917) Charles Stewart (30 October 1917 - 13 August 1921)	9 November 1905 22 March 1909 17 April 1913 7 June 1917
2) United Farmers of Alberta (1921-1935)	Herbert Greenfield (13 August 1921 - 23 November 1925) John E. Brownlee (23 November 1925 - 10 July 1934) Richard G. Reid (10 July 1934 - 3 September 1935)	18 July 1921 28 June 1926 19 June 1930
3) Social Credit Party (1935-1971)	William Aberhart (3 September 1935 - 23 May 1943) Ernest C. Manning (23 May 1943 - 12 December 1968) Harry E. Strom (12 December 1968 - 10 September 1971)	22 August 1935 21 March 1940 8 August 1944 17 August 1948 5 August 1952 29 June 1955 18 June 1959 17 June 1963 23 May 1967
4) Progressive Conservative Party (1971 -	E. Peter Lougheed (10 September 1971 -	30 August 1971 26 March 1975 14 March 1979 2 November 1982

Source: *The Canadian Parliamentary Guide* (Ottawa, various years).

a weak but developing Alberta based section of the Canadian business class and had considerable support in its early years from farmers and, to a much lesser extent, from labour. But the business interests with whom the Liberals were allied were less tightly tied to central Canadian capital than the Calgary-centred Tories, and more open to US capital. Following World War I and its aftermath, which led to increased class differentiation and political radicalism, farmers broke with the Liberals and pushed the United Farmers of Alberta into power in 1921. The United Farmers of Alberta (UFA) was mainly a farmer movement with some labour support, especially in its early years; however, its leadership moved into increasingly conservative positions and alignments as economic crisis deepened. The class polarization caused by the Great Depression led to a cleavage in the UFA between a radicalized formation that became part of the

Social Credit movement and a less defined 'socialist'-oriented formation that later became the base of the Cooperative Commonwealth Federation (CCF); both elements sought change away from the inaction and discredited learership of the UFA government.[63] In 1935, the Social Credit Party was swept to power, bringing with it a few years of unparallelled turbulence and vacillation in government direction. In its early, more radical phase, Social Credit was also a mainly petit bourgeois movement; however, with the accession to power of the Manning administration by 1943, the Social Credit government became aligned increasingly with US monopoly capital and shifted strongly to the right, especially during the years of the US-led Cold War. During the 1940s and 1950s, the old, established business groupings in the province, which had been weakened seriously during the Depression, regained some of their initiative and, in the wake of massive oil and gas development, new capitalist groupings were spawned. During the 1960s, stronger pressures emerged from these groups for a more urban, industrial, and "provincialist" orientation, culminating in 1971 with the election of the Conservatives. The Conservatives represented a higher level, more aggressive section of Alberta capital, with some ties to central Canadian capital and more ties to US capital, but chafing to advance their own independent position.

In highlighting some major trends in the evolution of the Alberta state it is useful to begin with a brief analysis of the composition of key legislatures.

(a) *Businessmen in Government.* The first Alberta legislature, elected on 9 November 1905, began the long series of "business" legislatures that have dominated the province's development. Of the total of 25 members, there were at least 12 merchants, 5 lawyers, a manufacturer, a financier, a livery stable proprietor, two doctors, and 3 farmers with interests in stockraising. Most members of the legislature had a diversity of entrepreneurial interests. Although only one MLA considered himself primarily a real estate agent, several were active in land dealings and many had substantial holdings. At least eight members—about one-third of the legislature—had significant interests in selling or producing lumber. Another sector of importance was stockraising and farming. In farming, however, it was a small and exceptional minority of the rural population who were able to break out of heavy indebtedness, expand their farms, and diversify their holdings to the point that they were able to establish for themselves a secure local base for major capital accumulation.

The first legislature was quintessentially colonist. Of the 25 members, 17 were born in Ontario, two were born in Quebec (Anglophone), one in New Brunswick, one in England, one in Ireland, one in Utah, and two in continental Europe. Members were overwhelmingly Anglo-Saxon, and several prided themselves in their "United Empire Loyalist" and upper class family background. However, Alberta's first legislature was also less established and much less economically powerful than its Ontario or Quebec counterparts or the Dominion parliament.

The first cabinet had five members, one of whom was "elevated" to the Senate within a few months of his appointment as Minister Without Portfolio. Alexandar C. Rutherford, the Premier, Provincial Treasurer, and Education Minister, headed the leading Strathcona law firm whose clients included the Alberta Grain Company. Among his personal interests were the Vogel Meat and Packing Company, the Great Western Garment Company, the Star Mining Company, the North-West Mortgage Company, the North-West Gas and Oil Company, and the Bulletin Company. Rutherford invested heavily in property and was solicitor for the Imperial Bank of Canada. The Minister of Public Works, W.H. Cushing, was one of the most important lumber manufacturers in Calgary, and was involved in several other businesses, including the Calgary Natural Gas Company and the Calgary Lime and Cement Company. The Provincial Secretary and Agriculture Minister, W.T. Finlay, was a lumber merchant, with interests in the Medicine Hat Printing and Publishing Company and the Medicine Hat Ranch Company. The Attorney-General, C.W. Cross, was an Edmonton lawyer, with interests in the Edmonton Iron Works, Edmonton Trust Company, and Le Courrier de l'Ouest Publishing Company. Like this first cabinet, the business interests of other early Alberta cabinets tended to be locally or regionally based.

Splits soon emerged as to the pace of development and the position of the provincial government in relations between local-provincial capital and central Canadian (and other outside) capital. On one side was a more independent, 'liberal', locally based grouping that was relatively more aggressive in defence of local-provincial interests and in the direct use of the state to promote its accumulation. These business interests pushed for a faster pace of development that would rapidly expand their own local markets and strengthen their position early on the scene against later arrivals and outside competitors. On the other side was a grouping with interests more closely allied with outside capital who viewed their position within the strategic objectives of Anglo-Canadian imperialism. Those business interests favoured less hurried and less independent development and a stronger alliance with the policies of central Canadian capital and the Dominion government. Thus, the latter grouping acted more as guardians (and benefactors) of ruling Dominion and Imperial interests than as representatives of particular local-regional business interests.

The United Farmers of Alberta, elected in the summer of 1921, appeared as a movement of the "pioneer farmer," but one distinctly white, Anglo-Saxon, and Protestant. While the Liberals were based mainly in the business and professional strata of the growing urban settlements in Alberta, the UFA drew its main support from rural areas among farmers, including their upper strata, and certain professionals. Of the 59 members of the legislature following the election, at least 35 were farmers (of which 31 were UFA, 2 were Independents, and 2 were Liberals). Of the 31 UFA farmers, who constituted not only most of the 39 UFA members but also an absolute majority of the legislature, a majority

(18) were immigrants from Britain and Ireland (9) and from the US (9). Only one immigrant was born elsewhere, in the Ukraine. Of the Canadian born, most came from Ontario; only two appeared to be of French Canadian background. Most UFA members had arrived in Canada and settled in Alberta between 1900 and 1910, but two senior leaders, Premier Greenfield and Agriculture Minister Hoadley, had arrived as early as 1892 and 1889, respectively. The UFA members were generally more established and better off than the average farmer, and several were engaged in other activities, such as livestock breeding and small commercial business. (The most powerful UFA premier, J.E. Brownlee, was a corporate lawyer.) With few exceptions they were strongly Protestant, including a significant group of Irish Protestant background; denominationally, they were overwhelmingly Presbyterian and, to a lesser extent, Methodist. With respect to education, many UFA farm members had secondary and even post-secondary education.

Despite its theories of "group democracy" and its sometimes radical reform rhetoric, the UFA governments were committed in practice to accepting the framework of capitalist private property relations. The UFA movement was by no means homogeneous, especially as many key members were not working farmers but urban professionals. Considerable differentiation occurred in Alberta between wealthier and poorer farmers and, sharply, in relations towards wage earners and the labour movement. Although the UFA was the first Alberta government to have a labour representative in its cabinet, the anti-labour position in the UFA was reflected, for example, in Premier Greenfield's statement that "The allies against the farmer are high freights, labour, machinery and money...."[64] In part, this can be explained by the role of farm labour during these years, and the fact that action on farm labour conditions and organization would have constituted a threat to a significant section of farmers hiring labour, some of whom were in the UFA membership.[65] The rightward drift of the UFA cabinet leadership and the growing politico-economic differentiation in the UFA led to deep cleavages and 'immobilism' over the party's general political direction. These conflicts were exacerbated by the Great Depression. The UFA was pushed aside and replaced by another petit bourgeois movement, although one less social democratic in character—Social Credit.

In the summer general election of 1935, the Social Credit Party demolished the UFA by winning 56 of the 63 seats then in the legislature. With respect to composition, the Social Credit representation had many more middle-level professionals and merchants than did the UFA and, in general, a larger urban component. No fewer than 12 Social Credit members of the legislature were teachers and 5 were clergymen. Several of the former were principals, and many in both groups were involved in other remunerative activities such as selling insurance and farming. As well, there were four lawyers, two engineers and doctors, and one chiropractor, dentist, and druggist. Approximately 10 members were primarily merchant-businessmen, and several others had side interests in commerce. Taken together with the relatively lower representation of farmers in Social Credit than in the UFA, it is significant that such a high proportion of Social Credit representatives were engaged in non-productive and service activities—the highly vulnerable, dependent, and 'squeezed' middle strata of the population. Of the Social Credit members, a little over half were born in Canada. About 20 were born in Ontario, but there was a small group of five who were Alberta born. The foreign born were about evenly divided between Britain and the US, with one each from Denmark and British India. Like the UFA, Social Credit representation was overwhelmingly Protestant although with a stronger fundamentalist strain. The largest single denomination was the United Church[66] followed by the Baptists, Presbyterians, and Mormons.

The first few years of Social Credit government saw the introduction of several "radical" measures which were potential threats to central Canadian banking and finance and which launched the most serious challenge to the Dominion Government and federal state structure that was ever to issue from Alberta. However, after a turbulent period of vacillation and compromise on Social Credit's sharpest anti-monopoly measures, climaxing with the 1937 backbench "insurgency," there was a period of backtracking and the seeking of "respectability" among previously reviled big business interests. With the elevating of Ernest Manning to the premiership following Aberhart's death in 1943, Social Credit took an even sharper turn to the right.[67] It soon became another small "c" conservative party, though one with a stronger "provincialist" as opposed to Anglo-Canadian "imperialist" orientation than the then existing Conservative Party. The political shift corresponded with the influx of US capital during World War II, in oil exploration and development, air transport, the Canol project, and the Alaska Highway. The Social Credit leadership, both as a government and as individuals, became increasingly tied to these interests. Crucial decisions in the late 1940s and early 1950s involving oil and gas export, pipelines, public ownership, leasing and royalties policy, and industrial development policy expanded the power of US monopoly capital in Alberta and generally subordinated economic development in the province to its aggressive leadership. These major changes in the direction of development in Alberta met some resistance inside the legislature from the Liberals and CCF, as well as among sections of the general population. But Manning Social Credit relied effectively on growing prosperity and the Cold War ideology of anti-communism and "national security" inspired by American military-industrial interests, coupled with its own now-respectable populist rhetoric, as a cover for the lurch towards continental integration with the United States.[68]

The success of the Conservatives in the general election of August 1971 marked the rise to power of a different group of business interests with substantial roots in the traditional Anglo-Canadian ruling class. However, they had developed some independence as a result of their own history of capital accumulation in Alberta, especially the wealth amassed in the wake of the post-World

War II natural resource boom and close relations with US capital. In composition, the Conservative representation was wealthier, more urban, and better educated than the previous Social Credit representation. Of the 45 Conservative members in the 75-seat legislature, the overwhelmingly largest group were businessmen and lawyers. Many of the lawyers had substantial corporate involvements, and constituted well over half the Tory representation. Peter Lougheed, their leader, was himself a corporate lawyer and graduate of Harvard Business School, who between 1956 and 1962 rose to become General Counsel, Vice-President, and Director of the Mannix (now Loram) Corporation, a major Calgary based construction and engineering firm. Other professionals, most with consulting or business interests, were the next largest group. Fewer than 10 members were primarily farmers or had significant interests in farming. With respect to birthplace, a high proportion—about two-thirds—were born in Alberta (typically in the inter-war years), and of the remainder all but two were born in other parts of Canada. Significantly, Saskatchewan rather than Ontario was in first place among those members born in the other Canadian provinces. Although general sociological evidence tends to indicate that religious affiliation plays a less significant role in politico-economic stratification than in earlier decades of the century, it is worth noting that this legislature was strongly Protestant in character. The largest denominations reported were the United Church, followed by the Anglican Church. However, the presence of seven Catholics marked a contrast with previous Conservative representations.

There were important differences in the Conservative government between the cabinet and "backbenchers." The cabinet members, particularly its 'inner circle,' were more urban and better educated and had more substantial business interests than the politically subordinate backbenchers. Virtually every cabinet member was a professional and/or businessman; however, unlike previous Alberta administrations, the cabinet had a significant number of members who had worked in senior positions in big business. The proportion of the cabinet born in the prairies was only slightly higher than that among backbenchers (but interestingly, in terms of religion, the cabinet was over one third Anglican, with a somewhat smaller United Church affiliation and a disproportionately low number of Catholics—typical of the 'old' Conservative Party).

(b) *Government in Business.* As the socio-economic profiles of the provincial governments since 1905 have undergone considerable changes without losing their essentially capitalist character, so also has government policy in terms of state development and intervention.

The general strategy of the Liberal government—and an underlying theme of succeeding governments—was to use the provincial state to promote and organize capitalist development in Alberta and thereby raise up a substantial business class in the province. The Liberals emphasized the growth of settlement and primary production and the massive extension of infrastructure. Under three successive Liberal administrations, provincial public expenditures on infrastructure mushroomed, most visibly in the areas of telephones, railways, highways, and irrigation.

The most important direct intervention was in the establishing of the first provincial public telephone utility, Alberta Government Telephones. As a result of high private rates and the unwillingness of the private utilities to extend unprofitable lines into remote and sparsely populated areas, the province authorized municipalities to establish their own telephone systems, built its own trunk lines, and purchased the Bell Telephone Company by 1908. In 1907, during what was then a wave of business and general public support for public utilities, the Minister of Public Works, W.H. Cushing, attacked Bell and argued that "the only way to regulate such a monopoly is to enter into competition and ensure low rates and proper service."[69]

The more typical form of state intervention, however, was through the process of public guarantees of the debt of private enterprises, notably in railways. In the first legislative session the provincial government began chartering railway promotions and, in 1907, gave itself the authority to acquire any railway under provincial jurisdiction. But in 1909 the Liberals proposed their major railway policy: provincial government guarantees of the private debt on branch lines of the Canadian Northern and Grand Trunk Pacific, and on the Alberta and Great Waterway (AGW) railway—but not on CPR lines. This policy created the provincial government's first major indirect liability (nearly $20 million) and gave rise to the most serious legislative confrontation in Alberta's first decade—the AGW controversy. Planned to connect Edmonton to the Mackenzie River system near Fort McMurray, the AGW was originally a promotion of two Kansas City bankers who claimed to have a vision of a railway line from the Gulf of Mexico to the Arctic. After the 1909 election, the CPR-oriented Conservatives, led an attack on the Liberals, allegedly to expose certain mismanagement and naive financial dealings that involved Morgan banking interests of New York. Premier A.C. Rutherford, who also acted as Minister of Railways, resigned in 1910 and was replaced by the Sifton administration.[70]

Despite some continued Conservative resistance, railway development, especially for northern Alberta, went ahead. Sifton began a new series of major guarantees in 1912, this time including the Edmonton, Dunvegan and British Columbia Railway. The 286-mile (460 km) AGW began construction in 1909 and was completed in 1922, although only after the province took over the company in 1920. The larger 423-mile (681 km) Edmonton, Dunvegan and British Columbia (1912-21) was also taken over by the province in 1920, then leased out to the CPR.

By 1921, total provincial financial obligations had climbed to about $59 million in gross direct debt and $30.4 million in indirect liabilities (guarantees). Added to this were the losing operation of the province's major telephone utility and a series of major current budget deficits between 1914 and 1921 (with the exception of 1919 and 1920). At the same time, Alberta had comparatively low taxes, largely as a result of farmer pressure against high property taxes and the unwillingness of the Liberals to shift the incidence of taxation towards corporate interests. A 1937 report of the Bank of Canada concluded:

To summarize, we find that the policies pursued in the ambitious and extravagant 1905-1922 period resulted in the accumulation of a heavy dead weight debt, and that no adequate effort was made to put the government and various government enterprises on a self-supporting basis, in spite of favourable opportunity presented by the general prosperity. Alberta consequently entered the following period [1922-30] under a handicap which was certain to create problems for the future, unless a determined effort was made to reduce debt.[71]

The general development strategy of the UFA government was more restrained if not 'conservative' than that of the Liberals, in the sense that the state was generally not as active in initiating programmes or expanding owner-ship in the economy. (However, since the UFA exhibited greater reluctance to use public finances as a means of expanding infrastructural development to the advantage of certain major capitalist interests, the UFA should not be considered as simply another small "c" conservative party.) The change in strategy was evident in the first budget speech of the Premier and Provincial Treasurer, Herbert Greenfield, in 1922: "Alberta now enters upon a new phase in its history in that it may be said that we have reached the stage where we must mark time in the trend of over-expansion that has overtaken by a considerable margin the extreme limit of our sources of revenue." A series of cutbacks, including in educational and social areas, was initiated. All the major capital projects, such as railways, telephones, and highways, were continued on from the Liberal governments, but expanded less rapidly. For example, total highway mileage grew only from 59,400 miles (95 600 km) in 1922 to 62,847 miles (101 120 km) in 1935, of which about 95 percent were local and farm highways. The number of telephones in use rose from 66,581 in 1922 to a peak in 1929 of 80,273, then declined during the Great Depression to 61,179. Moreover, provincial govern-ment ownership actually declined under the UFA, when in the late 1920s it sold off the Lacombe and Northwestern Railway to the CPR and transferred the remaining government railways to the Northern Alberta Railway Company, a company jointly owned and operated by the CPR and Canadian National Railways.

Probably the single most consequential event under the UFA was the settlement of the "Natural Resources question" and the transfer of Dominion Lands to the Province on 1 October 1930. When Alberta entered Confederation in 1905, the federal government had been adamant that federal ownership of natural resources was necessary to carry through the "successful settlement policy upon which the greatness and increase in the financial strength and resources of Canada depend." As stated by Clifford Sifton, federal Minister of the Interior, the federal fear of provincial ownership was that the prairie provinces would impede immigration and settlement: "instead of administering these lands for the purpose of settlement they would administer them for the purpose of revenue."[72] During the protracted federal-provincial negotiations of the 1920s the main issue, in fact, was settling compensation for forgone provincial revenues.[73] Besides providing for the transfer of the remaining Dominion Lands, the final compromise agreement, signed on 14 December 1929, increased the current annual subsidy in lieu of resources to a minimum of $562,000 in perpetuity. Also, because Alberta had substantial mineral and other revenue-producing resources, it was agreed to establish a commission to decide what supplementary compensation should be paid to put the province "in a position of equality with the other provinces" as from 1905.[74] The federal government was to retain Indian lands and national parks.[75]

Underlying the federal government's agreeing to provincial ownership was the fact that the bulk of prairie agricultural colonization centred on free homestead policy was now over—by 1928, only about 18 percent of the surveyed areas of Alberta remained "undisposed of."[76] In the difficult years of 1920 to 1925 the number of Alberta homestead entries not only declined but was exceeded by cancellations. However, with the improved economic conditions of the later 1920s, there was a limited resurgence in entries which reached a final peak in 1929. Most of this last wave of homesteading was directed northward, including into the Peace River country. The expansion of white settlement threatened to dispossess once again many Métis people who had become concentrated in north-central Alberta in the years following the Red River and North-West uprisings; it also compelled a renewal of the Métis people's national democratic struggle.[77] Unlike Treaty Indians, the Métis did not have even the limited protection of treaty reserves and were viewed as "squatters" on Crown Land, so Métis struggles centred on their rights to their land (and livelihood), which were rendered even more precarious by the transfer of its Dominion lands on which they lived to the province.

The overriding financial problem faced by the UFA government was its large debt load, yet few provincial measures were taken to change the province's relationship with outside banking and financial interests. Despite repeated calls from the UFA membership for government-initiated farm debt moratoria, the formation of a provincial bank, "the nationalization of our banking and credit systems," and even outright discussion of defaulting, the government appeared more concerned that "bond houses and those who deal in our securities are beginning to ask some very awkward questions."[73] As well, no major changes in taxation took place (but for the introduction of a gasoline tax in 1922), again leaving Alberta as one of the lowest taxed provinces in Canada. Adding to the problem, Dominion grants, which had declined from 50 to 20 percent of total provincial revenue between 1905 and 1921, fell to 16 percent in 1929-30. By 1929, the cost of debt charges as a proportion of total provincial revenue had risen from 22 percent in 1921 to 32 percent. In 1932, debt payments reached a staggering 48 percent of provincial revenue. Thus, by 1935, the UFA policies compounded by the Great Depression crisis had made the province increasingly subordinate to and dependent upon outside capital, particularly bank and finance capital.

The succeeding Social Credit government took some potentially stronger measures against "moneyed interests" in its early, more radical, phase. According to the *Financial Post*, with the Social Credit victory the "worst pre-election fears of Alberta bondholders were realized." Upon taking office the new government suspended payment on Alberta government savings certificates, which "caused panic prices for Alberta bonds."[79] In 1936, it defaulted on over $3 million on bond payments, unilaterally cut the interest rate on its own provincial bonds by half, and passed the Debt Adjustment Act and Settlement of Land Debts Act. All these actions were designed to ease the immediate financial crisis facing the government and private debtholders. The Social Credit Measures Act and the Alberta Social Credit Act were also passed in 1936, and $236,000 in government scrip, called "Prosperity Certificates" (or "funny money") was issued. In 1937, at the height of the radical backbench "insurgency," the Alberta Social Credit Act was passed, providing for the issuance and distribution of "Alberta Credit" to counteract "the unused capacity of industries and people of Alberta to produce wanted goods and services." In 1938, the Social Credit cabinet authorized the formation of the Treasury Branches system, a form of provincial bank.

These and other 'radical' Social Credit measures had little direct or major economic effect. Most were only weakly pursued by the Social Credit government which was dominated by the conservative wing of the Social Credit movement, and were successfully blocked by financial interests and the Dominion Liberal government of W.L. Mackenzie King.[80] Fully eleven Social Credit statutes were disallowed by the federal government. Strong opposition came also from powerful groups of Alberta businessmen such as those in the rightist "People's League" and in the Edmonton Chamber of Commerce and Calgary Board of Trade. Furthermore, given that the Social Credit government was cut off from needed credit and investment by hostile financial interests and given its general belief in the principle of corporate private property (which precluded nationalization or other major redistributive measures), Social Credit radicalism was soon stymied. Social Credit measures became simply typical conservative measures. By means of significant increases in taxation and continued austerity, the provincial government managed to obtain a slight current budget surplus in 1937 and a much larger surplus in 1938, thus ending a string of deficits going back to 1931.[81] Thereafter, the Social Credit (and, until recently, the Conservative) governments never faced another deficit budget, largely as a result of generally improved economic conditions and, later, the prolonged natural resource boom. The improvement of conditions permitted debt repayment to proceed "normally." Gross funded debt reached its peak in 1939 and

1940 at about $156.1 million, then declined almost continuously after World War II until its low point of only $11 million in 1968.[82]

With the decisive end of its radical phase by the early 1940s, the Social Credit leadership embarked on a programme of development which, with respect to its relationship with big business, was the most conservative Alberta had ever witnessed. In the crucial oil and gas sector, the provincial government subordinated itself to the private initiative of the major petroleum corporations, led by Imperial Oil, and was content to collect low rents on provincial natural resources, mainly through royalties and mineral lease sales.[83] During the late 1940s and early 1950s, policies gearing oil and gas production, export, and pipeline construction to a continentalist market were set in place with the collaboration of the oil and gas corporations, the provincial Social Credit government, and the federal Liberal government. Key agreements on oil and gas export had the effect of reducing opportunities to advance secondary industry in the province—by "exporting forward linkages." Provincial initiatives were of a limited regulatory nature and centred on the Petroleum and Natural Gas Conservation Board (1938), which was reorganized as the Oil and Gas Conservation Board in 1942. Indeed, the Manning Social Credit governments went out of their way to avoid public ownership, a stance vividly demonstrated in the formation of Alberta Gas Trunk Line Ltd. (AGTL). In establishing AGTL (1954), the Social Credit government actually created a major state-enforced private monopoly on gas transmission in Alberta, then bestowed control upon a small group of corporate interests who have now become, in the form of "Nova, an Alberta Corporation," the single largest Alberta-based corporation. Stepping into the tradition of the Hudson's Bay Company and Imperial Oil, AGTL found that monopoly is an effective path to capitalist supremacy, though all the while advocating "free enterprise."

While Social Credit was prepared to turn over this and other highly profitable monopolies and benefits to private corporate interests, and to leave the development of secondary industry to the latter's prerogative, the government did not resist extending public ownership in some highly unprofitable infrastructural developments to facilitate export-oriented production of natural resources. One notable example was the Smoky River coal project, a promotion of McIntyre Mines Ltd. In the late 1960s, the provincial government committed about $150 million for the construction of the Alberta Resources Railway (about $139 million) and the Grand Cache townsite so that McIntyre could export coal to Japan. McIntyre's commitment was less than $50 million and the province's royalty levels insufficient to meet even interest charges.[84] The badly constructed Alberta Resources Railway was the only major railway project of Social Credit. During Social Credit governments, total railway trackage had actually declined overall since 1935, as compared to its growth by 3,700 miles (5950 km) under the Liberals (1905-21) and by 1,000 miles (1600 km) under the UFA (1921-35). However, in highways, telephones, and municipal development, notably for new or reactivated 'resource towns',[85] major public investments expanded rapidly beginning in the late 1950s. This was handled mainly through provincial guarantees, especially of municipal debt, which rose to nearly $1.4 billion by 1971. Even gross direct debt rose from a low of about $11 million in 1968 to $105 million in 1971.

The Conservative government under Premier Lougheed, elected in the summer of 1971, took a much more aggressive position with regard to state intervention than did Social Credit. In particular, the Conservatives have tried to use the state most decisively to force industrialization, which is part of the government's general development strategy:

Since entering public life over nine years ago, my theme has been that this province's economy is too *vulnerable*, it is too dependent upon the sale of depleting resources, particularly oil and natural gas for its continued prosperity. We have perhaps another decade left to diversify our economy to become less dependent.... To me, it's obvious that an economy such as ours in Alberta with no national political clout relying upon the sale of unprocessed resources for its next generation's prosperity is folly in the extreme.[86]

The means employed by the Lougheed government have generally included the traditional methods such as tax and royalty concessions and the expansion of roads and telephones. However, the direct takeover of Pacific Western Airlines (PWA) in August 1974, in order to defend and consolidate Alberta's position as the "Gateway Province to the North," went well beyond Social Credit practice. So also did a more typical Conservative form of intervention— the "joint venture." In 1973, as a means of assisting the Syncrude consortium project in the Athabasca Tar Sands, the government formed the Alberta Energy Resources Corporation, to be half-owned by the province. But the Premier made a point of emphasizing that "It is our intention as government policy to have the minority of the directors appointed by the provincial government and the majority by the shareholders at large and to have as government appointed directors, businessmen and not public servants."[87] This Tory enterprise contrasted sharply with the Social Credit government's only comparable venture, the weaker and unsuccessful Alberta Investment Fund (1966), basically a loan fund, which did not take on any major equity ownership, including in the first major Athabasca tar sands project, the US-owned Great Canadian Oil Sands.[88]

In 1973, a profound shift took place in the international terms of trade for oil. Spurred by the Arab-Israeli War of October 1973, the OPEC countries succeeded in quadrupling the world price of oil within three months. (The price was doubled again in 1979-80.) The Alberta government together with the oil "majors" took advantage of the OPEC action to press for world-level prices for Alberta oil and gas. After several provincial-federal confrontations, the Trudeau government (which had controlled oil prices since September 1973), agreed to raise prices in stages to the world level. Alberta's provincial coffers were deluged with windfall oil revenues to the point that the Conservatives were faced with a major question: how to deploy the vast accumulation without significantly expanding public ownership, which would antagonize their corporate allies, and yet not openly giving away funds to corporate interests, which would be unacceptable to most citizens, or allocating funds to social programmes, which would be unacceptable to most corporate interests.[89] In 1976, the Conservatives formally established the Alberta Heritage Savings Trust Fund, which began with $1.5 billion and was planned to receive 30 percent of all future non-renewable resource revenue. As instituted, 65 percent of the funds were to be invested in projects that would yield a "reasonable" rate of return while helping to industrialize and diversify the Alberta economy. By 1979, the "Heritage Fund" had accumulated well over $4 billion and, by 1983, over $13 billion.

With major capital accumulation in the Heritage Trust Fund, the provincial government shifted decisively from a debtor to a creditor position. Previous surpluses were largely ploughed back into the operating or capital budgets of government programmes, or lent to municipalities or crown corporations as internal financing.[90] However,the use of "Heritage Funds" has gone well beyond this, to the extent that the provincial government surplus is being lent primarily to private (including foreign) corporations. For instance, in 1977, over $2 billion was in short-term securities, and nearly $101 million was in Gulf debentures (at 8 1/8 percent) and Canada-Cities Services debentures (at 8 3/8 percent). To a much lesser extent, loans are being made to outside provincial governments and crown corporations. For instance, in 1977 the Conservative government made a $50 million loan (at 10 percent) to Newfoundland. By treating its surpluses in this way, the government has become increasingly integrated into major capital markets as a part of the financial oligarchy. Furthermore, in its reaping of economic surplus—interest and dividend payments and capital gains—from both private corporations and individuals, and from other sections of the Alberta and Canadian state, the Alberta state has committed itself to the path of "state rentierism." Coupled with the provincial government's role in such large-scale operations as the Alberta Energy Company and PWA, and the multiplicity and intimacy of personal relations between the provincial cabinet and big business, the economy in Albera has become a paradigm of modern state-monopoly capitalism.

6. The Rise of US Capital in Alberta

Another important trend in the Alberta economy has been the remarkably rapid rise of US capital in the provincial economy. As a result of the pattern of natural resource development, particularly oil and gas, American and other foreign capital has taken commanding positions in many key areas of the economy. By the end of the Social Credit era in 1971, Alberta had the highest level of foreign (mainly US) ownership and control in Canada—55.8 percent (48.2 percent) of corporate taxable income was controlled by foreign (US) corporations. In 1976, after four years of Conservative government rule, 67.1

percent (58.5 percent) was controlled abroad, again the highest level in Canada, which averaged 49.4 percent (42.4 percent). Indeed, by 1976, foreign (US) ownership had reached 86.2 percent (76.0 percent) in mining and 80.6 percent (70.7 percent) in manufacturing.[91] In the late 1970s, largely as a result of take-overs of some medium-sized foreign firms and accelerated internal growth by Canadian government and private corporations in the petroleum industry, the proportion of foreign ownership in Alberta began to decline from the peak levels of 1974 to 1976. However, Alberta still had by far the highest proportion of foreign ownership in Canada and the absolute value of foreign capital was continuing to rise. In fact, during the later 1970s roughly 30 percent of all foreign (and US) corporate taxable income in Canada was located in Alberta.

This shift in the control of the Alberta economy is exemplified by the rise of Imperial Oil to its position as the most powerful corporation in Alberta, super-seding the CPR and, before it, the HBC. Imperial Oil was originally a Canadian firm formed around 1880 in south-western Ontario. In 1898, Imperial was taken over by Rockefeller's Standard Oil trust. By World War I, Imperial was actively exploring in Alberta. The 1914 discovery in Turner Valley by Calgary Petroleum Products (1912), a Calgary based company whose directors included William Heron, A.W. Dingman, R.B. Bennett, and James Lougheed, stimulated further interest. In 1921, a change took place which altered fundamentally the control of development in Alberta. The directors of the independent Calgary Petroleum Products, following a suspicious fire in October 1920 that destroyed the Com-pany's refinery, sold out a controlling interest to Imperial Oil, and the corpora-tion was reorganized as the Royalite Oil Company. Moreover, in 1920 Dominion Lands regulations were changed to permit foreign interests licenced or registered in Canada to prospect for oil and, in 1921, while James Lougheed was the federal Minister of the Interior, concessions were made to promote Imperial's activity in Alberta, on the urging of Imperial itself.[92] A major strike was made in 1924 ("Royalite No. 4") and, by 1929, through the continued technique of organizing several small companies with independents as minority owners, Imperial controlled three-fourths of the Turner Valley field.[93] The Turner Valley field had surpassed production in the older Canadian fields around Petrolia, Ontario, by 1925. In 1935, Turner Valley produced nearly 90 percent of Canadian output, although Canadian production in total provided for only about 5 percent of Canadian consumption.[94]

In 1928, the *Financial Post* reported that the four "really big" companies operating in Alberta were Imperial Oil, Canadian Western (acquired by Inter-national Utilities in 1925), the Alberta Fuel and Gas Company, and the Hudson's Bay-Marland Oil Company—all US majority-owned and controlled.[95] With the World War II activities of the oil majors, particularly in exploration and the Canol Project, followed by Imperial's 1947 Leduc find, the full significance of the developing trend made its impact on the Alberta economy. Major multi-national corporations engaged in a massive scramble for control of Alberta's resources, a process that has continued with almost no letup, and implanted a

Oil Pipelines and Resource/Resort Centres in Alberta

Rainbow Lake

ATHABASKA
OIL SANDS

Fort
McMurray

PEACE RIVER
DEPOSITS

Grande
Prairie

Swan Hills
Fox Creek

COLD LAKE
DEPOSITS

Whitecourt
Redwater

Grande Cache

St. Albert   EDMONTON

Hinton   Devon   Lloydminster
        Robb
Jasper   Camrose
        Drayton
        Valley
        Wetaskiwin

Red Deer

Drumheller

Banff

Canmore   CALGARY

● City

■ Metropolitan Area

◈ Resource/Resort Centre

— — — Major Oil Pipeline

░ Oil Sands or Heavy Oil Deposit

Medicine Hat

Coleman
Blairmore   Lethbridge
Bellevue

Figure I-2

series of producing operations such as Redwater (1948), Pembina (1953), Swan Hills (1954), Rainbow (1965), and West Pembina (1977).

In the late 1940s and early 1950s, there was a crucial period of pipeline promotion and development which gave rise to major political struggles over continentalism, culminating in the infamous "Pipeline Debate" of 1956.[96] During these years the basis of Alberta's pipeline infrastructure was laid. Imperial Oil organized the Interprovincial Pipeline Company (1949) for eastern continental markets and the Trans Mountain Oil Pipe Line Company (1951) for the Pacific Northwest. Natural gas transmission lines followed soon after, notably the Canadian-Montana Gas line south to Montana, the Westcoast Transmission Company to the Pacific Northwest, and the Trans-Canada Pipe Lines Company for eastern continental markets.[97] All these pipeline projects were executed in the perspective of a continental—mainly US—market and were majority-financed and owned by US capital. Despite opposition, Manning Social Credit was able to drive in the thin edge of the continentalist wedge against anti-export forces by using the intense Cold War atmosphere and the 'hot' war in Korea (1950-53). In March, 1951, the provincial cabinet authorized Alberta's first natural gas export. Premier Manning announced that the export, according to the *Calgary Herald*, was "purely for defense purposes to serve the needs of the vital Anaconda copper mining company operation in Montana."[98]

The massive influx of foreign, especially US, capital and the growing continentalization of the economy spawned a group of Alberta based capitalists in 'independent' oil and gas companies, natural resource-related service and consulting operations, construction, and land dealing and development. In particular, the government-initiated monopoly, AGTL, developed as a key centre for some Alberta based capital, although it was by no means fully controlled by Alberta capital. By the 1970s, AGTL had grown into one of the largest gas pipeline companies in Canada (with about 5,400 miles or 8700 km of pipeline). When the Conservatives came to power, the number of provincial government appointees on the Board of AGTL was increased from two to four to strengthen the position of Alberta capital, and AGTL was encouraged to diversify its operations. As the leading element of Foothills Pipe Lines Ltd., AGTL's most publicized success has been to win federal government approval to build and operate the first major northern gas pipeline in North America. However, the Foothills victory over the rival Arctic Gas Pipeline Ltd., a powerful continentalist consortium[99] from which AGTL broke away in 1974, has still to be realized.

The AGTL/Nova monopoly has also become heavily involved in efforts to "diversify" the provincial economy—and itself—such as in the development of a $350 million gas ethylene plant near Red Deer through its subsidiary Alberta Gas Ethylene Company Ltd. This is one of a series of "world-scale" petrochemical complexes geared to a continental market that are now under development. The growth of a major petrochemical industry in the later 1970s is dwarfing the limited petrochemical development under Social Credit, and marks an important

Alberta in North America - Pipelines

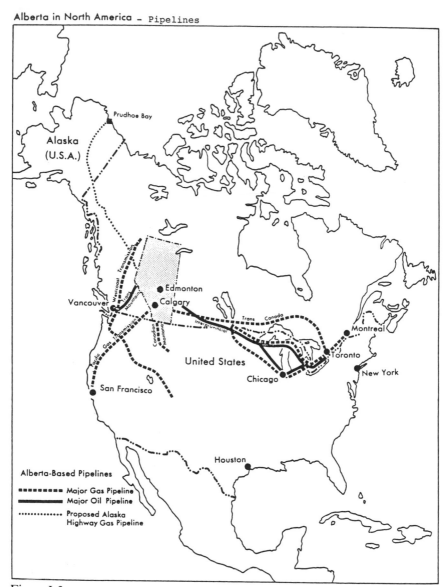

Figure I-3

new development in the Alberta economy. However, since the Conservatives' "diversification" programme is substantially dependent upon oil and gas production, their programme may actually be an "intensification of dependency."

Figures such as Robert Blair, president of AGTL/Nova since 1966 and the *Financial Post*'s "Businessman of the Year" in 1977, exemplify a prominent type of Alberta based capitalist.[100] Blair, who has also been a director of the Bank of Montreal, Dofasco, and Canron, is widely known as a 'nationalist,' presumably a Canadian nationalist. However, Blair and other 'nationalists' in the higher strata of the business class in Alberta have tended (like the continentalists) to have accumulated a significant part of their capital by promoting continental integration and they continue to support foreign investment and collaboration in joint ventures. They have found that facilitating continental markets and foreign access to Canadian resources, such as through the Canadian-US "gas swaps" and "pre-building" that are a vital part of the Foothills pipeline project, is highly profitable and, perhaps, their leg up on outside rivals.[101] This is an emerging English Canadian 'bourgeois nationalism' different from that of the early National Policy period, which was often allied with British imperialism, and also different from traditional labour calls for economic independence and sovereignty. Although the Nova-Foothills grouping has successfully mounted a challenge to the dominance of US capital in certain areas, it is unlikely that this or any other section of Alberta capital could supersede Imperial Oil and the other foreign majors without the support of strong, 'nationalistic' state policies, as long as private capital accumulation and continentalist collaboration dominates development.

Paralleling the rise of AGTL/Nova has been the rise of Dome Petroleum, also started in the 1950s and based in Calgary. Dome and Nova have become the two largest private Canadian oil and gas conglomerates.[102] Headed by Jack Gallagher, Dome has been especially aggressive in promoting development in the Beaufort Sea—"the high North." In its expansion Dome has been strongly supported by the federal government, for instance, in the "super-depletion" allowances on wells costing over $5 million bestowed in the 1977 federal budget[103] and in joint-venture support from Petro-Canada for the Arctic LNG (Liquified Natural Gas) Project. In 1981, under the stimulus of federal National Energy Programme incentives, Dome took over US-controlled Hudson Bay Oil and Gas.[104]

One of the most important signs of a shift in economic power in Canada came in 1978, when Dome took over the Toronto-based TransCanada Pipelines, then controlled by the CPR. Since TransCanada is collaborating as half-owner with Nova in developing an eastern natural gas pipeline from Montreal to Quebec and to the Maritimes (the Q and M Pipelines project), Calgary-based capital now has a commanding monopoly on gas transmission in Canada. Moreover, Petro-Canada, which also participated briefly with Nova in the Q and M project, has taken control of Westcoast Transmission, which means that

Canadian capital has effectively recaptured control of gas transmission in Canada from US capital.

Together with Nova and Dome, the federal Crown (state) corporation, Petro-Canada, forms the third member of what can be considered the leading "three sisters" of the Canadian-controlled section of the oil and gas industry in Canada. Established in 1975 with the goal of becoming Canada's "national oil company," Petro-Canada has risen to the position of being the largest Canadian oil and gas corporation and the fifth largest of all oil and gas corporations in Canada (behind Imperial, Shell, Gulf, and Texaco), mainly by acquiring existing operations. Petro-Canada's presence in Alberta began to be felt with the acquisition of US-owned Atlantic Richfield Canada Ltd. in 1976 and, more visibly, of US-owned Pacific Petroleums Ltd. in 1979. In 1981, under the added impetus of the National Energy Program, Petro-Canada took over the Belgian-controlled Petrofina Canada Ltd., paying $1.46 billion of public funds, an amount 37 percent over the trading value of Petrofina shares.[105]

Petro-Canada has also become involved in non-conventional (tar sands) oil development in Alberta. However, its main focus is on long-term development in the high North and offshore areas of Canada, not in Alberta, where conventional production is in decline due to depletion of this finite natural resource. Petro-Canada's involvement in high risk joint ventures like PanArctic Oils Ltd. and the Arctic LNG Project entail collaboration and support for central Canadian and foreign firms, as well as Alberta based firms like Dome.[106] The shift in the leading areas of development reflects not only geological and technological realities, but also the political concerns of eastern Canadian interests to command a larger share of future oil and gas development and to counteract Alberta's near monopoly on oil and gas production in Canada. (By the early 1960s, Alberta supplied 70 percent of Canadian output and the trend rose to 90 percent by the 1970s.) Despite Alberta's continuing importance in oil and gas supply, the main locus in the struggles for future sources of supply, in which Alberta and other Canadian interests are asserting stronger positions (relative to US and other foreign interests), is shifting northward and into coastal areas.

The rise of Nova, Dome, and other Alberta forces in the oil and gas industry has lessened but by no means ended the dominance of US capital, including in non-conventional "mega-projects" like Imperial Oil's projected Cold Lake heavy oil project or Shell's projected Allsands tar sands project. A more serious challenge to US capital came in the federal Liberal government's National Energy Program (NEP), which was announced in the October 1980 federal budget. On the surface, at least, there was little disagreement with the NEP goal of energy self-sufficiency by 1990—"Canadian energy independence"—which in itself was a significant change from the aggressive continentalism of the 1940s and 1950s. But a major part of the NEP involved "Canadianization"—at least 50 percent Canadian ownership by 1990—and this included an expanded role for Petro-Canada. This the Lougheed government opposed, especially the increased public ownership,[107] claiming the NEP was more interested in 'federalization' than Canadianization. There also occurred a major oil industry campaign, led by the multinationals but also involving most Alberta interests and direct US government pressure, to block the Canadianization and public ownership elements of the NEP. However, the Lougheed government's main objections to NEP were its pricing regime, which was said to underprice Alberta's resources, and the division of rents, which substantially increased the federal government share at the expense of the corporate and provincial government shares.[108]

A major confrontation erupted between the Lougheed government and the Liberal federal government. Lougheed's strategy had four parts: cutting back on Alberta oil output, stalling approvals on two major oil sands projects, launching a legal attack on the federal natural gas export tax, and mobilizing public opinion to the provincial government's position.[109] In retaliation against the province's staged oil cutbacks, which reached about 15 percent of Alberta production, the federal government imposed an oil surcharge to cover the higher cost of the additional imported oil. In September 1981, a five-year settlement was reached in which the federal government eased its position on certain provincial demands, for instance, the gas export tax was reduced to zero and higher oil and gas prices were agreed to, but retained its substantially increased rent share.

The federal NEP strategy tried consciously to split the Alberta oil and gas industry, to win over by lucrative incentives—tax bribes—the Canadian section of the industry from the US section. But the Canadian section was largely unwilling (at least initially) to "come on side;" most joined in with the foreign majors in denouncing the NEP.[110] Given the dominance of foreign oil interests in Alberta, it is not surprising that the continentalist tendency has predominated within Alberta, including in the Lougheed government, though Lougheed was caught increasingly in the tension as differentiation in the ranks of Alberta capital proceeded. Nor is it surprising that some Alberta based corporations with interests and ambitions going far beyond the boundaries of Alberta, like Dome and Nova, did take a more realistic approach to collaboration with central Canadian capital and the Canadian state.[111]

Similarly, central Canadian capital was prepared to compromise—to 'make a deal' with Alberta capital—and accept higher fuel prices.[112] Central Canadian interests did not include cheap energy alone. Heavy industry in central Canada, particularly steel, supported higher prices for Alberta oil at least partly on the assumption that higher prices would stimulate energy 'megaprojects' and thus create a market for their steel and related manufactures.

Although the federal-provincial energy truce was signed in September 1981,[113] the underlying economic situation was not stable. By 1982 it was evident that a general depression was taking hold and spreading to Alberta. The laws of the capitalist market system were soon undermining the NEP as well as the

Keynesian dream of a smoothly progressing 'regulated capitalism.' World oil prices were generally predicted to rise, but they actually began a large decline. Thus, after reaping massive tax privileges and the NEP acquisition splurge, Dome's acquisitiveness had left it in a classic crisis—overextended in declining markets. Oil and gas industry demands for relief became louder, the Allsands and Cold Lake megaprojects were halted, and large numbers of employees were laid off. In April 1982, the Alberta government reduced its revenues under the NEP agreement to 'ease' industry taxes by $5.4 billion. In May, the federal government, not without Dome's precarious situation in mind, announced similar aid to the industry in the amount of $2 billion. By now the NEP revenue projections were battered and, further, it was likely the federal government would have to take additional, special measures to bail out Dome. Finally, the federal government announced that it would not allow further acquisitions (of foreign firms) by Petro-Canada. The brief phase of rapid 'Canadianization' was coming to an end.

7. The Developing Working Class

In Alberta's early years, the drive for rapid capital accumulation intensified the exploitation of labour, exacerbating relations between labour and capital. Labour organization took root in railways, coal mining, and construction, especially in the main centres of Medicine Hat, Lethbridge, Calgary, and Edmonton. The first union in Alberta was probably a lodge of the Brotherhood of Locomotive Engineers, chartered September 1886 in Medicine Hat.[114] By the time of provincial autonomy, key local unions had been organized, municipal labour councils formed (Calgary in the early 1900s and Edmonton in 1906), and independent labour political activity was first appearing. In 1912, the Alberta Federation of Labour was formed at Lethbridge. These were important organizational advances for the working class in Alberta, particularly as they were won in the face of "the new and fiercely individualistic employing class in Western Canada who were Social Darwinists to the core."[115] For example, in 1903, following a strike against the CPR by the US-centred United Brotherhood of Railway Employees, the then Senator James S. Lougheed of Calgary attempted to amend the Canadian criminal code to provide for the arrest and imprisonment of non-British subjects who entered Canada and urged workers to seek an improvement in wages or conditions.

Union membership grew rapidly in the decade preceding World War I. A peak membership of 11,572 (in 171 locals) was reached in 1913, but this fell rapidly to 7,618 (in 149 locals) in the first year of the war.[116] There was an upsurge in organization during the general crisis that broke out during the war and led to the Winnipeg General Strike (1919), but the post-war depression and decline in coal mining cut into gains made in these years. This ended the first major phase in the development of the working class in Alberta.

Another major upsurge in organization took place in the later 1930s and

1940s, and saw the growth of industrial unionism, especially in meat packing. This renewed phase of advance reached a peak in the late 1940s with the onslaught of the Cold War. The aggressive anti-communist hysteria together with the continued decline in the coal mining sector was used to break much of the militant tradition in the Alberta working class. As in the aftermath of World War I, a period of reaction set in, led by capital and their political allies.In 1949, for example, the Alberta Minister of Labour and Industry, Dr. J.L. Robinson, could state openly that some employers were pressing for changes in the Labour Act that would ban communists from participating in negotiations and that "labour's outstanding achievement during 1948 was cleaning out Communist leadership."[117] As elsewhere in Canada, the 1950s and early 1960s were a period of slow growth and even decline, though it was of major significance for uniting labour that in 1956 the Alberta Federation of Labour was transformed into the single labour centre in Alberta representing both craft and industrial unions.[118]

However, another, the third, major phase of labour growth and activity appeared in the 1960s. In the fifteen year period from 1962 to 1977 total union membership in Alberta more than doubled (see Table I-6). A distinguishing feature of labour organization in this period has been the relatively low proportion of Canadian unions with membership outside government employ. This has given international unions a more prominent position in Alberta. Nonetheless, it is important to note that the proportion of workers in international unions is declining: unlike their corporate counterparts, who have generally promoted foreign ownership and opposed 'Canadianization,' Alberta workers (and Canadian workers as a whole) are becoming increasingly independent. A sign of this trend and an important event for Alberta labour occurred in 1979, when the Canadian section of the Oil, Chemical and Atomic Workers International Union achieved full autonomy, enabling it to merge with the Canadian Chemical Workers Union to form the Energy and Chemical Workers Union, with headquarters in Edmonton. Recently, in the face of deepening economic crisis and the increasing militancy and national consciousness in the Canadian labour movement, certain right-wing leaders and 'roadmen' in twelve US-run international building trades unions have tried to split the Canadian Labour Congress and, hence, the provincial federations of labour and local labour councils, by setting up another labour centre, the so-called Canadian Federation of Labor. However, this action, announced publicly in 1981, may actually bring about a new and sharper phase in the struggle for independent Canadian unions.

The ebb and flow of struggle between labour and capital as reflected in strike-lockout statistics (Table I-7) also indicates the existence of a three-phase historical pattern in working class development. Again, the first phase of growing militancy and unity culminates with a crescendo of activity in the late 1910s and early 1920s. The second phase reached a peak in the mid-1940s. The third phase emerged out of the Cold War and is developing at the present time.

Out of the rise of the working class and its struggles developed not only the

Table I-6

Alberta and Canadian Labour Union Membership for Selected Years, 1962-1979

	1962	1970	1978	1979	Percentage growth 1962-79
Canada					
1 Total					
Number of members	1,514,905	2,267,526	2,907,639	3,035,752	100.4
Number of locals	—	10,099	12,333	12,910	
2 International unions					
Number of members	1,011,676	1,383,181	1,527,052	1,573,807	55.6
% of (1)	66.8	61.0	52.5	51.8	
3 Canadian unions					
Number of members	324,050	622,864	897,737	966,777	198.3
% of (1)	21.4	27.5	30.9	31.8	
4 Government employees unions					
Number of members	179,179	261,481	482,850	495,168	176.4
% of (1)	11.6	11.5	16.6	16.3	
Alberta					
5 Total					
Number of members	78,034	125,079	186,567	195,774	150.9
Number of locals	—	587	659	749	
% of (1)	5.2	5.5	6.4	6.4	
6 International unions					
Number of members	49,034	68,921	99,077	103,671	111.4
% of (5)	62.8	55.1	53.1	53.0	
% of (2)	4.8	5.0	6.5	6.6	
7 Canadian unions					
Number of members	11,117	27,104	34,233	37,405	236.5
% of (5)	14.2	21.7	18.3	19.1	
% of (3)	3.4	4.4	3.8	3.9	
8 Government employees unions					
Number of members	17,883	29,054	53,257	54,698	205.9
% of (5)	22.9	23.2	28.5	27.9	
% of (4)	10.0	11.1	11.0	11.0	

Source: Statistics Canada, *Corporation and Labour Unions Returns Act*, Part II, Catalogue 71-202, 1970 and 1977 (Supplements), 1978, 1979.

organized labour movement but also independent class based political action. In its earliest years labour generally had sided with the Liberals over the Conservatives but the Liberals' allegiance to capital over labour, like that of the Conservatives, became increasingly evident as capitalism advanced, thus accelerating social and political differentiation. The first signs of independent political action appeared in the early 1900s. Probably the first independent labour candidate at the provincial level was A.D. McDonald, who ran as an Independent in Calgary in the first provincial election, held 9 November 1905. In a by-election held in Lethbridge in 1909, Donald McNabb, a Labour candidate, was elected

Table I-7

Strikes and Lockouts in Alberta, 1902 - 1980

	Alberta Provincial Disputes			Inter-provincial disputes affecting Alberta		Alberta Provincial Disputes			Inter-provincial disputes affecting Alberta
Year	Disputes	Employees affected	Lost days		Year	Disputes	Employees affected	Lost days	
1902	1	90	1,080	—	1941	8	1,451	10,479	—
1903	4	183	3,990	—	1942	17	4,461	7,223	—
1904	1	28	112	2	1943	41	7,025	33,536	1
1905	2	400	13,000	—	1944	19	2,458	7,943	—
1906	12	1,491	127,709	—	1945	17	2,729	6,260	2
1907	6	678	2,556	2	1946	23	9,308	27,871	2
1908	3	569	8,599	1	1947	11	1,243	14,742	2
1909	6	873	48,416	1	1948	5	146	1,573	1
1910	6	730	13,882	3	1949	8	687	4,865	—
1911	12	1,668	8,545	2	1950	12	1,963	13,643	1
1912	14	3,345	76,837	1	1951	9	1,409	8,882	—
1913	6	1,369	13,051	1	1952	11	1,666	13,874	—
1914	4	1,077	17,167	—	1953	5	956	2,559	—
1915	4	355	4,108	—	1954	6	1,032	59,220	—
1916	4	494	8,974	—	1955	3	225	1,625	—
1917	17	11,613	330,618	—	1956	4	1,121	11,935	—
1918	31	5,076	55,711	2	1957	2	405	2,085	1
1919	16	6,098	147,829	2	1958	8	1,321	27,570	1
1920	36	8,593	127,019	—	1959	5	559	11,090	—
1921	11	729	6,435	—	1960	5	1,684	27,610	—
1922	20	10,562	966,842	—	1961	8	2,413	17,390	—
1923	14	3,435	55,267	—	1962	9	1,073	21,300	—
1924	9	7,146	1,002,179	2	1963	7	1,127	23,520	2
1925	14	3,200	89,756	—	1964	2	68	6,300	—
1926	3	445	4,105	—	1965	9	1,123	6,170	1
1927	5	765	6,371	—	1966	15	2,350	46,780	2
1928	10	2,743	87,057	—	1967	9	1,428	17,920	—
1929	3	321	10,142	—	1968	10	2,279	58,622	1
1930	5	174	2,260	—	1969	15	2,221	64,000	2
1931	10	662	5,717	—	1970	10	2,511	37,160	2
1932	20	3,294	111,783	—	1971	19	9,773	83,020	7
1933	11	1,235	14,474	—	1972	9	932	25,870	6
1934	9	519	5,754	1	1973	25	8,405	181,430	6
1935	12	1,870	20,054	—	1974	44	22,237	203,850	8
1936	14	2,783	20,987	1	1975	34	16,979	374,940	7
1937	17	2,413	15,094	—	1976	27	7,532	106,910	5
1938	11	1,720	9,874	—	1977	13	4,819	66,810	1
1939	10	1,524	19,043	—	1978	51	21,685	447,340	5
1940	7	882	8,238	—	1979	27	2,245	62,560	4
					1980	43	24,269	538,680	4

Source: Compiled from issues of *The Labour Gazette,* Ottawa, Department of Labour, and *Report on Strikes and Lockouts in Canada,* Ottawa, Department of Labour. Under "interprovincial disputes affecting Alberta" is an estimate of the number of disputes in areas of federal jurisdiction in which employees in Alberta were involved. A few Alberta-B.C. coal mining disputes are included in this category, but most are under Alberta provincial disputes.

by acclamation. Although he was only a few months in office, McNabb was the first elected labour member in Alberta's provincial or territorial history. During the World War I crisis, a labour candidate was elected in the 1917 provincial election. Four were elected in 1921, six in 1926, four in 1930, and, finally, one in 1940.

Labour was active at the municipal level as well. Labour candidates were elected to several municipal councils and more than once the local boards of trade and their allied commercial press attacked labour and spread fears of "class dictatorship" (presumably, of working people, not themselves). Significantly, despite the less democratic franchise (which included property qualifications and multiple voting for property owners), municipal councils were more easily subjected to organized pressure than the provincial or federal levels of the state, and had considerable union activity among their own employees. For this reason also, higher levels of the state often have been inclined to take over directly various areas historically under municipal jurisdiction (such as taxation, policing, relief, and planning) rather than to provide greater indirect financial assistance or increased local powers, especially in the field of taxation: capitalist class interests have been less threatened by removing the allocation of public resources from this 'less responsible' level of government where anti-popular measures were more difficult to carry through because 'the mobs are at the gates.'

As capitalist development created the working class in Alberta, so its continued expansion brought the working class closer to the political centre stage. The Dominion government had established a Department of Labour in 1900 and was soon active in reporting and conciliation in Alberta. One of the most serious strikes in early Alberta, that of 500 Lethbridge miners against the Alberta Railway and Irrigation Company in 1906, actually gave rise to Mackenzie King's anti-labour Industrial Disputes Investigation Act (1907), the key piece of Canadian labour legislation during the succeeding two decades. The Provincial Liberals, who had "a good deal of hostility towards the demands of organized labour,"[119] were compelled by the Lethbridge strike and other bitter class battles erupting in the coal fields and rail centres to recognize that an important new question was on Alberta's historical agenda. In February 1907, on the motion of the Minister of Public Works, Cushing, the legislature approved the appointment of a commission "to make inquiries into conditions of labour interests with a view to obtaining all possible information with regard to any differences existing between capital and labour, in order that the government may be able to frame legislation looking toward the peaceful settlement of disputes of this nature." However, it was not until much later that the first major labour-related government agencies were created: the Workmen's Compensation Board (1918), Bureau of Labour (1922), and Minimum Wage Board (1922). The Minimum Wage Board was succeeded by the Board of Industrial Relations (1936) under the Minister of Trade and Industry (1936-48). Subsequently, the growing role of the province in labour matters was reflected in the formation of the Ministry of Industries and Labour (1948) and, finally, the Ministry of Labour (1959).

Over the course of many years, Alberta labour was able to win some concessions, especially during militant periods such as the late 1910s. For instance, in 1917, under considerable labour pressure, the legislature passed a Factory Act, the first, albeit limited, minimum wage legislation in Canada. However, for virtually all provincial governments since 1905, labour has been viewed as a force potentially threatening to propertied interests and the social status quo, particularly in its voicing of socialist concepts. Thus, the acceleration and maturing of capitalist development—and the working class—has carried with it a haunting fear for the Alberta establishment. Expressions of this theme can be found occasionally, and usually euphemistically, such as in Premier Lougheed's 1974 speech to the Calgary Chamber of Commerce: "I doubt it is necessary for me to point out that with this province and with this diversification will come also some problems and growing pains in terms of material and manpower shortages in the short term and in the longer term, greater propensity for labour disputes."[120] Less vague have been the series of specific anti-labour actions advocated and taken by the Conservative government, notably in support of federal wage controls beginning in 1975, in anti-strike legislation (Bill 41) against provincial employees in 1977, and in regulations further restricting the political rights of provincial public employees in 1978. It is apparent that the struggle between labour and capital has entered a new phase in which the provincial business class has chosen to make increased use of the state to weaken labour and control collective bargaining as a means of maintaining rapid capital accumulation. Whether in the next few years the working class in Alberta can be contained by the state and weakened by the ideology of 'provincialism' remains to be seen. The outcome, however, is crucial, for it will determine the long-run direction and alignments of Alberta's economic development.

8. Conclusion

The century of capitalism ascendant in Alberta has seen a generally subordinate and highly uneven form of regional development determined by both internal and external—including international—forces. In the formative years, development was dominated by central Canadian capital, but Canadian 'westward expansion' (which has been characterized, more accurately, as "internal colonization") was linked with the general expansion of British imperialism. The Confederation arrangements were worked out directly with the Colonial Office and approved in the Imperial parliament at London as part of British imperial strategy of the time. In particular, British ruling circles wished to curtail US economic and territorial expansion in northern North America, notably the vulnerable North-West, to consolidate their military and investment position in Canada, to secure a transportation and trade link with Asia, and to reduce their costs of colonial administration.[121] Throughout the era of the National Policy, which set the framework for internal colonization, the Canadian capitalist class and state were financially bound and generally subordinate to British imperialist interests. This subordinate relationship was exemplified in the compliance of the Canadian government with the Imperial government in the South African ("Boer") War (1899-1902) and World War I and the fact that a "Department of External Affairs" was not even formally established as part of the Canadian state until 1909.[122]

However, as capitalism in Canada advanced, Canada's relationship with the imperialist system changed. The rapid accumulation of Canadian capital, a substantial portion of which was appropriated in the process of internal colonization, pushed Canada partially out of its subordinate, semi-colonial status. Indeed, by the 1920s, following the cataclysmic changes of World War I, Canada itself had emerged as an imperialist power of lower rank. Increasingly, sections of Canadian capital were competing internationally, notably in their investments in the US and Latin America. By the beginning of the majority Liberal federal government of W.L. Mackenzie King in 1926, and conclusively by the close of World War II, the US had come to take the place of Britain as the leading capitalist country in the world, and Canadian capitalism had shifted its strongest ties from Britain to the US.

The achieving of provincial autonomy in 1905 reflected the growth of locally and regionally based business interests and some popular democratic pressures. However, certain features of internal colonization, exemplified by the federal government's retention of Dominion Lands (and resources) to control settlement and resource exploitation, lasted until "full autonomy"—an autonomy equivalent in legal terms to that of other provinces—was obtained in 1930. Despite changes in this internal 'semi-colonial' status of Alberta, and despite the dramatic development of industry, capital accumulation, and state intervention especially during World War I, the subordination and dependence of the provincial economy persisted, as revealed both in the post-World War I crisis and by the catastrophic impact of the Great Depression.

The 'pioneer' era based on extensive railway and agricultural development which reached its peak during World War I, came to an end with the Great Depression. During the 1920s, US penetration of the Alberta economy, based in oil and gas, had increased significantly, soon superseding British imperialism as the leading foreign force in Alberta, and weakening the position of central Canadian capital in Alberta. In the 1930s, the depression crisis greatly weakened the position of Alberta capital relative to outside capital, and facilitated the latter's expansion in Alberta.

With the 1940s and the beginning of a long period of growth heavily dependent on oil and gas development, Alberta entered an era of rapid and relatively mature capitalist development. Although still a subordinate economy with highly uneven development, the class structure, the degree of urbanization, the level of concentration of capital, and the diffusion of technology and techniques increasingly took on the proportions of a highly developed capitalist economy. The growth of Alberta capital, despite its setbacks in the 1930s, emerged as an important factor in the Alberta economy, often through junior alliances with US capital. With the 1970s, the latest phase of Alberta's development, the economy is still subordinate, primarily to American rather than central Canadian capital, but Alberta capital and its state have become a powerful force in determining future provincial development.

While recognizing the importance of these dominant forces, one must also emphasize the inadequacy of viewing the development of capitalism in Alberta as simply a history of rivalries and alliances among various competing capitals. A full picture needs to recognize the varying alignments of *all* politico-economic forces, particularly the relationship between labour and capital, which determines the fundamental structure and antagonistic dynamic of capitalist development. From this standpoint, the most consistent economic force pitted against the power of both central Canadian and US capital has not been Alberta based capital, but labour. Indeed, a measure of the degree of 'independence' of Alberta based capital has been its long history of collaboration with outside capitals in common cause against Alberta labour.

In its rivalry with central Canadian capital, Alberta capital has made considerable use of its most powerful lever for capital accumulation—the Alberta state. By maintaining various selected "provincial rights" postures, particularly with respect to the control of natural resource production and pricing, transportation, and taxation, Alberta capital has helped strengthen its positions—and those of US capital—against central Canadian capital. However, the westward shift in wealth and the locus of economic power in Canada has exacerbated tensions within the Canadian state structure and society (especially since the 1973 oil price increases and the 15 November 1976 election of the Parti Quebecois in Quebec), and weakened resistance to further takeover of the Canadian economy by American capital. During the course of the federal-provincial energy struggles certain internal divisions in Alberta capital became more evident. Some federal measures such as the National Energy Program and a turn towards 'Canadianization' in the oil and gas industry strengthened the portions of central Canadian capital but also the nationalist tendency in Alberta capital. Despite these developments, the continentalist trend, though somewhat weaker, continued to predominate in Alberta.

At the same time, Alberta capital is aggressively seeking a leading position over central Canadian and British Columbia capital, particularly in the scramble for the natural resources of northern Canada. Alberta capital aspires to a "place in the sun" as a continentalist "gateway province" to the north, making Alberta a transportation corridor and staging area for northern development. In this northward drive of Alberta capital, the people of Alberta and Canada, especially the Native peoples, are witnessing a pattern of development with which they have had a long and painful familiarity. Alberta capital is doing unto the north—the new North-West—what 'eastern' capital did unto them. The aggressors have changed a little, but the victims have not.

/David Leadbeater, An Outline of Capitalist Development in Alberta-/

Notes

[1] Olive P. Dickason, "A Historical Reconstruction of the Northwestern Plains," *Prairie Forum*, 5, no. 1 (1980), 21-22.

[2] In this context, 'primitive' carries the meaning of 'first' or 'original' and not 'crude' or 'unsophisticated.'

[3] Diamond Jenness, *The Indians of Canada* (Ottawa, 1972; 1st ed., 1932).

[4] For a discussion of aspects of the ideology of the 'expansionist movement,' which was "primarily an English Canadian phenomenon," see Doug Owram, *Promise of Eden: The Canadian Expansionist Movement and the Idea of the West, 1856-1900* (Toronto, 1980).

[5] Rupert's Land was the name of the vast territory granted freehold to the HBC in 1670, which was roughly defined as the area drained by the rivers flowing into Hudson Bay.

[6] The North-West Mounted Police (NWMP) became the Royal North-West Mounted Police in 1904 and the Royal Canadian Mounted Police in 1920.

[7] R.C. Macleod, "Canadianizing the West: The North-West Mounted Police as Agents of the National Policy, 1873-1905," in Lewis H. Thomas, ed., *Essays in Western History* (Edmonton, 1976), 106.

[8] Quoted in René Fumoleau, *As Long as This Land Shall Last: A History of Treaty 8 and Treaty 11, 1870-1939* (Toronto, n.d.), 24. English and Canadian authorities already had considerable experience in the techniques of usurpation. Fumoleau notes that between 1781 and 1902 in Canada 483 treaties, adhesions, and land surrenders were obtained; of these, 123 treaties and land surrenders had been signed with eastern Native peoples before 1867. A map showing the major treaties is on page 81 of this volume.

[9] For more background of the treaties in Alberta see Richard Price, ed., *The Spirit of the Alberta Indian Treaties* (Montreal, 1979 [?]).

[10] E. Palmer Patterson II, *The Canadian Indian: A History Since 1500* (Don Mills, Ont., 1972), 17.

[11] For example, clergy-directed villages such as Lac La Biche (1854), St. Albert (1861), Victoria (now Pakan, 1862), St. Paul des Cris (1866), and St. Paul des Métis (1896).

[12] V.I. Lenin, *Imperialism: The Highest Stage of Capitalism* (New York, 1969; 1st ed., 1917), 10.

[13] Joseph Pope, ed., *Correspondence of John A. Macdonald* (New York, 1921): letter to C.J. Brydges, managing director of the Grand Trunk Railway, 124-25. The railway, as promised to British Columbia, was to be completed within ten years of that colony's entry into Confederation on 20 July 1871.

[14] Ibid., 125.

[15] Quoted in Chester Martin, *"Dominion Lands" Policy*, vol. II of W. Mackintosh and W. Joerg, eds., *Canadian Frontiers of Settlement* (Toronto, 1939, 275-76).

[16] One such notable figure, in Calgary, was James A. Lougheed, a corporate lawyer and major land speculator.

[17] Tom Naylor, *The History of Canadian Business, 1867-1914* (Toronto, 1975), vol. I, 286.

[18] J. Lukasiewicz, *The Railway Game: A Study in Socio-Technological Obsolescence* (Toronto, 1976), 46. The peak growth of railway construction was reached around 1915 at about 39,243 net miles (63 142 km) of main track, which was about 35,000 route miles (56 315 km) or a record 4.5 miles (7.2 km) per 1,000 persons in Canada.

[19] Martin, *"Dominion Lands" Policy*, 302-303.

[20] Lukasiewicz, *The Railway Game*, 30. Investment includes cash, credit, and proceeds of land sales.

[21] Quoted in Martin, *"Dominion Lands" Policy*, 227.

[22] Ibid., 431. This figure for all Dominion Lands may be a low estimate of homesteader failures. For Alberta, out of 34.7 million acres under homestead entry between 1905 and 1930, 15.9 million were cancelled (about 46 percent). Figures are not yet available on how many homesteads were turned over to individual speculators and land companies once the patent was acquired.

[23] Alberta, *The Case for Alberta*, Submission to the Royal Commission on Dominion-Provincial Relations (Edmonton, 1938), pt. I, 52.

[24] Martin, *"Dominion Lands" Policy*, 495-501. Free homesteading included more than 2 million acres granted as 'military bonuses' to veterans of the South African and First World Wars. Even for those obtaining the 160-acre homesteads, the growth in farm scale was a factor encouraging the purchase of additional land. By 1926, 58 percent of the 77,130 farms in Alberta were larger than 200 acres.

[25] The actual pattern of land distribution was much less regular than the idealized 'checkerboard' pattern with odd-numbered sections going to railways and even-numbered sections going to homesteading. One geographer has gone so far as to comment that "there is no such thing as a 'typical prairie township'." See John Tyman, *By Section Township and Range: Studies in Prairie Settlement* (Brandon, 1972).

[26] Martin, *"Dominion Lands" Policy*, 319.

[27] Max Foran, "Early Calgary 1875-1895: The Controversies Surrounding the Townsite Location and the Direction of Town Expansion," in A. McCormick and Ian Macpherson, eds., *Cities in the West* (Ottawa, 1975), 26.

[28] Canada, *Grain and Rail in Western Canada*, The Report of the Grain Handling and Transportation Commission (The Hall Commission) (Ottawa, 1977), vol. 1, 274.

[29] During these years, the Canadian state was not alone in practising discriminatory regulation of freight rates to accelerate metropolitan capital accumulation: Imperial Russia and Imperial Germany had started even earlier.

[30] *Grain and Rail in Western Canada*, 275.

[31] D.H. Breen, "The Canadian Prairie West and the 'Harmonious' Settlement Interpretation," *Agricultural History*, 47 (January 1973), 65.

[32] A.A. den Otter, "Railways and Alberta's Coal Problem, 1880-1960," in A.W. Rasporich, ed., *Western Canada Past and Present* (Calgary, 1975), 86.

[33] Dominion Bureau of Statistics, *Canadian Mineral Statistics, 1886-1956*, Reference Paper no. 68 (Ottawa, 1975), 56, 105. The volume of coal is measured in short tons where 1 ton = 2,000 lbs. Figures in brackets are metric tonnes (1 t = 1.102 tons).

[34] Alberta, Publicity and Statistics Branch, *Statistics of Progress* (Edmonton, 1929), 148. In this context, "establishment" included all plants with 5 or more employees. In only 5 years—by 1910—there were 290 establishments with 6,930 employees (or 24.1 per establishment) with a capital investment of $29.5 million (or $101,737 per establishment) and a gross output of $18.3 million.

[35] Ibid., 144-45.

[36] H.A. Innis, *Settlement and the Mining Frontier*, vol. IX of Mackintosh and Joerg, eds., *Canadian Frontiers of Settlement*, 309-310.

[37] *Census of Canada*, 1911, vol. III, ix.

[38] Stanley B. Ryerson, *Unequal Union: Confederation and the Roots of the Conflict in the Canadas, 1815-1873* (Toronto, 1968), 276-77. Beginning in the late 1840s the ascendency of the older and more conservative merchant and allied banking interests was superseded by the newer and more dynamic industrial (including railway) and allied banking interests.

[39] Gustavus Myers, *A History of Canadian Wealth* (Toronto, 1972; 1st ed., 1914), 265-66.

[40] W.T. Easterbrook and Hugh G.T. Aitken, *Canadian Economic History* (Toronto, 1956), 383.

[41] Herbert Legg, *Customs Services in Western Canada, 1867-1925* (Creston, B.C., 1962), 10.

[42] For some material on the role of Winnipeg in early prairie trade see Donald Kerr, "Wholesale Trade on the Canadian Plains in the Late Nineteenth Century: Winnipeg and Its Competition," in Howard Palmer, ed., *The Settlement of the West* (Calgary, 1977), 130-52.

[43] H.M.P. Eckardt, "A Quarter Century of Canadian Banking," *Journal of the Canadian Bankers Association*, 26 (1918-19), 30.

[44] See, for example, Donald G. Paterson, *British Direct Investment in Canada, 1890-1914* (Toronto, 1976), 64-69. There is evidence that in certain areas the presence of large land companies not only aroused hostility from settlers but actually had a discouraging effect on settlement. See, for example, Bruce E. Batchelor, "Economy and Society in Central Alberta on the Eve of Autonomy: The Case of the SLHC," *Canadian Papers in Rural History*, III (1982), 148-55.

[45] Naylor, *The History of Canadian Business*, II, 29-30.

[46] Canada, *House of Commons Debates*, 12 March 1875, I, 656. One elected representative was to be added for every one thousand non-Indian adult males in an area not exceeding 1,000 square miles (2589 sq km).

[47] Eric J. Hanson, *Local Government in Alberta* (Toronto, 1956), 31.

[48] A typical reflection of this reality is the following comment from "The Review" newspaper of Bow Island (c. 1911-12): "The difference between a live town and a dead

town is often the difference between a live Board of Trade and a similar institution in the last stage of decomposition. As a general rule in western towns and cities the business men of the town form the Board of Trade and what is good for the business men is good for the town and vice versa. In the development of a going town the Board of Trade is a great factor and has at its command for bringing to a town institutions that will be a benefit to that place.... Not only is the Board of Trade effective in building up the town but in coadjument [sic] with the Village Council they are a large factor in the government and welfare of the people who are already there." Quoted in *Silver Sage: Bow Island 1900-1950* (Bow Island, Alberta, n.d.), 117.

[49] See A.A. den Otter, "Coal Town in Wheat Country: Lethbridge, Alberta, 1885-1905," *Urban History Review*, 1-76 (June 1976), 5. For more on the early development of Lethbridge, especially the role of the Galts, see, by the same author, "Lethbridge: Outpost of a Commercial Empire, 1885-1906," in Alan F. Artibise, ed., *Town and City: Aspects of Western Canadian Urban Development*, Canadian Plains Studies 10 (Regina, 1981), 177-202.

[50] "Boosterism" has been defined as "the campaign to stimulate economic and population growth by advertising, lobbying, and offering incentives to development." See Paul Voisey, "Boosting the Small Prairie Town, 1904-1931: An Example from Southern Alberta," in Artibise, ed., *Town and City*, 147.

[51] Hanson, *Local Government in Alberta*, 32. By 1913, Alberta city debenture debt had risen to $41.9 million, as compared to the total provincial direct debt of $15.3 million and guarantees of $37.2 million. Edmonton had a total debenture debt of nearly $22.3 million by the end of 1913.

[52] The figure for incorporations includes incorporation by Companies Ordinances as well as by Cemeteries Ordinances, Butter and Cheese Ordinances, Mutual Fire Insurance Ordinances, Masonic Lodge Ordinances, and special private ordinances. Extra-territorial companies, or "foreign companies" as they have also been called, include companies incorporated by the Dominion government, by provincial governments, and by other countries. Of the 302 extra-territorial companies registered to the end of 1905, 100 were incorporated in Canada (36 by the Dominion, 4 by British Columbia, 31 by Manitoba, 26 by Ontario, 3 by Quebec), 73 in other countries (30 by Britain, 42 by the US, and 1 by the Netherlands), and in 129 the place of incorporation was not stated. Banks and railway companies were not required to register.

[53] A key figure in the decision was Frank Oliver, an Edmonton publisher, Liberal MP (1896-1917), and Minister of the Interior under Laurier (1905-11).

[54] For instance, in 1973, Alberta overtook Ontario in having the highest personal expenditure (on consumer goods and services) per capita in Canada. In 1979, taking average per capita personal expenditure as 100, Alberta had 148.9 compared to Ontario at 105.6, Quebec at 87.4, and Newfoundland at 54.9. (Canada, Department of Finance, *Economic Review*, April 1981, 129.) Such figures must be read with care since by themselves they say virtually nothing about income and wealth disparities *within* provinces, nor about poverty in Alberta, nor about the wage level or standard of living of the average worker. As it happens, Alberta wage and salary earners in larger firms (20 or more workers) on

average do have higher average weekly earnings than workers in all provinces except British Columbia (in June 1981, the industrial average for Alberta was $394.17 while for Ontario it was $348.86, for Quebec $352.43, and for Newfoundland $325.96) and they do have lower taxes (Alberta has generally lower rates of income tax and no retail sales tax). However, any accurate comparison of the standard of living must also take into account the generally higher level of prices in Alberta and factors contributing to the social wage, especially the cost and availability of educational, health, and social services.

55   Statistics Canada, *Survey of Production*, 1978 (catalogue no. 61-202). The comparable figures for Ontario are 43.5 percent (1935), 43.6 percent (1970), and 37.4 percent (1978).

56   Alberta Land Use Forum, Technical Report 11, *Structure of Alberta Farms* (Alberta Department of Agriculture, 1974). The census farm has been defined roughly as a tract of land of one acre or more producing agriculture products valued at $50.00 or more in the last year.

57   See Libbie and Frank Park, *Anatomy of Big Business* (Toronto, 1973; 1st ed., 1962), chapter V.

58   Potentially, a major challenge to central Canadian financial power would have been the organization of bank workers, but almost no progress has been made in this area. For all their alleged dislike of 'eastern bankers,' the Alberta government and Alberta based business interests have never deigned to support the unionization of banks or other financial institutions.

59   Naylor, *The History of Canadian Business*, II, 167.

60   In the Edmonton area, a large practice of comparable significance was established by H.R. Milner in 1912. Milner was instrumental in advancing the takeover and expansion of International Utilities Corporation of the US, which owned Canadian Utilities, Northwestern Utilities, Canadian Western Natural Gas, and Alberta Power. These latter firms as well as Calgary Power were recently taken over by the Calgary based multinational, Atco, another indication of the growing power of Alberta capital.

61   In 1981, according to advance census information, the labour force had risen to 53.4 percent of the population for Alberta, compared to 48.8 percent for Canada and 51.2 percent for Ontario, while the number of those receiving labour income was 91.7 percent of the labour force for Alberta, compared to 92.9 percent for Canada and 93.8 for Ontario. These figures for the receiving labour income include self-employed persons in incorporated companies; the figures in Table I-4 for wage and salary earners do not.

62   C.B. Macpherson, *Democracy in Alberta: Social Credit and the Party System* (Toronto, 1962; 1st ed., 1953), 15-16.

63   The formation of the Social Credit movement in Alberta and of the CCF can both be dated from 1932.

64   Hon. H. Greenfield, *Budget Speech*, 1922 (Alberta Department of Treasury).

65   To this day, farm labourers remain among the least organized and most poorly treated groups of workers in Alberta. For instance, although minimum wage regulations have existed for groups of industrial workers for more than 60 years, farm labourers have yet to receive even this minimal protection.

66   Formed in 1925, the United Church combined mainly the Methodists, Congregationalists, and part of the Presbyterians.

⁶⁷ In the important 1944 wartime election, which occurred two months after the June victory of the CCF in Saskatchewan and in the face of a strong challenge from the CCF and Labour Progressive (Communist) Party, Manning told voters they were choosing between "state socialism as represented by the C.C.F. and Christian democracy represented by the Social Credit party" (*Edmonton Journal*, 5 August 1944). As a sign of the emerging entente between big business and Social Credit, the Tory *Edmonton Journal*, once a vociferous enemy of Social Credit, now supported the government: "What was necessary above everything else was the decisive defeat of the C.C.F." (Ibid., 7 August 1944.)

⁶⁸ The oil industry was especially prominent in the "military-industrial complex" and the drive to create a "Fortress North America." There were numerous oil company-government ties. For example, John Foster Dulles, the US Secretary of State during the 1950s, was Chairman of the Board of Trustees of the Rockefeller Foundation, a director of the International Nickel Company of Canada, and a member of the Wall Street law firm of Sullivan and Cromwell, which represented, among other large corporations, Standard Oil of New Jersey, the parent company of Imperial Oil.

⁶⁹ Archibald O. MacRae, *History of the Province of Alberta* (Calgary, 1912), 461. Bell Telephone was chartered by the Dominion Government in 1880.

⁷⁰ Although a definitive history of this, the first of Alberta's two best publicized provincial railway scandals (the second surfaced in the 1960s, with the Alberta Resources Railway and the Social Credit government), has yet to be written, a brief account is available in Douglas R. Babcock, *A Gentleman of Strathcona: Alexander Cameron Rutherford*, Historic Sites Service Occasional Paper no. 8 (Edmonton, 1980), especially chapter 3.

⁷¹ Bank of Canada, *Report on the Provinces of Manitoba, Saskatchewan and Alberta* (Ottawa, 1937), p. 10 of the Alberta report.

⁷² Canada, *Debates of the House of Commons*, 1905, p. 3096. Prime Minister Laurier foresaw a grave setback for federal goals if, for instance, Alberta or Saskatchewan "under the strain of financial difficulty, were to abolish the free homesteads, which have proved so beneficial and so great an inducement to immigration...Or if the price of government lands for sale were to be increased over the present very moderate rate." However, he did note that the western provinces "in being deprived of the public lands, are deprived of a valuable source of income" and suggested compensation. (Ibid., p. 1434.)

⁷³ As early as 1922, when formalized negotiations began between the four western provinces and Ottawa, the federal government, then under Liberal Prime Minister King, had accepted the general principle that Dominion Lands should be transferred to provincial ownership. Premier Brownlee's discussion of the main stages of the negotiations is reported in the *Edmonton Journal*, 16 December 1929, p. 7. A secondary issue was the transfer of School lands and the School Lands Fund, whose disposition was at times a subject of severe tension, at least partly due to the federal Liberal government's desire to protect the Roman Catholic Church's interest in separate schools.

⁷⁴ The annual subsidy to Alberta was to jump to $750,000 when the provincial population (then 640,000) reached 800,000 and to $1,125,000 when it reached 1,200,000. The Royal Commission on the Natural Resources of Alberta (the Dysart Commission), which was

appointed in 1934, recommended a supplementary payment of $5 million plus accrued interest. The provincial Department of Lands and Mines in its first annual report noted that on the date of transfer there were 17,219 petroleum and natural gas leases in force covering an area of 2.3 million acres; in the six months alone after 1 October, the government collected $198,339 in revenue from rentals, fees, and royalties on petroleum and natural gas.

[75] Federal administration of the national parks was attacked by the then Conservative leader R.B. Bennett, who supported provincial administration. In then (as now) prevailing political conditions in Alberta, provincial control would have created a situation more favourable to corporate exploitation of national park resources.

[76] Martin, *"Dominion Lands" Policy*, 498. The undisposed of area amounted to 15.4 million acres; the total surveyed area of Alberta amounted to 87.9 million acres. The *Report* of the Royal Commission on the Natural Resources of Alberta (1935) estimated the total land area of Alberta was 159.2 million acres of which the total arable land was 87.5 million acres (p. 16).

[77] A recent book argues that "The native people most threatened by this expansion of settlement were the semi-nomadic Metis and former treaty Indians who depended on the bushlands to support their traditional economy. And it was these people who would initiate the rejuvenation of the Metis national liberation movement dormant since 1885." Murray Dobbin, *The One-And-A-Half Men: The Story of Jim Brady and Malcolm Norris, Metis Patriots of the Twentieth Century* (Vancouver, 1981), 56.

[78] Carl F. Betke, "Farm Politics in an Urban Age: The Decline of the United Farmers of Alberta after 1921," in Thomas, ed., *Essays in Western History*, 187.

[79] *Financial Post*, 31 August 1935. Even before the election, the Aberhart campaign had had "a depressing influence on Alberta bonds for months."

[80] Right from the outset of the Social Credit government there were leading financial interests who felt that the Social Credit movement could be contained by the federal state system. The *Financial Post* on 31 August 1935 editorialized that: "If Alberta were a self-governing country, its election results of last week could be interpreted only as a popular mandate for a complete transformation of the political and economic system. But Alberta is only a province with limited powers and with almost none of the powers that its new political leader will require to carry out his programme. So instead of a social revolution Alberta faces only chaos."

[81] Of the 17 budget years under the Liberals, 9 ended in deficit; of the 14 budget years under the UFA, 9 ended in deficit.

[82] Government of Alberta, *Public Accounts*, 1971-72 (Edmonton), Statement no. 19, 81.

[83] About 85 to 90 percent of the mineral rights in Alberta have been owned by the provincial government since 1930, when Dominion Lands were transferred to the province. This high proportion of state ownership of mineral rights resulted from the fact that most land grants in Alberta did not include mineral rights; after the land regulations of 17 September 1889, the Dominion government retained mineral rights in all grants.

[84] While the province suffered considerably from the Smoky River project (as was partially revealed in a 1973 commission of inquiry chaired by N.R. Crump, former CPR

president), Manning himself obtained a position on the board of McIntyre after retiring from the provincial legislature in 1968.

[85] For example, Drayton Valley, Hinton, Swan Hills, Fort McMurray, Rainbow Lake, Grande Cache, and Fox Creek.

[86] Premier Peter Lougheed, Speech to the Calgary Chamber of Commerce, 6 September 1974 (Edmonton, Office of the Premier), 3.

[87] Ibid., 9. By 1980, the Alberta Energy Company had assets of $703 million, which is about one-fifth that of Nova and one-ninth that of Imperial Oil.

[88] GCOS Ltd. was controlled by Sun Oil Ltd. of Pennsylvania. In 1979 the two companies were merged as Suncor Inc.

[89] Social programmes, such as public education, health, welfare, housing, and culture, tend to redistribute income and raise expectations; hence, they can weaken the capitalist social structure and incentive system.

[90] With $1.8 billion of guaranteed debentures in 1977, the Alberta Municipal Finance Corporation has for many years been the provincial government's largest single "indirect liability." The AMFC was followed by Alberta Government Telephones, at $.9 billion in 1977. Besides AGT and AMFC, "Heritage Funds" have been used to finance the Alberta Home Mortgage Corporation, the Alberta Housing Corporation, the Alberta Agricultural Development Corporation, and the Alberta Opportunity Company.

[91] Government of Canada, *Corporations and Labour Unions Returns Act* (CALURA), catalogue no. 61-210, Report for 1971, pt. I, 147, and 1976, pt. I, 353. The figures for 1975 were even higher in all the above categories (see *CALURA*, 1975, pt. I, 259). In 1979, foreign (US) control of corporate taxable income was 60.6 percent (53.7 percent) for Alberta—which was still higher than the 1971 level—compared to 43.1 percent (36.9 percent) for Canada as a whole.

[92] Martin, *"Dominion Lands" Policy*, 458-59, and order-in-council PC 105 of 1920. Beginning in 1914, at the urging of the British Admiralty and Colonial Office, the Canadian government had restricted oil and gas development on Dominion Lands to Canadian and British companies. See D.H. Breen, "Anglo-American Rivalry and the Evolution of Canadian Petroleum Policy to 1930," *Canadian Historical Review*, LXII, no. 3 (September 1981), 283-303.

[93] Henrietta Larsen, E.V. Knowlton, and C.S. Popple, *New Horizons, 1927-1950*, vol. 3 of the *History of Standard Oil Company (New Jersey)* (New York, 1971), 110.

[94] Herbert Marshall, F. Southard, Jr., and K.W. Taylor, *Canadian-American Industry: A Study in International Investment* (Toronto, 1976, 1st ed., 1936), 107-108.

[95] Ibid., 108. By 1935, the dominant petroleum companies in Alberta were Royalite Oil and Foothills Oil and Gas Company, Ltd., both controlled by Imperial.

[96] Fierce debate surrounded the Trans-Canada pipeline, which was to extend from the Alberta-Saskatchewan border to Montreal. This gas pipeline was promoted by US interests and proposed to have part of its route (after Winnipeg) go south into US territory. Under the leadership of the Liberals, particularly C.D. Howe, and with the support of the Alberta Social Credit MPs and Alberta Conservative MPs, the project was driven through parliament using closure against the Conservative-CCF opposition.

In the end, Trans-Canada, with generous support from the Canadian and Ontario governments, developed an all-Canadian branch as well as a US branch. Gulf Oil was originally a major interest behind the project.

97 It was not until after World War II that natural gas came fully into its own as a major industry. Prior to then most gas was wastefully flared off as a superfluous by-product of oil drilling activity, though some gas was transmitted and distributed through pipelines by utility companies for local heating and lighting purposes beginning as early as the decade before World War I. James Gray suggests it was the discovery of the huge Pincher Creek Field, especially the Gulf Pincher Creek Walter Marr #1, which came in during August 1949, that provided the main impetus to the gas pipeline promoters. See J. Gray, "The Pincher Creek Gas Field," *Canadian Historical Review*, LXII, no. 3 (September 1981), 369-72.

98 *Calgary Herald*, 22 March 1951.

99 Arctic Gas Pipeline Ltd. included Imperial Oil, Gulf, several other major US oil and gas companies, Shell, the Canada Development Corporation, Consumer's Gas, Canadian National Railways, and Canadian Pacific Investments. The consortium claimed to have expended over $100 million in its bid to develop its proposed Mackenzie Valley pipeline. Toronto based TransCanada PipeLines was a major backer of the Arctic Gas project.

100 For a brief discussion of some other figures, particularly the "Patio Group" around the Premier, Peter Lougheed, see, for example, Peter Newman, *The Canadian Establishment* (Toronto, 1977), I, 245-53. Lougheed and several key Conservative figures represent in Alberta what is relatively 'old money,' though much Conservative backing comes also from 'new money.' One journalist suggests that "Probably three-quarters of all the significant oil fortunes in Alberta have been made in the 1970's." Peter Foster, *The Blue-Eyed Sheiks: The Canadian Oil Establishment* (Don Mills, Ont., 1980), 351.

101 For a discussion of the Alberta prebuild see François Bregha, *Bob Blair's Pipeline: The Business and Politics of Northern Energy Development Projects* (Toronto, 1979).

102 According to the 1982 *Financial Post 500*, as of the end of 1981 Dome was larger than Nova measured by assets and profits but smaller than Nova measured by sales (or operating revenue) and employees. Nova has a bigger presence within Alberta itself.

103 At the time, such costly wells occurred almost exclusively in the Beaufort Sea, Dome's special interest. The budget became known in certain circles as the "Dome budget" and its super-depletion section as the "Gallagher amendment," though later Imperial Oil also benefitted.

104 The Hudson's Bay Company's ownership of 4.5 million acres of mineral rights (after 1889, the HBC and the railways, like the Dominion government, retained mineral rights) was leased out in 1926 to US interests who formed the Hudson Bay Oil and Gas Company. The HBC retained a minority interest in HBOG which in later years became even more lucrative than its retailing operations. The CPR still controls its oil subsidiary, Pan-Canadian Petroleum Ltd.

105 Such lavish compensation was another indication of the 'bourgeois national' character of the NEP, which had as its goal a strengthened Canadian capitalism (not 'socialism' as some critics alleged), even if it meant using public resources to enrich a small, privileged

section of Canadian capital. Lucrative patronage also played its part. For a few "consulting services" in acquiring Petro-Canada, the federal government paid a $1 million fee to Sogener, a Swiss bank whose vice-president was the long-time Liberal supporter, Maurice Strong. The Alberta government's practices meet about the same standards of ethics. See, for example, Don Smith, "The patronage game champs," *Toronto Star*, 25 July 1981, p. B-5.

106 However, this has not ended all rivalry or some private sector hostility to Petro-Canada, as was demonstrated in 1978, when AGTL/Nova outmanoeuvred Petro-Canada in the expensive battle to take over US-owned Husky Oil Ltd, or in the efforts of some oil interests and the Conservative Party to "privatize" Petro-Canada.

107 In the federal general election of February 1980, the nine-month old Conservative government of Albertan Joe Clark, which had generally supported the "provincialist" positions of the Lougheed government on energy matters even before the NEP, was replaced by the Trudeau Liberals, in part because of Conservative plans to "privatize" Petro-Canada. Even public opinion polls confirmed that the Conservative position flew in the face of strong popular support for Petro-Canada as a government institution— including in Alberta. Nevertheless, the federal government's support for 'Canadianization' and public ownership should not be exaggerated, for the NEP studiously avoided the takeover of Imperial Oil, the keystone of US corporate imperialism in Alberta and in Canada.

108 According to the federal Finance Minister, Allan MacEachen, the NEP would increase the federal/provincial/corporate percentages to 24/43/33 from 10/45/45.

109 Premier E.P. Lougheed, television talk on 3 September 1981. The Lougheed strategy was not supported by all Albertans. Notably, the Alberta Federation of Labour opposed the oil cutbacks.

110 One outgrowth of the anti-federal, anti-'socialist' oil industry agitation was the appearance, especially since 1980, of so-called western separatist organizations, which have tried to act as vehicles for right-wing protest. In February 1982, an official separatist candidate, Gordon Kessler, was elected in a provincial by-election in Olds-Didsbury, a fading Social Credit riding. Kessler, who owns a firm that does oil scouting (industrial spying) for oil companies, claimed that his firm fell from 13 to 3 employees as a result of the NEP, which he called the "national extermination policy."

111 Thus, Dome participated in the acquisition boom stimulated by the NEP when it took over Hudson Bay Oil and Gas.

112 One of the justifications used for developing Petro-Canada was that the higher prices for oil would 'not sell' to the public unless there was a perceived change in who was getting the revenue. The political idea, which played on working people's genuine feelings of social responsibility and patriotism, was that ordinary consumers would be more willing to accept price hikes if some of the revenues went to a publicly-owned company rather than to wealthy private oil company owners and if areas of Canada outside Alberta got a bigger share of the taxes.

113 The two other western provincial governments involved in the energy struggles, British Columbia (Social Credit) and Saskatchewan (NDP), soon after concluded

agreements with the federal government in line with the Alberta agreement. Political partisanship was not necessarily decisive in determining responses to the NEP. The Ontario provincial government, a Conservative government, actually provided some support to the NEP: in 1981, it bought a 25 percent shareholding in Suncor, with options to buy further shares (up to 51 percent) if other Canadian buyers were not found.

114 Warren Caragata, *Alberta Labour: A Heritage Untold* (Toronto, 1979), 9.

115 Irving Abella, *The Canadian Labour Movement, 1902-1960*, Historical Booklet No. 28, The Canadian Historical Association (Ottawa, 1975), 5.

116 John Blue, *Alberta Past and Present: Historical and Biographical* (Chicago, 1924), I, 391, 392.

117 *Calgary Herald*, 9 March 1949.

118 Before 1956 the umbrella organizations were the Industrial Federation of Labour of Alberta (associated with the Canadian Congress of Labour in Canada and the Congress of Industrial Organization [CIO] in the US), which had grown out of the rise of industrial unionism in the 1930s, and the craft based Alberta Federation of Labour (associated with the Canadian Labour Congress in Canada and the AFL-CIO in the US). By 1952, the Industrial Federation had about 8,000 members while the Alberta Federation had 18,430 members; in 1957, the year after merger, the united Alberta Federation of Labour had 32,000 members.

119 L.G. Thomas, *The Liberal Party in Alberta: A History of Politics in the Province of Alberta, 1905-1921* (Toronto, 1959), 49.

120 Lougheed, *Speech*, 6 September 1974, 8.

121 Some indication of the importance of British imperialism in Canada is evident in the fact that throughout the 25 years prior to 1914 about 70 percent of Canadian capital imports originated in Britain and that in some years as much as 22.6 percent of all British capital exports went to Canada. See Paterson, *British Direct Investment*, 3-4.

122 The very naming of the province (1905) and the provisional district (1882) after Her Royal Highness Princess Louise Caroline Alberta, the fourth daughter of Queen Victoria and the wife of the Marquis of Lorne, Governor-General of Canada from 1870 to 1883, reflects the role of British imperialism in Alberta's past. Unfortunately, while the name can one day be changed, the carnage of these imperialist wars cannot be so easily undone.

Indian Land Policy and the Settler State in Colonial Western Canada

A.D. Fisher

I say that we have been patient a long time, and when we say that, mild words only serve as covers for great ones to do wrong, it is time when we were justified in saying that robbery is robbery everywhere, and the guilty ones are bound by the force of public opinion to take notice of it.

Louis Riel

1. Introduction

It has been suggested by some Albertans that it is their pioneer heritage and the natural wealth of their province that have created their present state of economic well-being. Such is the accepted myth of the settler colony. This myth finds expression in conventional Alberta histories, for example, in James MacGregor's popular history which is dedicated "To the fur traders, farmers and financiers who have made Alberta what it is." MacGregor writes:

As a white man's haven Alberta's morning had dawned. The Indians had been elbowed aside. The tide of settlement was starting to lap at its edges. Year after year the scurrying surveyors were coming to know more of Alberta's interior and were marvelling at its soil's richness, while away in the East, dawdling politicians held out the promise of a railroad.

Later he concludes:

In opening up our province the pioneers of seventy-five years ago chose to follow a rough road and stuck with it until they set sunny Alberta on the highway to our modern riches. Today's youth, having no less courage but infinitely more know how, have the opportunity to choose their own rocky path of sacrifice and patience which, pursued quietly and persistently, could lead them and the world to witness the swiftest expansion of human well-being that has ever coloured men's dreams.[1]

Unfortunately, this myth exists to legitimate the present political economy—*the status quo*. It does not refer either to actual geography or to history. It neglects a number of important historical matters and through this neglect distorts the contribution of the original Albertans and their environment to the present state of affairs. It misrepresents the Native peoples of Alberta and their role in the pioneer past: the myth concentrates selectively on cultural matters and thereby manipulates the ties between the particular pioneer culture of the colonizer Canadians and the pre-existing culture and economy of the Indian and Métis—hunting, freighting, and fur trading.

Basically, today's myth derives from an earlier era of national 'internal' expansion (1860-1900). This era was the one that saw the purchase of Rupert's Land and the building of the CPR; it also set a pattern for expansion in the present day. The recent expansion is exemplified by the proposed northern natural gas pipeline development, by the James Bay development, and, in Alberta, by the construction of the Big Horn Dam and the effects of the W.A.C. Bennett Dam on the Peace-Athabasca Delta. For the Native peoples concerned, this modern expansion will likely have results that are as unfavourable for them as were those of the expansion that affected their grandparents.[2] Thus the mythology of the settler colony is more than a historical curiosity. It is an explanation of contemporary political relations, one that ignores the implications of the unequal costs of national expansion in the West, in either 1870 or 1970.

The settler myth ignores historical government policy towards the Native peoples, the land, and its resources, and it evades the governmental view of its own responsibilities in economic development. In doing so, the myth obscures the successful pre-settlement economy, the successes of reserve Indians, and how or why the outcome of reservationization turned out to be Indian underdevelopment in "the bountiful land" of Alberta. It is these issues this essay addresses.

2. The Fur Trade Era

During the fur trade era in the eighteenth century, there developed in western Canada a cluster of institutions related to the interdependency of trader and Indian as well as to sporadic conflict between free traders and the monopolistic Hudson's Bay Company. This interdependency and conflict influenced modes of production, transportation, and dissemination of fur trade products, financial management, and, indeed, domestic matters such as marriage patterns, family size, and location of residence. These institutions created a number of sub-cultural adaptations to the ecology and geography of the West, some of which came to bear names such as "Home Guard" Indians, "far" Indians, Métis, Voyageur, etc. These institutions accompanied the rapid spread of fur trade culture towards the West during the mid-eighteenth century. In 1754 Henday's trip west led him just north of Red Deer and then west of Edmonton in Alberta. He was followed west by Smith, Deering, Le Blanc, and Pink from 1756 to 1764. In the 1770s, Pond, Pidgeon, Blondeu, Tomison, and Longmore travelled the western prairies. All this activity eventually brought about conflict between the traders and the Blackfoot, Gros Ventre, Assiniboine, and Cree. In 1777, three traders were killed in a skirmish in western Saskatchewan, and another was killed in 1779. In 1780, also in Saskatchewan, Peter Pond's trade fort, Sturgeon House, was burned. In 1781, Longmore was attacked by the Gros Ventres, prairie fires became common around the western trade forts, and six traders were killed in the Manitoba country.

To counter this hostility, the Hudson's Bay Company in the 1780s sent Thompson, Fidler, and Gaddy to winter with the hostile Blackfoot confederacy, but they were unable to engage the Blackfoot more fully in the fur trade. By the 1800s the western prairies had been penetrated by the established fur trade institutions, which led to the building of Buckingham House, Edmonton House, Chesterfield House, and Rocky Mountain House. However, as illustrated by the attack of the Blackfoot on Lewis and Clark in 1810, conflict caused by these changing circumstances lurked in the wings, so to speak, and threatened to burst forth to centre stage.

In the early nineteenth century the political economy of eastern Indian life was changing; the Crown no longer needed Indians as military allies. The fur trade, as we have noted, had moved further to the west, and so the eastern Indians had value neither to state nor to corporate citizen. Furthermore, the fur companies of Canada had become interested in land acquisition through land companies, such as the Canada Company and the British-American Land Company, and in banking, such as through the Bank of Montreal.[3] About the same time, timber began to replace fur as the leading export commodity and the Hudson's Bay Company reorganized itself internally to cope with these political, economic, and geographical changes.

These changes were reflected in Indian policy, too. Canadian Indian lands, formerly protected from expropriation or purchase by the Proclamation of 1763, became vulnerable to alienation by the Indian Department of the Governor General's Office. Eleven and one quarter million acres belonging to nine eastern Canadian tribes were given up *to pay for Indian annuities* between 1818 and 1838. Reflecting on this land policy and the parallel responsibility for administering Indian band funds, L.S.F. Upton characterizes the Indian Department with the word "fraudulent."[4] Upton also notes that in the 1830s Sir Francis Bond Head attempted to remove the Hurons, Ottawa, Ojibway, and other Indians to Manitoulin Island by accepting a surrender of their lands which amounted to three million acres. In reaction to these changes in land and trade policy the Colonial Office issued an official statement on Indian policy in 1838: "The document was a comprehensive statement of the duty to civilize the natives."[5]

3. Confederation

The new policy for Indian affairs derived from changes in British mercantile policy in the mid nineteenth century, changes that were also expressed in the process of confederation and the subsequent National Policy in Canada. Confederation was based upon a strong centralized state organization which would on occasion intervene in commerce in order to organize and direct national expansion. While doing so it would favour the existing commercial enterprises of land companies, railroads, and banks.[6] The Robinson-Superior Treaties of the 1850s exemplify these influences of centralized mercantilism on Indian affairs as do the subsequent numbered treaties on the prairies. This colonial settlement policy was extended to the Northwest Territories after the Crown's purchase of Rupert's Land in 1869-70. Zaslow summarizes this extension as a continuation of the Indian Policy of central Canada. It continued to regard the Indians in need of protection as before, and it emphasized that the Anglo-Saxon way of farming was to be the standard of civilization for the prairies.[7] The continuation of these policies is not surprising as the Hudson's Bay Company, the Grand Trunk (and later the Canadian Pacific), and other land and banking interests of central Canada were not-so-silent partners in the transfer of Rupert's Land to the Crown.[8] The 1860s transfer left the new Dominion government in much the same position as the English Crown had been in 1763, holding title to a vast expanse of land occupied by the disgruntled Indians and mixed-bloods.

The central government proceeded to carry out the following measures: to pass the Manitoba Act (1870) to control the land; to follow Robertson-Ross' advice concerning a police force to control the Indians and Métis and create the Mounted Police (1873)—placing the Indian Department under the Department of the Interior and the Secretary of State for the Provinces (1873); to enact the North-West Territories Act (1875) to regulate those lands and communities not under the Manitoba or other Acts; to enact the Indian Act (1876) to regulate the Indians and their lands. As a result, the opening of the western frontier in Canada was not done by free trader or independent settler. It was opened as a corporate enterprise of the central government, controlled *by* members *of* and *for* the benefit of a central Canadian corporate elite.

In 1875 the Half-breed Land and Script Commission was operating in Manitoba to extinguish the claims to land by the Métis. In this way the mixed-bloods' claims could be removed to make way for the eastern capitalists' Grand Trunk and Canadian Pacific railways and subsequent settlement. The year 1876 saw the signing of Treaty No. 6 and 1877, Treaty No. 7. These agreements were based in part on the experience obtained in the Robinson and earlier numbered treaties (see Figure II-1). The purpose of the treaties was to extinguish the claims to land by Indian people and to open up to settlement the remaining habitable land in the western North-West Territories.

4. The Land To Be 'Surrendered'

The land to be surrendered had been studied by two government expeditions, a British one headed by Captain John Palliser in 1857-59, and a Canadian one in 1857-58 which included Henry Youle Hind as geologist-geographer. These studies, although contradictory, established the idea that the western territories contained two types of land. The first was called "true Prairie land—Sterile or with scanty pasture." It was bounded on the north and east by another type, a "Zone of Ancient forest cleared by fire—soil fertile and rich."[9] These studies were later transformed and led to the concepts of the Great American Desert for the southern zone and the fertile zone for the northern zone of the western prairies.

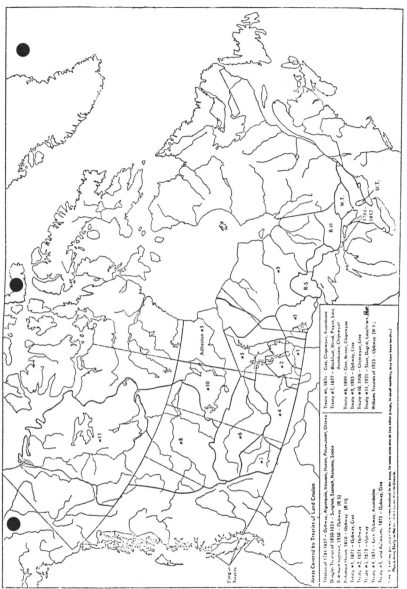

Figure II-1

The fertile zone is especially interesting in that it is in this "Zone of Ancient forest cleared by Fire" that the soil itself had been made valuable by "The crackling flames of fires set by the Indians...."[10] Charles and Ralph Bird report that David Thompson recorded how the aspen parkland (the Ancient forest) was regularly burned by the Indians to increase the range available for buffalo. They say further:

Throughout the era of the early explorers and the fur traders, it seems likely therefore that the grasslands within the aspen parkland were considerably more open and extensive than they were after the bison had disappeared and settlement began.[11]

The Birds buttress this statement by noting that during the initial stages of settlement it was the grasslands within the parkland that were first broken for crops. Indeed, they say that it was not until World War II and the introduction of the bulldozer that Albertans could complete the assault on the aspen parkland (which had become considerably enlarged by this time due to the suppression of Indian burning).

It was in this zone that the national development scheme was to emphasize the Anglo-Saxon farming complex, while to the south in the true prairie zone the policy chose cattle ranching. Treaty No. 6 covered most of the fertile zone in Alberta while Treaty No. 7 covered the true prairie (see Figure II-2). The fertile zone was occupied primarily by Crees and Stoneys, while the prairies were held by Blackfoot, Stoneys, and Sarcees. In the southern zone the financial friends of the Conservative government had interests. There was the CPR syndicate which would choose the southern route through Kicking Horse Pass instead of the northern Yellowhead Pass route. Next, there were the land speculators attached to the CPR and Hudson's Bay Company, and, finally, there were the supporters of the Canadian military and hence the North-West Mounted Police. These friends of the Government were represented by Lieutenant Governor David Laird and Colonel James F. Macleod at Blackfoot crossing where they negotiated the surrender of the true prairie zone of southern Alberta to the central government.

These negotiations with the Blackfoot-speaking bands were not entirely smooth. At first, the Bloods and Peigans refused to meet at the place chosen by the Treaty Commissioners.[12] In the Blood and Blackfoot camps there was resistance to making treaty. Nevertheless, when on 21 October 1877 Crowfoot said "I will sign the Treaty," the Blood and Peigan war chiefs bowed to consensus and agreed to sign. They and the other signatories, the Stoneys and Sarcees, surrendered the prairies and foothills from the Milk River to the Battle River, from the Cypress Hills to the Rocky Mountains, for reserves whose size was based on the formula of one square mile of land per family of five. This formula meant that the signatories of Treaty No. 7 retained approximately three percent of the land of southern Alberta. Also, they retained the right to practise their "vocation

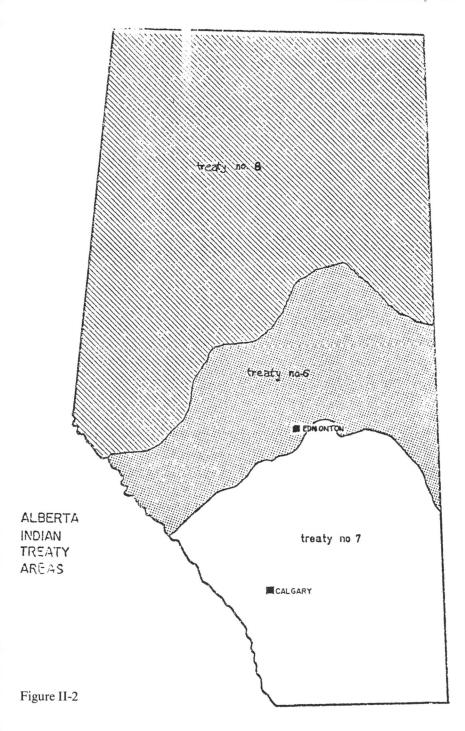

treaty no. 8

treaty no. 6

EDMONTON

treaty no 7

CALGARY

ALBERTA
INDIAN
TREATY
AREAS

Figure II-2

of hunting" throughout the surrendered tract. Both of these treaty rights were to be abrogated by the subsequent settlement policies of the central government.

The reserve awarded to the Bloods on Treaty day was deemed uninhabitable by them. For this reason they moved near to Fort Macleod where they stayed until a new treaty was signed in 1883.[13] At the same time, indeed, in the middle of the new reserve in one case, the friends of the government were founding cattle ranches.

5. Early Settler Society

These ranches were based on 21-year leaseholds of up to 100,000 acres of the surrendered Indian lands. The leases were granted at 1¢ per acre per year or approximately 10¢ per cow per year. Many ranches were owned by the merchant/banker establishment of central Canada. The first on the scene, the Cochrane Ranch Company, was incorporated in 1881 by Senator M.H. Cochrane of Compton, Quebec.[14] The Oxley Ranch Company was owned by Alexander Stavely-Hill of the UK. Other ranches of note were the Northwest Cattle Company, the Walrond Cattle Ranche Limited, the Stewart Ranche Company, the Military Colonization Company, the Halifax Ranche Company, and the Winder Ranch Company. The last was owned by Captain William Winder of the North-West Mounted Police. All of the ranchers were closely affiliated with the Conservative party in Canada or the UK.[15]

The ranchers shared the ideology and the politics of the legal arm of the central Canadian government, the North-West Mounted Police. Modelled on the Royal Irish Constabulary,[16] designed to be the Canadian military *and* the arm of central authority in the West,[17] the Mounted Police were led by the sons and comrades of the central Canadian elite. Eighty percent of their officers were Canadian born, upper class, well educated easterners with connections in high society.[18] Ranch employees and ranch managers were often ex-policemen or ex-Hudson's Bay employees. This was the pioneer or settler society that enveloped the Treaty No. 7 Indians of the true prairies.

This was not a frontier society of political radicalism or social innovation. The settler society that grew in southern Alberta in the last decades of the nineteenth century was a hierarchical, orderly, western example of the Victorian *status quo*.[19] This society had been created by the supporters of the government in central Canada. This government had helped its supporters by underwriting railway ventures, by creating a special western military police force, and by granting investment opportunities in land speculation (with the railroads and land companies) and land leases for cattle ranching. It was this society that made and enforced the treaty obligations of the southern Alberta Indians.

6. The Emergence of Enforced Dependency

At first, while elements of the earlier fur trade economy remained, the Indians had priority over the cattlemen or railwaymen.[20] Then, with the destruction of the remaining constituents of that earlier society after the North-West Uprising (1885), the attitude of the Mounted Police and ranchers changed. An example of the change can be seen in the attitudes of the Acting Indian Agent on the Blood Reserve, W. Pocklington. During the early years of the reserve, when land matters were unsettled, the police and Indian Agent turned a blind eye to war parties against the Cree and horse raids into Montana.[21] The Agent said at that time regarding rations, "It has afforded me much pleasure to find such [reducing Indian rations] is not the present intention of the Department; if it were, very serious trouble would be the result, as these Indians are a powerful tribe, rich in horses, with many warriors, well armed, and a large supply of ammunition."[22] During the North-West Uprising, rancher and policeman did their utmost to prevent the Blackfoot, Blood, and Peigan from becoming involved. The employees of the Cochrane Ranch pulled down Indian tepees found off-reserve while the ranch owners bribed the Bloods to stay at home and off the Ranch.[23]

After 1885, "serious trouble" seemed less likely and, therefore, the Mounted Police could become more coercive towards the Indians. In a sense, the ranching frontier in southern Alberta had encircled the Treaty No. 7 Indians cutting them off from their traditional "vocations" of hunting and trading, and closing off a number of alternative economic adaptations which might have presented themselves decades earlier. It has been claimed that the collapse of the buffalo economy created starvation and economic dependency among the western tribes, but it might just as logically be claimed that the post-fur trade expansion of mercantile Canada, which depended on Mounted Police, Treaty Commissioners, surveyors, railways, and cattle ranchers, simply occupied all of the available life-sustaining space in southern Alberta, thus making it impossible for the Treaty No. 7 Indians to pursue *any* vocation let alone their traditional one of buffalo hunting.

Because the Indians could no longer hunt, because there were no buffalo, and because the Mounted Police were charged with protecting the ranchers' cattle from marauding Indians, the government had to feed its "wards." In the words of the government, it was "cheaper to feed the Indians than to fight them."[24] Feeding the Indians was good business, too, and beef and rations were provided to the Blackfoot, Blood, and Peigan by the Walrond Ranche Company, the Cochrane Ranch Company, and the I.G. Baker Company of Fort Benton, Montana. The habitat of the vocationless Indians became further restricted with the arrival of the Mormon settlers near the boundary line. The Bloods allowed them to winter along Lee Creek in 1886.

In the north, settlers were organizing to oppose the cattle rancher political elite. Until 1896, the ranchers controlled the economy and politics of Alberta. D.W. Davis, the first MP from the Alberta region of the North-West Territories, was a former trader and a former employee of the I.G. Baker Company of Montana. These connections made him sympathetic to the ranchers' economy.

In 1896 he lost his seat to Frank Oliver, a Liberal from Edmonton who would eventually become Minister of the Interior and hence Minister of Indian Affairs. Oliver's support came from the fertile zone north of the prairies, and from northern railroad interests and land speculators.

7. The Indian Struggle Against Dependency and Land Surrenders

Although the Indians within the enveloping settler society were now largely on rations, they continued to seek from among the residue of post-fur trade activities an economic pursuit that would sustain them, both mentally and physically. The search was given impetus by the government's insistence that Indians be self-supporting. This insistence was a longstanding policy based on the reluctance of the government to spend lavishly on the West and on the customary conversion of royal gifts and trade gifts for Indians into administrative and subsistence monies.[25] In southern Alberta the search led to the establishment of an Indian cattle industry on reserve which parallelled that of the eastern-owned ranch enterprises. In the north this option was frustrated by the absence of open land for husbandry or agriculture. Much of the fire-wrought meadowland had been surrendered at treaty time, and much reserve land was aspen-poplar 'bush' land. When faced with such conditions frustrated reserve superintendents perversely recommended the surrender of more Indian land in order that it might be sold and the money used to reduce the cost of rations, annuities, and administration.

The Indian cattle industry began in earnest in 1894 when Red-Crow and Crop-Eared-Wolf exchanged part of their horse herds for cattle. These horses, the Indian's 'capital' of the buffalo fur trade era, were exchanged for the capital of the leasehold ranching era, cattle. However, this economic conversion was not accomplished without resistance. Just as at Treaty time, conservative elements resisted the change. On all three Blackfoot-speaking reserves (see Figure II-3) the introduction of cattle created an uproar among the conservatives.[26] By this time the former hunters were coal miners, freighters, scouts for the Mounted Police—primarily a cheap labour force supplying casual labour and hay to the ranchers' society in southern Alberta.[27] The labouring activities, however, did not fit into the structure of the fur trade-reserve society on reserve.

The introduction of cattle met with varied success: the Bloods were the most successful and the Blackfoot were the least. The reason the Bloods were so successful was their direct association with the cattle elite, their experience of the combined power of Police and rancher, and their recognition of the prestige of the paramilitary rancher elite.[28] It is little wonder that the leaders of the "Kainah" (many-chiefs) sought to emulate the powerful cattlemen and aspired to their prestige by affiliating with their enterprise. Their Indian Agents agreed with their choice and the annual reports testified that cattle ranching was the way of the future for these Indians.[29] Also, they indicated that "The principal occupation of those Indians, after seeing to their cattle and horses, is hay-making and freighting of coal, flour and other supplies." "$1400 was realized from the

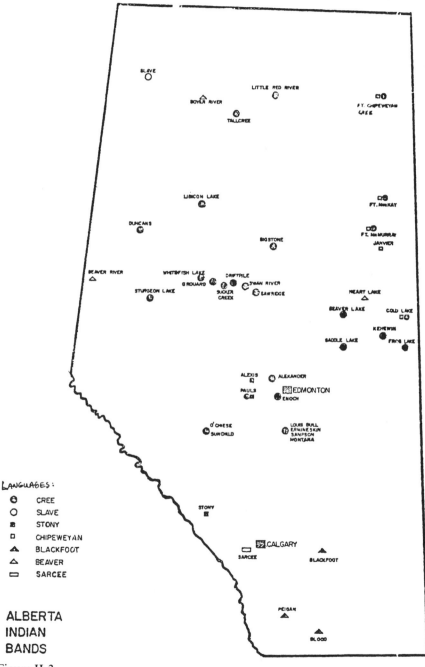

LANGUAGES:

- ● CREE
- ○ SLAVE
- ▣ STONY
- ▢ CHIPEWEYAN
- ▲ BLACKFOOT
- △ BEAVER
- ▭ SARCEE

**ALBERTA
INDIAN
BANDS**

Figure II-3

Mormon Colony for freight," but stock raising, "...is fast assuming a most important place."[30] In 1901 the Bloods had more than 2,500 head of cattle in their operation. Such was not the case on the Blackfoot Reserve.

The conservatives among the Blackfood had resisted the introduction of cattle fearing a reduction in their rations. In 1901 their fears were realized. Their new Agent, A.J. Markle, having come from a posting on a more easterly reserve, was personally appalled at the conditions on the prairie reserve and, "...acting on his conviction the only way to make an Indian self-supporting was to make him work, inaugurated the work-or-starve policy." The Blackfoot responded in three ways. Some just died of a broken heart. Others began begging and stealing. Almost all the rest tried to avoid everything associated with the white man, including the cattle industry.[31] They stayed away from the cattle economy because it implied a personal obligation to the oppressive Indian Agent.

On the Peigan Reserve in the foothills of the Rocky Mountains there was mixed success at ranching. Due to its climate the reserve was not thought to be particularly suited to farming, so the Peigans worked at haying, freighting, and stock raising. They had 775 head of cattle in 1901.[32] In 1903 there were nearly twice that many at 1,423 head. In 1905 they went into grain farming "on a limited scale." In 1910, in order to provide the capital to enlarge this enterprise and to provide funds for Blackfoot rations and farming, two land surrenders were engineered. Indeed, throughout the first decade of this century the government had been attempting to achieve new land surrenders on all three Blackfoot-speaking reserves. The first of these attempts on the Blood reserve was defeated by a 3 to 1 margin,[33] and similar attempts were voted down on the other reserves. In 1910, however, the Blackfoot surrendered 125,000 acres, and the Peigans surrendered 11,192 acres.[34]

Today, it might be concluded that these land sales were necessary to provide development capital to advance the economic development of these reserves. It might also be presumed that the pressure of pioneer settlement led to calls for more and more Indian land. However, this does not seem to have been the case.

The land surrendered by the Blackfoot in 1910 remained largely unsold until 1917 when the Soldier Resettlement Programme caused the sale of most of the remaining land. The capital derived from initial sales was not enough to lift the Blackfoot from the depression caused by the "work-or-starve" edict.[35] The land of the Peigan Reserve was never thought to be especially suited to Anglo-Saxon farming, and it too went unsold until 1913. Therefore, pioneer land needs do not seem to have been behind the 1910 land surrenders. On the contrary, it seems that land surrenders were forced on Indian groups in a punitive or retaliatory manner, on bands reputed to be uncooperative or unwilling to become "civilized" or self-supporting.

This retaliation against conservative bands was often couched in terms indicating that land surrender was being considered for the band's own benefit.

For example, Was-hat-a-now's band lost its reserve near Fort Victoria because it was a small band that was "going backwards," "…the majority hunt or fish as the fancy takes them."[36] They were amalgamated with Chief Blue Quill's band in 1893. Blue Quill's band was also small but had the virtues of being settled and 'progressive.' A second example was Sharphead's band, another band that "…did very little but hunt." They were broken up and amalgamated with Paul's band, west of Edmonton, and with Sampson's band at Hobbema in 1897. A third example was that of Chief Pa-pas-chase's band in Strathcona or south Edmonton. Pa-pas-chase was mentioned in 1886 as having quieted the excitement and "boastfulness" of the Indians around Edmonton during the uprising in 1885.[37] Patriotism notwithstanding, Pa-pas-chase lost his reserve because it stood in the path of the Calgary-Edmonton railway. His followers joined Enoch's band, Sampson's band, and one or more bands at Saddle Lake Reserve.

There were other bands unlike Pa-pas-chase who communicated with the insurgents at Frog Lake and Duck Lake. Bobtail's band near the Bear Hills is thought to have done this and also to have burned the missionary's house and the Hudson's Bay warehouse at Battle River.

In 1909, the remaining sixty-three residents of Bobtail's Reserve agreed to a complex land surrender which amalgamated them with Sampson's band while at the same time allowed their relatives in the Montana band to retain ten square miles of their former reserve for themselves.[38] This Indian community had been archetypically recalcitrant. Not only had they participated in the general unrest accompanying the 1885 uprising, some of them had joined the exodus to Montana to avoid retribution after the uprising collapsed. Still others of the band at first opted for half-breed or Métis status by accepting land scrip in 1886, then they recanted the following year and asked to revert to reserve Indian status. Finally, in 1896, the United States deported the members of the Bobtail group who were then known as the Montana band, and they returned to their Alberta reserve.[39]

The notorious Agent Markle serving as Inspector of Indian Agencies appears to have engineered most of the early twentieth-century land surrenders. In the Bobtail case there were attempts to gain surrenders in 1904, 1905, 1906 and 1908. Success was achieved in 1909. Bobtail's band had agreed to surrenders in 1904 and 1906, but the conditions that they demanded were unacceptable to the government. (In 1906, the responsible minister was Frank Oliver of Edmonton.) In 1906 these unacceptable conditions included:

1. a sale price of $10 per acre
2. no further requests for land surrenders
3. an increase in freedom of movement for individual members of the band, and more Indian involvement and responsibility in band management
4. greater openness in the granting of permits to sell products off the reserve
5. guaranteed support for the aged and infirm band members.[40]

But in 1909 surrender was achieved by Markle under acceptable terms. Bobtail's band ceased to exist, and their collective resistance to expansion was stilled.

8. Government Duplicity

The government's attitudes towards the Indians and their land are indicative of the climate in which Indian development was supposed to occur. Hayter Reed, Deputy Superintendant of Indian Affairs (1893-1897), typified these views. He said that it was the government's duty,

...to redeem from a state of partial savagery a horde of Indians dominated by tribal law and aboriginal customs and to transform them into competent agriculturalists, ranchers, or mechanics.[41]

It was officially recognized that redeeming the Indians would be difficult:

...the Indians, so far from having availed themselves of the machinery provided for enfranchisement, had rather shown a inclination to adhere to tribal customs.

But there were ways of achieving it:

There seems little room for doubt that a workable plan for enfranchisement may enable the Indian to make a start in the direction which Indian legislation has at any rate for its theoretical object, viz.: the breaking up of separate racial communities which have in whole or in part reached the highest point of development under tutelage, and their amalgamation with other national elements.[42]

Optimum redemption or development was impeded to some degree by envelopment of the Native economy by the National Policy. This then led to the rations system to avoid fighting the western Indians and to views such as the following:

...hopes may be entertained of making these moral weaklings good citizens and a credit and a profit to our country, and less a burden and expense...for in my mind nothing withers and eventually destroys true manhood more surely than the gratuitous issue of food to those who have the strength to earn it themselves.[43]

Here, the entanglement of ideology and action is clearly stated by Agent Markle. One must recall the response of the Blackfoot people to the imposition of his "work-or-starve" policy. In order to resist the imposition of Markle's "manhood" and to preserve their pride, they starved. There are other entanglements in the policy of "enfranchisement"[44] of the still "partially savage" Indians. Recall that self-sufficiency was a primary goal held for the western Indians by their Federal administrators. Because, as in many cases, the Indians were actively resisting assimilation as agriculturalists, ranchers, and mechanics, the only basis for achieving self-sufficiency was the sale of their land. Assimilation, enfranchise-ment, and the amalgamation of smaller bands were some of the motivating factors lying behind the active advocacy of Indian land surrenders. At the very best, these motives were opportunistic and short-sighted.

Worse yet, this official government rationale conveniently ignored certain aspects of the Treaty-making process. For example, Treaty No. 7 was uncondi-tional. It was a permanent, irrevocable surrender of Indian lands which bound both parties to the conditions of the surrender. One of the conditions was that the Indian signatories had the right to practise their vocation of hunting throughout the surrendered tract. This was a permanent condition subject to minimal regulation from time to time.[45] This permanent obligation was gradually abrogated by the introduction of the institutions of eastern Canada, the CPR, the Mounted Police, and grazing leases. It was not abrogated by the Blackfoot, Blood, or Peigan. The government was obliged to establish a policy of supplying rations to prevent the Indians from starving (in addition to its other Treaty obligations). The Blackfoot accepted them and became dependent on rations, in part because they could no longer hunt. Then rations were removed by the agents of the Crown. Since rations had replaced hunting, the removal of rations must have seemed to the Blackfoot a violation of the Treaty agreements regard-ing hunting rights.

The Treaties also had specified a formula for allocating reserve lands, one square mile per family of five. On this basis the various bands agreed to surrender the *remaining* lands. Sharphead agreed, Was-hat-a-now agreed, Pa-pas-chase agreed, Crowfoot agreed, all the Treaty No. 6 and Treaty No. 7 Chiefs agreed to these terms—one square mile per family of five as recorded in the treaty census. All these Chiefs agreed to these terms despite their knowledge that the number of their band members had lately become reduced. They agreed knowing, as did the Crown, that they could not ask for more land if they once agreed to the surrender. (This is illustrated by the fact that the Bloods had to agree to a second treaty in 1883 to confirm their new reserve along the Belly River. At that time another census was taken, as it was every year.)

Nowhere in Treaty No. 7 was it indicated that the reserves could be subse-quently expanded or contracted to reflect the actual numbers of Indians in the annual census. The land was to be reserved for them during the process of civilization—no matter how long that took. Indeed, it was to be held for them by the crown permanently. Alexander Morris felt that this reserve system would be of great value to the Indians of the prairies. He judged the Canadian system better than the American one, and said, "Any premature enfranchisement, or power given them to part with their lands, would inevitably lead to the speedy breaking up of the reserves, and the return of the Indians to their wandering mode of life…"[46] The Treaties said nothing of the Indians' requirements, nothing about financing changes in their life-ways. The rationalization of post-treaty land surrenders was in clear violation of the Crown's agreement with the Indian Chiefs. The rationalizations indicated that the so-called "civilized" civil servants were opportunistic. Indeed, the moralizing of Agent Markle was a grotesque insult to the once-powerful Blackfoot. It was *he* who introduced the "work-or-starve" policy that turned the Blackfoot against the Crown, a policy that appears to have impeded the successful change in their life-ways. (Note in contrast the successes of Bloods and Peigans to the south.)

One must conclude from these forced post-treaty land surrenders that at least some of the wealth of modern Albertans was directly extorted from Indian Albertans and their lands by opportunistic, amoral, pioneer civil servants. This extortion was in violation of the Treaties (Nos. 6 and 7). The Treaties were understood to have said in effect "...to have and to hold unto the use of the Indians forever." But possibly the post-treaty land surrenders were more fundamental policies than mere opportunistic 'mandarin' manipulations. The pressure for continued land surrenders is quite probably a continuation of the earliest expansion of central Canada into the West.

Returning to the example of the economically successful Blood Indians, after they began farming in 1907 their economy continued to grow until their Agent could claim "a fair portion" were self-supporting. The Bloods became economically 'successful,' a tribe of successful grain farming, cattle ranching, and hay-making Indians. While this success was being achieved, however, Canada had become involved in a European war. As a result, the federal government enacted special wartime legislation, such as the Greater Production Programme and the Soldier Resettlement Programme, which by revivifying the lagging National Policy in the West increased pressures on the Indians to surrender more of their reserve lands for sale. This renewed pressure was reflected in the land surrender referenda held in 1916 and 1918 on the Blood Reserve. The one held in 1916 was defeated and no land was surrendered, but the one held in 1918 was successful.[47]

It appears that the success achieved in the referendum was based upon a gross subversion of the democratic process which was in turn related to the destruction of the successful economy of the Blood Reserve. This occurred in a situation already complicated by the Indian Act's imposition of electoral majority rule upon a group who customarily decided matters by informal consensus. The Blood's former Agent, R.N. Wilson, documented the disruption of their way of life in a memorial entitled "Our Betrayed Wards."[48] Although not all of his accusations can be verified it seems clear that the Blood Agency did do the following. First, it refused to allow any more reserve land to be broken for Indians to cultivate unless the band agreed to a land sale. Then the Agency refused to disburse any of the band money derived from existing leases as agreed to at the time of the lease. Then the Agency stopped giving rations to the "permanently destitute" members of the band, while providing support for those band members who advocated the land sale (recall Bobtail's unacceptable conditions of surrender). Finally, Indians who opposed the referendum and sale were denied access to their own funds which were held by the Agency.

In 1918 the Bloods agreed to lease land near Cardston to non-Indian farmers on condition that the money derived from the lease be distributed to them on a per capita basis. Wilson charges that once the lease was arranged the Agency distributed only one third of the funds, reserving the remainder to itself. Also in 1918, the Minister of Indian Affairs—and soon to be Prime Minister— Arthur Meighen, announced a change in Indian administration. To overcome the difficulties faced in land surrenders or enfranchisement, the government that year claimed the right to lease Indian land with or without the approval of the Band concerned:

Whenever...land...is uncultivated and the band or individual is unable or neglects to cultivate the same, the Superintendent General may..., without surrender, grant a lease of such lands for agricultural and grazing purposes for the benefit of the band or individual.[49]

This order-in-council empowered the Superintendent to lease Indian lands even if the band, "...through some delusion, misapprehension or hostility..." vetoed a surrender, sale, or lease.[50] In 1918, the Superintendent authorized a second lease of 90,000 acres above and beyond the two leases assented to by the band, ignoring the Blood Agency's refusal to break more land for Indian cultivation.

The granting of this new lease caused those Indians living in the leased areas (50,000 acres at the north end of the reserve and 40,000 acres in the south-western area) to lose their homes. The new lease was also located in part on the winter range for the Blood cattle herd. Furthermore, the Agency and the lessees immediately fenced the better south-western range land, while leaving the northern range open, allowing the lessees' cattle to wander into the remaining band range. It was an unfortunate coincidence that many of the Bloods who were dispossessed of home and grazing land were opponents of the forthcoming referendum.

Bloods who objected to the lease of reserve lands were threatened with prosecution under the Indian Act by the Commissioner and by the Mounted Police. And the Agent refused to assist or support the band in its spring round-up, thereby adding to the confusion and worsening an already bad situation. The upshot of all this was that the reserve became over-grazed. Even the Blood Agency itself warned that there was insufficient hay and grazing land for the stock for the winter of 1918.[51]

According to the published reports of the Department for 1919, the Bloods had in the spring of that year [1918] a total of 3,742 cattle which would not include the fall calves lost through mal-administration...In the following spring the survivors were counted and found to number 1,200.[52]

Wilson states that these losses were not the same as those suffered in the winters of 1908 and 1910. The latter were caused by blizzards and frozen ground. The 1918 disaster was caused by the lack of feed on the reserve. The lack of feed, argues Wilson, was caused by the continuing campaign to obtain a successful land surrender referendum from the Bloods. His contention is supported by the fact that at the time of the disaster the Agency said leased land at the south end of the reserve was to be held "until after the next land sale vote." Further, when the Bloods protested their economic disaster (no crops had been grown on the reserve during that time either) they were told that the 90,000 acres of land leased without their consent would be held by the government until they voted to surrender it, and that out of the money raised by selling the surrendered land they would be compensated for their losses. During all this the Bloods voted to surrender some of their land.

In 1921, the Commissioner, supported by a force of ten Mounted Policemen, held another land sale referendum at the Blood Agency. The referendum lost by forty-five votes. In three out of four attempts to achieve a successful land surrender the Bloods resisted the Department's coercion. In 1883 the Blood Reserve contained 548 square miles and 2,043 residents. Today the Reserve contains 517 square miles and more than 4,000 residents. These figures testify to the wisdom and the courage of the Blood band members who resisted forced leases and land surrenders.

Land surrenders, some agreed to under considerable duress and some willingly acceded to, took place all over the Province. Pa-pas-chase's Reserve, Sharphead's Reserve, Was-hat-a-now's Reserve, Bobtail's Reserve, and the Montana Band's Reserve have disappeared since 1885. Almost all of Alberta's Indian reserves have been reduced in size. From the 125,000 acre Blackfoot surrender to smaller ones on the smaller reserves, each surrender has continued the reduction of the Indian land base since the earliest Canadian expansion. This process began with the treaty surrenders, followed by the pre-World War I surrenders, and finally the leases and surrenders associated with the war years. The continuing reduction of Indian economic alternatives supports Sander's judgement about the negative effects of national expansion upon Indian well-being.

9. Land and Underdevelopment

Historically, we can see how the Indian land question was closely intertwined with Indian economic *under*development. Indians were asserted to be detrimental to the growth of settlement. Therefore, economic sanctions were used to coerce Indian land surrenders in order to further non-Indian settlement. However, there was no continuous demand for the land leased and sold by the Department of Indian Affairs. Despite this, the federal government had to update the National Policy from ranching and railroading to soldier resettlement and amalgamation of Indian bands, which again produced land surrenders, a surplus of surrendered land, and a new challenge to the National Policy from the West.

Basically, the Indian people have not prospered because their economic and political unity was destroyed by their encirclement by economic institutions that were beneficial to central Canada. Both Indian and non-Indian westerners have fitfully resisted this encirclement. The most spectacular resistance was the uprising at Batoche and the associated Indian unrest. Less spectacular forms of resistance were those that led the government to retaliate with attacks on the land base of the Bobtail, Blackfoot, and Blood bands. The recalcitrant Indian bands who persisted in the pursuit of fur trade economic activities, the conservative element of the Blackfoot band who rejected cattle, the Bobtail and Montana bands, the Bloods who fought against land surrenders and leases are examples of this other kind of resistance.

It should be recognized by now that the underdevelopment the Indians have suffered has not been a consequence of their ignorance or backwardness. To the contrary, underdevelopment of Indian reserves has been both a cause and a consequence of federal land policy and federal Indian policy. Indirectly, non-Indian settlement has been a direct consequence of government suppression of Indian economic activities, a suppression made necessary by the belief that Indians and their land stood in the path of settlement.

10. Conclusion

Albertans have been able to move into the economic void left by the suppression of the fur trade-buffalo economy just as they initially moved into the fire-cleared meadows of the fertile zone, and into the lands surrendered by the Indians impoverished by the restrictions placed on their customary vocation of hunting (like other vocations of the fur trade era). Albertans have occupied the political void left by the suppression of continued Indian-Métis resistance under the British North America Act, the Manitoba Act, the Indian Act, and the numbered Treaties.

The Pioneers who colonized Alberta were from a hierarchical, Victorian, mercantile central Canada. In the last part of the nineteenth century these pioneers elbowed aside Indians and Métis, and installed the institutions of the National Policy. This policy favoured the merchant and financier friends of the central government.

During this pioneer period in the West there was a general battle in Canada between merchant and industrial capitalism. Unlike central Canada where merchant capital gave way to industrial capital, in the West it did not. At most, the battle led to the modification of mercantile institutions and relationships. This was because in central Canada civil society could impose social constraints on merchant capitalists (the banks, land companies, and transportation companies).

In western Canada these constraints were absent because the leaders of civil society were the cattlemen and developer allies of merchant capital. The representatives of government were also allies as was the infrastructure of colonial rule itself, the Royal Canadian North-West Mounted Police. Thus, when the western battle of 'modernization' was fought, merchant capitalism was only slightly transformed while the pre-existing Indian-Métis economy of fur trade and transportation was extinguished or rendered underdeveloped.

The National Policy allowed its agents to occupy all the available economic niches in the west. None was left over for the Indians or Métis. The accompanying land legislation and policy left them nowhere else to go. Surrounded by mounties and cattlemen, they traded their fur trade capital for a down payment on merchant commodity capitalism: ponies and land were exchanged for cattle or rations and reserved land.

Occupation or settlement opened up Indian land to speculators and took from the Indians and Métis the right to hunt on their land and the independence this implied. It took from them the means of production, the land, in return for promised treaty money and other annuities or land scrip. Then as the earlier fur trader economy evaporated and the Indians became dependent on rations, the scrip was sold and more surrenders coerced in order to pay for rations and annuities. These latter surrenders were rationalized by thoughts of transforming Indians into "competent agriculturalists, ranchers, or mechanics."

During the settlement of western Canada, pioneer Albertans received a 'leg up' from central Canada's National Policy and its effects on fur trade institutions. The pioneers' "rough road" referred to by MacGregor was smoothed somewhat by the capitalists of central Canadian society. This road led the new Albertans to the fertile meadows of the Ancient forest zone, enlarged by Indian fires, or to the vast open grasslands to the south. Their homestead or cattle lease was in part guaranteed by the Treaties, the rations, and the subsequent Indian land surrenders. Early colonial Indian policy was directed towards keeping European and Indian apart. From the 1870s until World War I Indian policy and government settlement policy parallelled one another. However, from the early 1900s Indian policy began to whittle away the remaining Indian land base, and this policy was justified by the use of the money from the sale of Indian lands to pay for Indian annuities and other Treaty benefits. This too was of benefit to the settler government. Eventually the Indians of Treaties No. 6 and No. 7 became wholly dependent on the Crown due to the loss of their lands and privileges. They had become an underdeveloped segment of western Canadian society, an unskilled casual labour force isolated on reserve.

Notes

1   James G. MacGregor, *A History of Alberta* (Edmonton, 1972), 127, 315.
2   Douglas E. Sanders, "Native Peoples in Areas of Internal National Expansion," *Saskatchewan Law Review*, 38 (1974), 23.

[3] R.T. Naylor, "The Rise and Fall of the Third Commercial Empire of the St. Lawrence," in Gary Teeple, ed., *Capitalism and the National Question in Canada* (Toronto, 1972), 5-7.

[4] L.S.F. Upton, "The Origins of Canadian Indian Policy," *Journal of Canadian Studies*, VIII, no. 4 (November 1973), 56.

[5] Ibid., 59.

[6] Naylor, "The Rise and Fall," 14.

[7] Morris Zaslow, *The Opening of the Canadian North, 1870-1914* (Toronto, 1971), 14-15, 18, 20.

[8] Naylor, "The Rise and Fall," 16-17.

[9] Leonard Wartkentin, "Steppe, Desert and Empire," in Anthony W. Rasporich and Harry C. Klassen, eds., *Prairie Perspectives 2* (Toronto, 1973), 116.

[10] Charles D. Bird and Ralph D. Bird, "The Aspen Parkland," in W.G. Hardy, ed., *Alberta: A Natural History* (Edmonton, 1967), 136.

[11] Ibid., 135.

[12] Hugh A. Dempsey, *Crowfoot Chief of the Blackfeet* (Edmonton, 1972), 95.

[13] Hugh A. Dempsey, "The Blood Indians," Glenbow, V. no. 3 (1972), 4.

[14] David H. Breen, "The Cattle Compact: The Ranch Community in Southern Alberta, 1881-1896," MA thesis (University of Calgary, 1969), 15-17.

[15] Ibid., 18-20.

[16] S.W. Horrall, "Sir John A. MacDonald and the Mounted Police Force for the Northwest Territories," *Canadian Historical Review*, LIII, no. 2 (June 1972), 181-82.

[17] David H. Breen, "The Turner Thesis and the Canadian West: A Closer Look at the Ranching Frontier," in L.H. Thomas, ed., *Essays on Western History* (Edmonton, 1976), 150.

[18] R.C. Macleod, "Canadianizing the West: The North-West Mounted Police as Agents of the National Policy, 1873-1905," in Thomas, ed., *Essays on Western History*, 105.

[19] Breen, "The Turner Thesis," 153.

[20] Macleod, "Canadianizing the West," 103-104.

[21] H. Dempsey, "The Blood Indians," Canada, Sessional Papers XIX, no. 4, *Sessional Paper 4* (1886), 74.

[22] Canada, Sessional Papers XVIII, no. 3, *Sessional Paper 3* (1885), 88.

[23] Breen, "The Cattle Compact," 49.

[24] Canada, Sessional Papers XXIV, no. 15, *Sessional Paper 18* (1891), 166, 167, 169.

[25] Upton, "The Origins of Canadian Indian Policy," 16.

[26] Lucien M. Hanks and Jane Richardson Hanks, *Tribe Under Trust* (Toronto, 1950), 29-30, for example.

[27] Ibid., 28, and Canada, Sessional Papers XXIII, no. 12, *Sessional Paper 14* (1899), 128.

[28] The Bloods or Kainah abandoned their first reserve on the Bow River near that of the Blackfoot and relocated further south near the RCNWMP post at Fort Macleod and the Cochrane Ranch Company.

[29] *Sessional Paper 14* (1899), 128-29.

[30] Canada, Sessional Papers XXXIII, no. 11, *Sessional Paper 14* (1900), 133.

[31] Hanks and Hanks, *Tribe Under Trust*, 33.

32   *Sessional Paper 14* (1900), 170.

33   Dempsey, "The Blood Indians," 7.

34   Canada, Sessional Papers XLV, no. 19, *Sessional Paper 27* (1911), pt. II, 5; and Hanks and Hanks, *Tribe Under Trust*, 35.

35   Hanks and Hanks, *Tribe Under Trust*.

36   *Sessional Paper 18* (1891), 52.

37   Canada, Sessional Papers XIX, no. 4, *Sessional Paper 4* (1886), 71.

38   David Lupul, "Indians on the Reserve: A Study in the Administration of Indian Affairs in Western Canada in the 20th Century," unpublished paper, Department of History, University of Alberta, 1976.

39   Ibid., 29.

40   Ibid., 37-38.

41   Canada, Sessional Papers XXVII, no. 10, *Sessional Paper 14* (1894), xvii.

42   Canada, Sessional Papers XL, no. 12, *Sessional Paper 26* (1906), xvii-xviii.

43   Hanks and Hanks, *Tribe Under Trust*, 40.

44   "Enfranchisement" has meant a number of things in various Indian Acts. Generally it may be taken to mean loss of treaty rights to hunting and fishing, to education and health care, and the assuming of the duties and privileges of a rate-payer or elector.

45   "And Her Majesty the Queen hereby agrees with her said Indians, that they shall have the right to pursue their vocations of hunting throughout the Tract surrendered as heretofore described, subject to such regulations as may, from time to time, be made by the Government...." "Copy of Treaty and Supplementary Treaty No. 7," Queen's Printer, 1966 [1877], 7.

46   Alexander Morris, *The Treaties of Canada with the Indians* (Toronto, 1971 [facs. ed.]), 287-88.

47   Dempsey, "The Blood Indians," 8.

48   R.N. Wilson, "Our Betrayed Wards," reprinted, *Western Canadian Journal of Anthropology*, VI, no. 2 (1974), 35.

49   Canada, Sessional Papers LIV, no. 9, *Sessional Paper 27* (1919), 20.

50   Ibid.

51   Wilson, "Our Betrayed Wards," 48.

52   Ibid., 58.

The Labour Movement in Alberta: An Untold Story

Warren Caragata

Ten thousand times has the labour movement stumbled and fallen and bruised itself, and risen again; been seized by the throat and choked into insensibility; enjoined by courts, assaulted by thugs, charged by the militia, shot down by regulars, traduced by the press, frowned upon by public opinion, deceived by politicians, threatened by priests, repudiated by renegades, preyed upon by grafters, infested by spies, deserted by cowards, betrayed by traitors, bled by leeches, and sold out by leaders, but, notwithstanding all this, and all these, it is today the most vital and potential power this planet has ever known, and its historic mission of emancipating the workers of the world from the thralldom of the ages is as certain of ultimate realization as the setting of the sun.

Eugene Debs

The cloak of conservatism draped over Alberta politics since the late 1940s has effectively hidden one of the province's richest traditions—a tradition of working class militancy at one time unequalled in Canada but for British Columbia. The myth remains that workers played a minor or, at best, supporting role in the historical development of Alberta,[1] a myth given some credence by the relatively quiet and politically conservative nature of the labour movement in Alberta over the last generation, by a society dominated by a single industry and a single political party.

Albertans in the early years flirted with the radical syndicalism of the Industrial Workers of the World, elected a socialist coal miner to the legislature, came close to putting a communist in the legislature in the same election that brought William Aberhart and Social Credit to power, and won one of the first provincial minimum wage laws in Canada. The country's first police strike, strikes by members of the Mounted Police, a miner's strike that led to passage of a key piece of federal labour legislation, a mining town that named its main street after the leader of the Communist Party—all are part of Alberta's labour heritage.

The history of any labour movement is a history of a struggle for power, a struggle that pits employers against employees—capital against labour—frequently with government as an active participant on the side of employers. It is a struggle for both democracy and dignity in the workplace and a struggle over the fruits of production, for a just division of wealth. The fundamentals of that struggle have not changed in almost 100 years of labour history in Alberta. The stage, the actors, and the intensity of the struggle may have changed, but the drama remains the same.

1. The Beginnings to World War I

The workers who fought Alberta's first battles with employers did so against the backdrop of a vast, largely unsettled prairie. In the earliest skirmishes, there were no unions to assist workers in their conflicts with all-powerful employers. According to the first major census of the North-West Territories, taken in August 1885, the population of the area later to become Alberta stood at only about 16,265 people, more than half of whom were Natives. There were only 60 industrial establishments and they employed only 215 people, all but three of them men.[2]

The coming of the Canadian Pacific Railway changed the face of the territories, bringing settlers and leaving industry in its wake. The railway, a key element of National Policy, reached Calgary in 1883. Not coincidentally, 1883 was the first year of any recorded labour disputes in the Alberta territory.

Railway construction meant the creation of new fortunes and the consolidation and growth of existing ones, but for the railway workers—navvies, as they were called—there was little glory and always tough, demanding, physical work. They laboured long hours for little pay, slept in filthy boxcars or tents, packed their own blankets and supplies or bought them at inflated prices from company stores. Mostly eastern Canadians or Americans, they were thousands of miles from home, hundreds of miles from any settlement, watched by the Mounted Police, and working in virtual indenture to their employers. A frequent complaint was failure by the sub-contractors to pay them wages owing.

Adding to their woes was the absence of any organization to help them in their struggle, not for a share of the great wealth they created every day, but at best for a clean bunk, a heated tent in winter, the wages owed them. In the late nineteenth and early twentieth centuries, labour organizations, where they existed, represented only skilled workers—printers, skilled construction workers, train engineers. The unskilled, such as the navvies, were left unprotected. It was a time when industrial development was in infancy, when cyclical swings in economic performance were sharp and violent. Even unions of skilled workers had trouble maintaining their membership rolls when depressions struck.

The Mounted Police had been formed by the federal government to bring order to the territories. Keeping order also meant keeping labour controlled during railway construction, "During the building of the C.P.R. main line, the Mounted Police allowed nothing to interfere with construction, even if it meant forcing down angry mobs of strikers single-handed."[3] Given the array of forces against them and the absence of a union behind them, it was little wonder that the spontaneous rebellions by the navvies were easily defeated.

In June 1883, about 130 navvies struck and the dispute threatened to spread to a nearby Indian camp. More than 25 Mounties were immediately sent to the work-site near the Alberta-Saskatchewan border where the leader of the strike was jailed and work resumed.[4] Some months later, after the rail line had reached Calgary, the Mounties were again involved on the side of the CPR in a labour dispute. This time, the strikers were not navvies but engineers and firemen protesting a wage cut. "Every engine which pulled out on the line was guarded by Mounted Police.... what for a time threatened to be a general railway strike was completely quelled."[5]

But the Mounties, who could always be relied on to keep the railway workers in line, were themselves not immune to grievances against their conditions of work. At Fort McLeod in September 1883, one troop refused to obey orders, complaining about overwork and bad food. Most of the problems leading to the short-lived dispute were settled and there is no record of disciplinary action being taken against the strikers.[6]

The 1883 strike in Calgary by railway engineers and firemen had been fought without any union backing. But unlike the situation for the unskilled navvies, there were unions operating in Canada and the United States that worked on behalf of the running trades like engineers, firemen, and conductors. Without these trades, the companies could not run the railways; because of their higher pay, better working conditions, and greater status-consciousness, these and other skilled workers came to be known as the "aristocracy of labour." The first unions organized in the Alberta territory were locals of these "aristocrats." A local of the Brotherhood of Locomotive Engineers was formed in Medicine Hat in September 1886. A local of the Brotherhood of Locomotive Firemen and Enginemen, was set up some months later, followed soon after by two other locals of the running trades.

Next to the railway running trades, the earliest union in the province was founded in Calgary in December 1886. The success of Assembly 9787 of the Noble and Holy Order of the Knights of Labour was short-lived with no records of its existence after 1888. But the establishment in the city of the Knights, one of the strangest labour organizations ever to make its imprint on North America, was warmly welcomed by the *Calgary Herald*, which wrote: "We have no doubt but this organization will long become an honor to Calgary and an object of important interest throughout the territories."[7]

The Knights, started as a secret society to protect itself from employer reprisals, was begun by nine Philadelphia garment workers in 1869. For a time, it vied with the American Federation of Labour as the premier labour organization in the United States. In Canada, it played an active role in the Trades and Labour Congress, especially in Quebec.[8] Generally, the Knights scorned strike action, preferring arbitration instead. They set up as cooperatives and believed strongly in the education of their membership, including the establishing of reading rooms and newspapers.

At a time when unions were formed to protect the interest of the skilled, the Knights organized the unskilled. At a time when unions were formed along strict lines according to craft or trade, the Knights organized "mixed assemblies" of workers in a particular location; these assemblies organized workers into one unit regardless of their workplace or occupation, and they included both skilled and unskilled workers. Mixed assemblies "were specially adapted to the needs of small towns where there were not enough workers of any one occupation to make a sizable trade union."[9] At a time when unions were loath to organize blacks and women, the Knights accepted them as members. The constitution refused membership only to a few: "no person who makes his living by the sale or manufacture of intoxicating drink; no lawyer, professional gambler or stockbroker."[10]

The Calgary assembly of the Knights was organized from Winnipeg, and although records of its activities are sparse, it was probably based on the CPR shops, both because it was one of the few industries in Calgary at the time and because the Winnipeg assembly was also based on CPR employees. The Calgary Knights, following the lead of other assemblies, started a newspaper called the *Northwest Call*, "intended, to be our organ as far as possible." The Calgary Knights also tried to organize American coal miners coming into the district to work in the newly opened mines in the Banff-Canmore area. One of their best preserved contributions, however, was a record summarizing the wages in the Calgary region in 1887. Clerks were earning $25 to $60 a month, cowboys and stablemen $30 to $45 a month, sawmill workers $40 to $75 a month, tailors $1.50 to $2.25 a day, carpenters $2.50 to $3 a day, and, at the top of the scale, stonemasons were making $4 to $4.50 a day. According to the Calgary Knights, for $6 a week, a worker could get good board and room.[11]

Following the construction of the main transcontinental rail line, attention turned to building the branch lines, bringing ever more territory under the control of the nation-builders in the East, anxious to keep American influence at bay. One of the most important lines was the Crow's Nest Pass line tying Calgary to the Kootenay region of southeastern British Columbia. Started in 1897 by the CPR with financial help from the federal and British Columbia governments, the line opened up the coal and mineral riches of the Crow's Nest and Kootenays. About 4,500 navvies were brought in to complete the task, living and working under such harsh conditions that two royal commissions were established to examine their frequent grievances. According to one police report:

> There are numbers of men who are totally unfit for the work and what will become of them during the winter is hard to surmise....No provision has been made by the company for returning these men to their homes, winter is coming on and there is likelihood of much hardship and destitution.[12]

Wages were $1.50 to $1.75 a day but men were paid only for the days they actually worked. If sickness or bad weather prevented them from working, they received no pay, but the board charges of $5 a week were fixed and constant. Blankets and other goods were sold at company stores where contractors made as much as 20 to 40 percent profit. Boots were sold at double their cost. One of the royal commissions estimated generously that after a year of work, a navvy might have $115 in his pocket.

In another account of the situation, Superintendent Deane, of the Mounted Police, reported to his superior in 1897 that all police patrols "when passing near construction work (on the branch line) have orders to go, out of their way if necessary, and look in upon working parties, enquiring of the foreman if there are any complaints."[13] The Police Officer on duty at Crow's Nest Pass reported in September 1897 that: "There are at present some half dozen of these men [the contracted navvies] in the Guard Room at Macleod undergoing sentence for desertion or refusal to work, and others at large." In the officer's view, construction work was going on satisfactorily without any significant trouble: "This is true in great measure to good luck and the presence of the police."[14]

Illness was also a constant in the over-crowded, dirty camps:

The number of men working upon the road who became ill, is, I think, abnormally large....How does it happen that there should be in the neighborhood of 1,500 men requiring treatment in a total aggregate of from 2,000 to 4,000, and all within the space of a year?

There must have been an utter disregard for the simplest laws of health somewhere and I think it may be found in the lack of sanitary conditions in the camp. How is it possible that sickness could be avoided where 50 or 60 men occupy a bunkhouse, say 24 by 40 feet, with a seven-foot ceiling and no ventilation provided.[15]

As one of the commissions summarized the evidence before it: "Instances were proved of violations of [employment] agreements, threatenings and illegal arrests by contractors, lack of medical attention...unsanitary houses, tents without stoves, overcharges for supplies, bad methods of wage payments and other abuses."[16]

The commission reports did have an effect. Under pressure, the federal government passed a Public Works Health Act in 1900 regulating housing and health care for workers employed on railway construction and other public works. The government even hired an inspector to enforce the legislation—two years later. The legislation and its feeble enforcement did not make much of a difference. Five to ten years later, employees working on the Grand Trunk Pacific and the Canadian Northern (now Canadian National) railways still complained about the same bad housing and poor sanitary conditions discovered by the Crow's Nest Pass royal commissions.

Construction of the Crow's Nest Pass line and an earlier branch line from Calgary to Lethbridge gave a major boost to the coal mining industry in the territory, an industry that was to provide the foundation for labour militancy in the province for almost 50 years. Although coal mining in Alberta was centred in three main areas—the south-west, the Drumheller region, and the Coal Branch in the Hinton-Edson vicinity—it was in the south-west, in the Lethbridge area and the Crow's Nest Pass, that Labour militancy in early Alberta was centred. And although coal in the Lethbridge area was being mined in the early 1880's, it was the construction and completion of the CPR's Crow's Nest branch line that provided the impetus to development in the region. The line began from Lethbridge in July 1897 and reached the Blairmore area by November 1898.

The Alberta coal towns were generally isolated communities with only the bosses and the coal miners. The class lines so clearly drawn were reinforced by the dangerous and miserable conditions faced by the miners. Alberta mines were among the most perilous in the world; fierce competition and the marginal nature of some mines encouraged operators to take chances with the lives of their employees. Timbers used to keep the mines from caving cost money and the miners were pressured not to use too many of them. Many complained that horses used before mechanization received better treatment. The miners and their families lived in crude shacks, often uninsulated, or in bunkhouses that usually had as many lice and vermin as miners. Families were forced by tight budgets, or occasionally by the death of a father in a mine accident, to send 12-year-old children into the dust of the mines. In a sad irony, the children worked in the dirtiest jobs, cleaning and sorting coal, because underground work was considered too dangerous.[17]

It was little wonder that miners looked to unions. One miner said the operators forced their workers into strong unions. "If they treated us good, I'd have never been involved in a union because there'd be no damn reason to be involved."[18] More than 60 percent of all strike activity in Alberta was accounted for by coal mining, up until the near-death of the industry in 1950s.

The first union the miners turned to was the Western Federation of Miners (WFM), a tough, militant organization born in the metal mines of Montana in 1893. The first Canadian local was formed in Rossland, British Columbia, several hundred miles west of Lethbridge, in 1895. The union had already been established in Lethbridge,[19] when it led the first coal miners' strike in the Alberta territory in 1897. The 200 miners walked out when the company cut wages by 17 percent. As was the case with the railway workers, the miners had to contend not only with the company, but also with the Mounted Police. Said the coal company president in a letter to Prime Minister Wilfrid Laurier: "Several hundred coal miners of mixed nationalities are employed at Lethbridge who were recently on strike and whose good behavior was largely the result of the presence of a considerable force of police which acts as a deterrent upon such disturbing influences."[20]

The mine owners hated the militancy and socialist rhetoric of the WFM and did their best to clean it out of the coal camps. Under heavy pressure from the mine owners, the Lethbridge miners allowed the WFM charter to lapse in the fall of 1902 and for about four years had an 'independent' union, which appears to have been under company control. Early in 1903, the owner of three Crow's Nest Pass mines withdrew recognition of the union, resulting in an immediate strike. The WFM was also under great pressure from coal and railway strikes that threatened to become a general strike in British Columbia.[21] The federal deputy minister of labour, William Lyon Mackenzie King, said in a Royal Commission on Industrial Disputes, which was established as a result of these strikes, that there was a difference between "legitimate" unions and unions like the Western Federation of Miners which were "revolutionary socialist." King's report which was attacked as "biased and partial" by the Canadian Trades and Labour Congress, recommended that American labour organizers should be prohibited from getting involved in Canadian labour disputes.[22]

The Western Federation of Miners was primarily a union of metal miners and was more interested in dealing with the complaints of that group than with those of the coal miners. At the same time, the WFM was involved in some 30 labour disputes, including the bloody Colorado labour wars. The dissatisfaction of its coal mining membership, coupled with the fact that the union was under heavy pressure elsewhere and was being attacked by the federal government, led the WFM to withdraw from the Canadian coal fields and ask the United Mine Workers Union (UMW) to replace it.[23]

The UMW made rapid progress in organizing the coal miners of the Kootenays and the Crow's Nest Pass though it could not gain a foothold in Lethbridge. By the end of 1905, the UMW had established a separate district for the Alberta and eastern British Columbia miners with about 2,200 members.[24]

As the coal miners were laying the foundations for trade unionism in the coal camps, railway shopcraft workers and construction workers in the growing urban centres were also organizing.

In most cases, the railway workers, even with the power of a union behind them, found themselves no match for the CPR. Too often, the company was able to play off one group of its employees against the other. And as long as the running trades were kept happy with relatively high wages, the trains would keep running despite strikes by other employees.

In 1900, shopcraft workers (including machinists, blacksmiths, and boiler-makers) in Calgary and Winnipeg 'hit the bricks.'[25] A year later, CPR trackmen (maintenance-of-waymen) went out demanding recognition of their union and a 10 cent increase, which would have raised their wages to $1.25 a day. In July 1901 it was reported with alarm in Winnipeg that "Indian labourers were holding a council or war and thinking of joining the strike."[26]

The Calgary trackmen received the support of all other CPR employees, including the running trades. The company, meanwhile, was refusing to negotiate with the new union and was hiring strike-breakers to replace the strikers. After two months, the walkout ended without winning the recognition, though with the company promising the strikers they could have their jobs back. The leadership of the powerful railway brotherhoods had attempted to mediate the strike and there were immediate charges that the trackmen had been sold out by the running trades. The Winnipeg labour newspaper, the *Voice*, said the CPR had "tampered with the heads of the brotherhoods." An official of the trackmen's union said the running trades leaders had been used by the CPR to get the strikers back to work on less than favourable terms.[27]

The strikes pointed out a failing in the way labour across North America was then being organized by the American Federation of Labour and its Canadian counterpart, the Trades and Labour Congress. The problem of organizing workers into compartmentalized unions based on a singular craft or skill (hence, the term "craft unions") was illustrated by the trackmen's strike: a massive enterprise like the CPR could only be challenged effectively by all its employees acting together. Only if the CPR employees were organized into a single union—an industrial union representing that industry—could the employees fight on somewhat equal terms. "After the trackmen's strike and other defeats, C.P.R. employees and workers in other industries began to realize they could solve their problems if they organized industrial unions.... It was a fight that would absorb workers in the West for more than fifty years."[28]

While workers in the West were mulling over the idea, some American labour activists were putting a plan for industrial organization into practice. Led by Eugene Debs and others, including leaders of the WFM, the American Labour Union was established in 1902,[29] with an industrial railway union as an affiliate. Debs had learned a bitter lesson about the danger of taking on the railways in the great defeat of the Pullman strike in 1894.[30]

The United Brotherhood of Railway Employees (UBRE) faced its first test in Canada in 1903 when CPR clerks in Vancouver walked off the job demanding recognition of the union and an end to harassment of UBRE organizers. On 9 March, Calgary railway clerks and baggage handlers joined the spreading walkout. The strikers were up against formidable odds. The railway itself, its secret police, the federal government, the running trades, and the courts were all on side against the new union. The rail strike in combination with WFM strikes in British Columbia coal fields led to the formation of the Royal Commission of Industrial Disputes. That report did not pull any punches against the WFM or the UBRE. They were led, stated the commission, by "socialistic agitators of the most bigoted and ignorant type."

The CPR police so successfully infiltrated the UBRE that one agent initiated four new members into the union. Even the union's general organizer was found later to have been on the CPR police payroll. According to testimony before the 1903 Royal Commission, "... Paid hirelings of the C.P.R. had worked their way into the union, taken a leading part in its deliberations, initiated new members and duly reported all that had taken place to their masters."[31] The US president of Boilermakers Union threatened expulsion for any member participating in the strike and the US based Brotherhood of Railway Trainmen printed a savage denunciation of the UBRE in its union paper.[32]

By the end of June it was all over, and this time the CPR could go ahead with reprisals. Jobs were filled by strikebreakers and most of the strikers found themselves blacklisted. But though the strike was broken and the UBRE finished in Canada, the idea that industrial unions were superior to craft unions prevailed. In 1907, the shopcraft workers attempted an alliance with the running trades, but the CPR headed off the federation by giving the trades an 8 percent increase and refusing the demands of the other workers.

Later that year, the company announced it would hire Japanese railway workers and early in the new year offered the boilermakers and other shop trades a cut in wages. The fear of being replaced with cheaper immigrant labour and the wage cut pushed the industrial unionism idea further towards realization. Heading the new joint bargaining committee was a Calgary machinist, R.J. Tallon. Tallon and his committee immediately began fighting over a series of layoffs at CPR shops that had cost 800 workers their jobs. When the company followed the layoffs by a 7 percent wage reduction, the shopcraft workers walked out. Their main demand was company recognition of the shopcraft federation but their main fight would be whether they would keep their jobs.

The company immediately set up employment bureaus in eastern Canada and Britain and within days there wer reports that Japanese strikebreakers were working in the Calgary and Lethbridge shops. The *Calgary Herald* of 19 August reported from Lethbridge that some of the strikebreakers had been hired by a detective agency in Chicago some months before the strike began and paid $120 a month to do nothing until they were needed to replace strikers. A little more than a month after the picket lines were up, there were about 300 strikebreakers in Calgary, living in boarding cars guarded by special police. Although hiring foreign workers as strikebreakers was clear violation of the Alien Labour Law, the federal government said it would not prosecute the cases. Again, government played not a neutral role but assisted the company, this time through an act of omission. It was a role that trade unionists were becoming familiar with, and would continue to see as a feature of Canadian labour relations.

Railway employees were to play a key role in the urban labour movement, as were the construction trades. Calgary's population had increased from 300 at the time the CPR main line was being built across Alberta to more than 4,000. Edmonton's population had grown from 700 to about 2,000 by 1901.[33] Population growth created a steady demand for construction work but as was the case with railway employees, it was the most highly-skilled trades like stonemasons and brick layers that were the most successful. Their members earned higher wages and their unions were more stable. Locals of stonemasons were formed in both Calgary and Edmonton in 1903.[34]

The masons' locals were formed a year after carpenters in both Edmonton and Calgary and smaller centres joined the United Brotherhood of Carpenters and Joiners (UBCJ). The masons' locals were to have a little more success in keeping their charters than the first construction union organized in the Alberta territory: Local 75 of the UBCJ was formed in Calgary in 1892 but had dissolved within the year.[35] One of the first unions formed in Edmonton was a local of the Bricklayers and Masons International Union (BMIU). The Edmonton group was the first BMIU local formed in Alberta and was chartered 16 May 1903.[36] The bricklayers and masons in Lethbridge were one of the first craft groups in that city to organize, on 10 June 1905. A local of the plumbers' union, Local 488, was formed in Edmonton in 1904 with seven charter members; Calgary plumbers organized in early 1905. A local of the Hodcarriers and Builders Protective Union (now the Labourers Union), Local 92, was established in Edmonton in 1906, but it had ceased functioning by World War I.

A significant number of locals outside construction and the main industrial sectors, generally small craft unions, also appeared in this period of rapid urban growth. The Calgary local of the International Typographical Union was organized in 1902. Reflecting the slower growth of unions in Edmonton, the typographers were not organized there until the following year. By 1913, the United Brewery Workers had three locals in Alberta, at Lethbridge, Calgary, and Edmonton. In fact, by 1913, barbers, bookbinders, cement workers, cigarmakers, hotel and restaurant workers, letter carriers, machinists, musicians, stage employees (including moving picture machine operators), and tailors all had small locals in Calgary or Edmonton (or both) and a few had locals in Lethbridge and Medicine Hat.

The large commercial and public buildings of the day were constructed of stone. Cutting and setting the stone was a highly specialized skill that guaranteed the stonemasons and cutters both higher wages and more secure employment than the carpenters. Carpenters too had a skill but there were enough other people around who could handle a hammer and saw, so carpenters could not establish the kind of monopoly the masons and cutters established. The stone workers buttressed their craft with strict apprenticeship and seniority provisions of the same type that allowed the running trades to claim their place as "aristocrats" of labour. The seasonal nature of construction work affected all workers in the industry but the hardest hit were those with least skill (since their skills were in greater supply) who could be treated more cavalierly than could the stone workers.

However, among the construction unions, the carpenters' union probably played the largest role in the Alberta labour movement. In 1902, when carpenters again tried to organize, the movement started in Frank, a town of some importance before a large chunk of Turtle Mountain fell on it—the "Frank Slide" (1903). The Frank local of the United Brotherhood of Carpenters and Joiners hired an organizer who that year founded locals in Calgary and Edmonton. The Calgary carpenters' union local was organized in 1902, when the UBCJ organizer, Robert Robinson, travelled to Calgary on an Alberta organizing trip. There he told a meeting of local carpenters that their organized counterparts in Nelson, British Columbia, were earning $3.50 a day for an eight-hour day, compared to the Calgary rate of $2.75 for a ten-hour day. Twenty-nine members enrolled and Local 1055 was formed 2 April 1902. Later that same year, Robinson travelled to Edmonton where he organized Local 1325 on 11 November. By 1907, Local 1325 had 405 members. In 1904, carpenters' locals were formed in Lacombe, Wetaskiwin, Medicine Hat, Coleman, Lethbridge, and Strathcona. A local was also formed in Red Deer, and in 1913, the carpenters of Athabasca Landing in northern Alberta were organized. But many of these locals were to have short life spans—by June 1915, only six locals, in Edmonton, Calgary, Diamond City (near Lethbridge), Athabasca Landing, Lethbridge, and Strathcona still existed.[37]

The organization of Calgary Local 1055 of the UBCJ did not come without a fight. The newly organized union called a two-week strike and pulled about 90 workers employed by 13 companies off the job for two weeks. This time the union was successful and won a reduction in the hours of work to nine hours a day and set a standard rate of $2.50 a day. The following year they were not to be so fortunate. The union called and won a short strike over the use of non-union labour but a short time later decided to come to the aid of the teamsters' union which had called a strike against the Builders' Exchange over hours and wages.

The carpenters and teamsters were to become the first group of Alberta workers to feel an effect of the conciliation and mediation efforts of deputy labour minister Mackenzie King. The experience almost ruined them. When the carpenters decided to refuse to handle building materials brought to sites by strike-breaking teamsters, the Exchange locked them all out. Construction labourers then joined the dispute and construction projects throughout Calgary fell silent. When the stonemasons local refused to support the strike, it was suspended from the Calgary Labour Council for its display of disunity. But despite the fact that the masons were working and some carpenters had drifted back to work, the strike was still on.

So Mackenzie King came to Calgary to straighten things out. His most recent assignment had been an examination of the UBRE and coal miners' strikes, an examination that had led to a ringing condemnation of sympathy strikes. King's settlement of the sympathy strike in Calgary construction broke the back of the young carpenter's union, which was not reorganized until 1904.

The agreement King worked out contained a so-called "non-discrimination" clause that allowed the employers to hire non-union workers. It prohibited employers from discriminating against union and non-union members, a discrimination the companies had no problem at all living with. But for the carpenter's union, which had won a union shop in its first contract in 1902, King's clause was a definite step backwards. Non-discrimination clauses in labour agreements enforced open-shop employment and they were to become a prominent feature of most settlements in which King was involved. Workers again found the role of government to be far from neutral when it became involved in clashes between labour and capital.[38]

King continued his activity in Alberta labour disputes. In particular, it was his involvement in a strike by Lethbridge coal miners that was to have a lasting impact on labour across the country.

The United Mine Workers had made rapid progress in the Alberta coal fields but the big Lethbridge mine of the Alberta Railway and Irrigation Company remained an important hold out. While the Lethbridge miners had been the first to organize, they had left the WFM to form an independent association. By 1906, however, they were ready to get back into the mainstream of labour activity in the coal fields. On 9 March, about 500 workers walked off the job, protesting wages and working conditions and demanding recognition of the UMW. The company tried to ignore the strike and keep the mine running. That decision resulted in violence. Fist fights and brawls were common and a detachment of Mounties was sent to the city to guard mine property and protect the strike-breaking miners. One house was reported burned down and several more occupied by strike-breakers were dynamited. The union charged that the explosions were the work of a Chicago detective agency, the same agency that had recruited strike-breakers for the CPR during the 1903 shopcraft dispute.

As the strike continued into the fall, the federal government began to receive complaints from the West that the dispute was cutting off coal supplies needed for the approaching winter. King was sent out to see what he could do to get the strike settled. The company at first refused his arbitration offer but later relented. King was then able to get the two sides to make concessions and end the strike by 2 December 1906.

The workers did manage to win a 10 percent wage increase, bringing the company rate to 30 cents an hour. They even received a promise that they would receive preference over the strike-breakers in getting their jobs back. But their major demands for union recognition and a check-off, where the company would deduct union dues from paycheques, were lost. The contract was signed not by the UMW but by a committee of the miners. And there was King's handiwork in the form of a non-discrimination clause.[39]

King returned to Ottawa to ponder the effect of the strike, confident that he had won the support of the Lethbridge miners and the UMW. Frank Sherman, president of District 18 of the UMW, wrote the deputy minister that he hoped "in the near future, with the help of men like yourself, that we will be able to devise a plan whereby we shall not have to call upon you to assist us in settling strikes."[40]

King drafted legislation that would become the key labour law in the country for the next 20 years. The Industrial Disputes Investigation Act provided for compulsory arbitration in disputes affecting railways, mining, and utilities, on the application of either party. Once the legislation had been invoked, however, there could be no strike or lockout until the arbitration board had completed its report. There was no time limit set on how long the arbitrators could deliberate. King had established a legal roadblock in the way of workers seeking to press their claims against employers who already held most of the cards.[41] According to one labour relations specialist:

...there were no effective restraints placed on employers to prevent the familiar practises of imposing yellow-dog contracts [where employees promise not to join a union], black-listing, discriminatory discharge of union members, and employment of non-union members or strikebreakers. On balance, it appears to have operated adversely to the strength and effectiveness of organized labour in Canada.[42]

An American who examined the legislation for US president Theodore Roosevelt said the act had "accomplished the main purpose for which it was enacted, the prevention of strikes."[43] But the legislation did not, as King had hoped, bring industrial peace to the coal towns of Alberta and south-eastern British Columbia. As long as conditions remained as they were and as long as employers continued to resist union organization, turmoil and strife would continue.

The Disputes Act was tested only a month after its passage when the coal companies, recently organized as the Western Canada Coal Operators Association, refused to recognize the UMW. The miners struck only to discover that, since arbitration under the act had been requested, the strike was illegal. King journeyed to the scene, and a month later the mines were back in operation with limited recognition of the UMW. The non-discrimination clause remained in the new contract.

The miners were on strike two years later in 1909 and again in 1911. The 1911 strike involved about 7,000 miners, lasted about eight months, and was one of the largest strikes in the country in the pre-war period. The Disputes Act was again invoked, over the union's objections, and a four-year contract saddled the miners with the non-discrimination clause and a continued open-shop.[44]

After the Act was passed in 1907, it was widely approved in labour circles in both eastern and western Canada. In 1907, a resolution demanding repeal of the Disputes Act was voted down at the Trades and Labour Congress convention. But experience with the law convinced workers that it operated to the employer's benefit. The first to be convinced were workers in western Canada, including the president of District 18 who had, at first, applauded King and his legislation. The TLC stand on the legislation became one of the issues that split the organization, roughly, into a more moderate East against a more militant West.[45] It took nine years of experience with the 'neutral role of the state' to convince the majority of Canadian trade union leaders that the act was discriminatory to organized labour. In 1916, the TLC convention passed a resolution demanding repeal of the act.[46]

The 1911 strike had one important effect on Alberta coal miners, for the first time bringing them into conflict with their international union. Because they had walked out after the legislation had been invoked, the strike was illegal. That did not bother the miners, but it bothered the international. The international threatened to withdraw its support from the strikers and, while it eventually backed down, it sowed seeds of discontent that would be reaped later.

Not all of labour's battles were fought on the picket line. There was an early realization that laws passed by all levels of government affected workers, their families, and their way of life. Too often, political decisions were taken by businessmen, lawyers, and other professionals who either ignored the concerns of working people or legislated against them. The desire for political action was one of the factors leading to establishment of central bodies like the Calgary and Edmonton labour councils and, later, the Alberta Federation of Labour. A Trades and Labour Council was established in Calgary on 19 February 1901, and in Edmonton on 16 January 1903. In 1905, at the first formal meeting of the Edmonton and District Trades and Labour Council under a charter from the Trades and Labour Congress, unionists representing the plumbers, carpenters, typographers, lathers, and bricklayers were present. At the outset, the council represented about 285 workers. In 1912, there were 30 affiliated organizations with a total membership of about 3,500.[47]

Political effort was rewarded early in Calgary when R.A. Brockelbank, president of the carpenters' local, won election to city council in 1902. Brockelbank was the the first labour representative elected to any level of government in Alberta. The success was short-lived, however, as he was defeated the following year. Edmonton workers were not able to elect any of their number to city council until 1914 when carpenter, J.A. Kinney, won an aldermanic seat.[48]

The issue of compensation for workplace injuries was an important spur to political activity at the provincial level. Until 1908, workers either had to live off the proceeds of private insurance (if they could afford the premiums), ask for charity, or try to sue their employers. Following the report of a provincial royal commission, the provincial legislature did pass measures to provide a scale of benefits for injuries and death. But companies were still allowed to use private insurance if they preferred and the courts were still involved in assessing liability.

In the 1906 strike at Lethbridge, one of the issues was the reduction in hours of mine work from nine to eight, but in 1908 this issue was removed from the bargaining table after legislation passed the Alberta Legislature setting the hours of work in the mines at eight. In 1912, the government established mine rescue stations in different parts of the province, but these rescue stations did not stop the slaughter of miners in the mines. In one of the worst mining disasters in Canadian history, on 19 June 1914, an explosion of gas at the Hillcrest Collieries mine in the Crow's Nest Pass killed 189 of the 235 workers in the mine. From 1905 to the writing of his book (published in 1924), John Blue records that 481 miners lost their lives. "Every 100,000 tons of coal produced in the last fifteen years has cost a human life."[49]

The first provincial labour member of the legislature was Donald McNabb, a Lethbridge miner and socialist. McNabb sat only for several months, having been elected in a by-election and defeated in the general election. Labour activists found it was more difficult to unite workers around political demands than around economic demands. Although McNabb came last in his riding, labour did maintain its toehold at the legislature. Charlie O'Brien, another miner, took the riding that included the Crow's Nest Pass by a slender 35 vote margin. O'Brien, a member of the Socialist Party of Canada (a forerunner of the Communist Party), was described by a comrade as a "genial chap." But his Liberal and Conservative colleagues in Edmonton saw him in a very different light. In 1910, when the legislature was pushing through a motion of condolence after the death of King Edward VII, O'Brien asked the legislature to include in the motion condolences for the families of 300 miners killed in a British mine disaster. He was rewarded for his suggestion by a shower of books and inkwells. O'Brien's antics in the legislature were not rewarded when the next election rolled around. Like McNabb, O'Brien found political unity an ethereal matter.[50]

In 1912, as O'Brien's term in the legislature was drawing to a close, Alberta workers tried a different tack in their efforts to influence the political process. McNabb chaired a Lethbridge meeting of about 40 delegates who were meeting to establish a provincial federation of labour. The meeting, held 14 and 15 June, was the first of the Alberta Federation of Labour (AFL) and, in its first year, it had about 20 affiliated unions, representing more than 4,000 workers.[51] Looking to expand their political base, the meeting's organizers invited 13 representatives from the United Farmers of Alberta (UFA). McNabb said that "the interests of the farmers and the city toilers are identical...If organized...they would be in a position to go to the legislative halls as a united band..."[52] The federation in its first constitution reserved several executive posts for the UFA; the posts were filled in 1912 but not thereafter. Farmers and workers would cooperate in future political battles but never with the organic unity that McNabb and others had hoped for.

McNabb had discovered the illusive nature of working class political solidarity in his losing election campaign. He encountered it again at the meeting he chaired. McNabb wanted the new federation to become a lobbying body, pushing for "legislation of a reform character." Many of the miners thought such a position did not go far enough. Their leader, Clem Stubbs, said the federation should aim at abolishing the "wage system." Stubbs told the convention that if the federation aimed at abolishing the wage system, the miners would be all for it. At its 1913 convention, the federation decided that its political groups were too numerous to hammer out a single political position and it confirmed itself as a lobbying body.

Sometimes it must have seemed to people like McNabb that there were as many strains of political thought as there were workers. There were, of course, Liberals and Tories but they seemed to spend more time voting than they did

attending labour conventions. There were reform Liberals and moderate socialists like McNabb, people who today would be considered social democrats. And
there were the hard-line left-wingers of various affiliations, including the Socialist
Party of Canada (SPC), the most influential. The SPC had built a large following in the coal camps.

There were also the syndicalists, people whose criticisms of the existing
social and economic order were almost identical to those coming from SPC
members but who parted company on the question of how to bring the old
order tumbling down. The syndicalists knew what McNabb and O'Brien had
painfully discovered: that it was a far simpler task to unite workers around
economic issues, to unite them on the picket line, than to unite them on political
questions. But while many of the SPC members were theorists, there was one
group of syndicalists who were staunch activists—the IWW.

The Industrial Workers of the World (later widely known as the "Wobblies"), was born in Chicago in 1905, with the WFM as one of its largest
affiliates. While its leaders were capable theorists, they were also activists and
the union they founded was built on action. Joe Hill and Ralph Chaplin, who
wrote most of the labour anthems still sung today, William D. Haywood, Helen
Gurley Flynn, Mother Jones, and Eugene Debs—all were at one time associated
with the IWW, three initials that struck fear into the hearts of businessmen and
politicians until the union was finally crushed in the late 1910s by severe
government and employer repression on both sides of the border.

Its message—"Abolition of the wage system"—that exploitation could only
be eliminated by the abolition of capitalism through a general strike was carried
across North America by some of the most capable union organizers ever seen
on this continent. Unlike the American Federation of Labor, and the Canadian
Trades and Labour Congress, the IWW believed that unionism was for all
workers, not just the skilled and the relatively secure. They organized everywhere
and everybody. They pioneered the sit-down strike; in one American mining
town, they organized the whole town, they travelled the rails to organize the
itinerant farm workers, making the IWW red card of membership an unofficial
railway ticket.

The chairman of the IWW was "Big Bill" Haywood, of the WFM. In 1908,
Haywood journeyed into western Canada on an organizing drive. He spoke in
Fernie and visited Calgary. The Wobblies succeeded in signing up some Alberta
workers, and in 1914 there were two locals in existence, one in Calgary, the
other in Edmonton. The Wobblies had some following in the coal camps, but its
real base in Alberta was built in the immediate pre-war years following its
organizing efforts among the navvies building the two northern transcontinental
lines through Edmonton and the Athabasca River valley in the Rockies. It was
during a work stoppage on one of these lines (that would later become the
Canadian National) that Wobbly organizer Joe Hill wrote the labour song
"Where the Fraser River Flows."

The IWW conducted its first Alberta strike in 1912 when it took over the leadership of a dispute involving about 250 Edmonton city labourers putting in sewer lines. (As was the case with the railway construction workers, most of the unions of the day who belonged to the AFL and its parent, the TLC, were not interested in taking up the cause of the unskilled, such as the city labourers.) The strikers were asking for a nickel an hour increase to bring their wage to 35 cents. The militia was put on alert and roving bands of pickets were met at construction sites by police exhibiting their revolvers. The police also arrested the secretary of the Edmonton IWW. The Wobblies and the city labourers lost the strike but the IWW in Edmonton maintained a high profile in the city and in Calgary until about 1914.

The Wobblies reached their peak of activity in the relief fights of the unemployed before World War I. In the pre-war depression, thousands lost their jobs. About 7,000 in Calgary were without work in 1914 and the *Labour Gazette* estimated that unemployment in Edmonton would reach the same number as winter set in.[53] As they had with the city labourers, the Wobbly organizers moved into the breach, organizing the jobless to demand better relief and jobs. And, as had been the case in the city labourers' strike, the police and authorities dogged their steps.

The coming of war ended the crisis, and the IWW in Alberta. But for the establishment, the legend of the IWW remained. Throughout the war, as political and economic unrest assumed epic proportions, the IWW was thought to be behind much of the turmoil. With the battle in Europe almost ended and the battle in western Canada at fever pitch, the federal government outlawed the ghost of the IWW.

2. World War I and its Aftermath

The war was to have far-reaching effects on the country. The demand for *matériel* created a large manufacturing base while sharpening class antagonisms. Rising prices, war profiteering, and the fear of post-war unemployment pushed workers to increasingly militant action. Moderate trade unions and moderate trade union methods were tossed aside by the rank and file who saw the failure of those methods. The fight against conscription and labour registration pushed new, more radical leaders to the fore. Those leaders could draw sustenance from the events in Russia in 1917, but the catalyst for working people was inflation.[54]

Between the start of the war and 1918, the cost of living increased 72 percent. By the end of June 1920 prices were double their 1914 level. Inflation made radicals of the moderates. Even skilled workers like machinists, who were in great demand to churn out the goods of war, could not keep pace. Machinists' wages rose by only 62 percent in the 1914-18 period, 10 points behind the cost-of-living increase. Rising prices not only heightened labour militancy, they swelled labour's ranks as more and more workers turned to trade unionism to help them battle relentless inflation. Between 1914 and 1919, trade union membership in Alberta increased by about 50 percent. The organization of women also advanced; in 1914, a local of the United Garment Workers of America was formed in Edmonton at the GWG clothing plant.

The first major strike of the war took place in the coal camps. During the summer of 1916, about 3,600 miners walked off the job demanding a 10 percent war bonus. They received a 7.5 percent increase, enough to get them to return to work but not enough to keep them there. The UMW then demanded either a 25 percent war bonus or a commission that could set increases tied to the cost of living. The demand was also supported by strike action, this time involving about 5,000 miners. The federal government, anxious to get production resumed, passed an order-in-council establishing a cost of living commission. The miners returned to the pits but were in no mood to wait. After several weeks back at work, the promised cost-of-living adjustment was still unpaid and again the District 18 miners walked out, this time for two weeks. The companies finally gave in and paid a $1.75 per week bonus.

During negotiations in the pre-war depression, their backs against the wall, the miners had agreed to a clause that allowed the companies to fire miners involved in wildcat strikes. Now, with war demands pushing the coal mines to peak production, the miners decided to get out from under the penalty clause, as it was called. The mines were closed for three months in 1917 with about 7,500 miners on strike. Losing patience, the federal government appointed a director of coal operations who would run the mines for the coal companies during the war. The director ordered the mines to reopen and got rid of the penalty clause. The miners also won regular cost-of-living adjustments and a 7.5 percent hike on top of an earlier 15 percent increase. These measures brought labour peace to the coal camps for the duration of the war.

While the miners accounted for the bulk of the strike activity in the late years of the war, workers in other occupations who had never before been on strike found themselves on the picket lines in the scramble to keep abreast of rising prices. Packing plant workers in Edmonton and Calgary organized unions and Calgary packing house workers went on strike. Street railway workers in Edmonton, Edmonton teachers, lumber camp workers in northern Alberta, restaurant workers, Edmonton fire fighters—all joined what was becoming a strike wave. In the two and one-half years ending 30 June 1919, more than 600,000 working days were lost in Alberta due to strikes, almost two-thirds of all man-days lost in the first 20 years of the century.[55]

Increasing willingness to organize and take strike action was not the only indication of rising militancy. The change was also reflected in debates within the Trades and Labour Congress. Strains in the Congress that had been evident before the war—over the issue of opposition to the Industrial Disputes Investigations Act, for example—became more pronounced as more radical leaders moved to the front of western trade union ranks. The battle was drawn over what response the TLC should take towards the war and conscription. Before the war began, the TLC had voted to hold a general strike to stop the war, a position taken in concert with trade union bodies in Western Europe. But when hostilities began, the TLC changed its mind. The move angered some western leaders, who were opposed to war on political grounds.

In 1916, the federal Conservative government appointed Calgary lawyer R.B. Bennett to carry out an inventory of the country's manpower resources, which required workers to register with local boards. Registration was seen as a prelude to conscription and western trade union leaders wanted nothing to do with it. The Calgary Labour Council, for instance, said it would not cooperate "until modern industry was re-organized to conscript all wealth and production...for use and not for profit."[56] The TLC, however, urged all workers to comply with the registration scheme.

In May 1917, the government followed the registration programme with conscription and the schism created by the registration battle grew wider. Despite earlier opposition to conscription, the TLC executive urged its members to comply with the law. Meanwhile, the Alberta Federation of Labour was polling its unions to find out whether it should call a general strike to fight conscription. The TLC executive's position was ratified by the 1917 convention of the Congress. It decided to fight the issue at the polls and moves were made to establish a broadly based working class party including the Socialist Party of Canada (SPC).

The new party (which came to be known as the Canadian [or Dominion] Labour Party) was not in place in time to fight the 1917 election. In Alberta, both the SPC and the moderates put up candidates, the labourites receiving assistance from the rump of Laurier's Liberal Party. Robert Borden's Conservative-Unionist coalition won the election handily, helped in part by the Wartime Elections Act which disenfranchised many immigrant voters. None of the labour candidates across the country won a seat.

The defeat strengthened the hand of those trade union leaders who saw electoral political action as futile and who looked to the general strike as the best method to win labour's aims. Traditional democratic methods were also being closed off, as the governments moved to head off what it thought was a pre-revolutionary situation in western Canada. In 1918, Montreal corporation lawyer, C.H. Cahan, was commissioned to study the cause of western discontent. Cahan found it to be the result of Bolshevik agitation. In September, the federal government then appointed him Director of Public Safety, charged with keeping civil order in Canada, particularly in the West. That same month, orders-in-council under the War Measures Act were used to outlaw the IWW and 13 other organizations. The government banned strikes, prohibited radical literature, and even outlawed the use of 14 alien languages.

The general strike was discussed during a 1918 strike of city fire-fighters in Edmonton; later the same year, Calgary unionists not only discussed a general strike call but issued one. Many leaders of western labour saw the general strike as a weapon to overthrow the capitalist system; for the rank and file, it was a weapon to win traditional collective bargaining aims—recognition and wage demands. The Edmonton fire-fighters strike was not revolution but about promotions and seniority.

Another dispute, foreshadowing the general strikes that occurred in 1919, involved unorganized freighthandlers in Calgary, who struck the CPR in 1918 over the issue of seniority and unfair discharge. The strike began when the local CPR superintendent fired a shed checker, allegedly for trying to organize a union, and then disregarded seniority in hiring a new checker. The freighthandlers subsequently walked off the job, striking over the issues of recognition and seniority. It was the second chapter of a battle started in 1903 during the UBRE strike, a strike that ended in nearly total defeat. This time, the workers received the backing of Canadian Division 4 of the Railway Employees Department of the American Federation of Labor, headed by Calgary machinist R.J. Tallon. The Calgary Labour Council backed their strike completely, declaring it was a battle for the right to organize against "profiteering corporations."[57] The Council issued a general strike call, answered in the affirmative by 19 of 21 unions. But within 24 hours, five of the strikers from the CPR's shops were in jail for violating the recent order prohibiting strikes. While the local unions were behind the freight handlers, their international leaders wanted nothing to do with general strikes. The arrests, the presence in the city of Public Safety Director Cahan, and the pressure from international union headquarters left Calgary labour divided. A settlement to the strike was reached on 23 October, but not before the *Calgary Herald* urged citizens to "obstruct the 'volcano of class reign' imposed by labour unions."

But the short-lived Calgary dispute drew national attention as the first test of the general strike. It also divided more workers in the West from their international unions and deepened divisions in the TLC between the moderate East and the militant West.

At the TLC's 1918 convention, western delegates were outvoted on every issue important to them. Resolutions favoring industrial organization were defeated, conscription was endorsed, and a resolution opposing Allied intervention in Bolshevik Russia was tabled. The westerners demanded release of conscientious objectors from prison but were outvoted. Discontent, felt even by western moderates, was becoming an open schism. Western delegates met in a separate caucus and decided to hold a Western Labour Conference in Calgary the following March.

Months later, in January, the radical shift of western labour was confirmed at the 1919 convention of the Alberta Federation of Labour where delegates unanimously declared their "full accord and sympathy with the aims and purposes of the Russian and German socialist revolutions."[58]

That was the backdrop for the meeting of the Western Labour Conference of March 1919, a conference that the moderates thought got out of hand.[59] This was not to be a meeting where grievances against the TLC would be aired. The conference sent greetings to Moscow and approved a resolution from British Columbia delegates accepting proletarian dictatorship "as being absolute and efficient for the transformation of a capitalist private property to communal wealth."[60] The convention then confirmed the schism with the TLC and international labour by voting to establish a new union, an industrial union to be called the One Big Union (OBU). In Alberta, a referendum of union locals saw a majority of workers voting for the new union, with near unanimous support from the miners. But on a union-by-union basis, the OBU came out on the short end. Of 57 locals voting, a majority voted to stay with their internationals. The moderates, out-organized by the left at the Calgary conference, soon recovered their wits and fought back.

The March meeting had decided to call another conference for early June to get the OBU off the ground but events in Winnipeg were to overtake the decision. The Winnipeg General Strike began in May over the issue of recognition. The mood of the West guaranteed that it would not remain a local matter and general strikes spread quickly. In Edmonton, a general strike was called for 26 May and, for a time, assumed proportions of the Winnipeg strike.[61] Street railway workers, taxi drivers, restaurant employees, civic workers, machinists, telephone operators, and power plant employees were numbered among the workers who walked off the job. Police and firemen offered to join the strike but were asked to stay at their posts by the general strike committee. The walkout lasted several days, until Mayor Clarke, who was sympathetic to the strikers, convinced the workers they had made their point.

In Calgary, the strike call was less successful. Most railway workers, postal workers, street car employees, and hotel and restaurant workers joined in a sympathy strike but the efforts of the Calgary Labour Council to push the idea of a general strike floundered when the majority of Calgary unionists, including the building trades, rejected the notion. The local strike committee conceded that local workers have "no grievances with their own employers...[but that] labour men were duty bound to stand by their class brothers in Winnipeg."[62] The employees of the CPR's Ogden Shops were the largest unit out. Postal workers in that city also joined the walkout but were fired by the government for their action.[63] Marshalling their forces, the moderates on the Labour Council were able to expel OBU supporters, ending radical control of the Council.

As all this was unfolding, the authorities and the business community were not inactive. In Winnipeg and other centres, "Citizens' Committees" were established whose main function was to picture the strikers, not as workers anxious to establish bargaining relationships with employers, but as the shock troops for a Bolshevik revolution. In Edmonton, the Mounted Police contacted the armed forces about the possibility of military assistance and machine guns were fired in the horse stables to acquaint the mounts with the sound of gunfire. The federal government, in one day, pushed through an amendment to the Immigration Act allowing for the deportation of foreign born Canadian citizens.[64]

Coincidence of timing, the propaganda from the Citizens' Committees, and the attitude of the federal government that discontent was based not on domestic issues like inflation and the desire to establish the rights of union recognition and collective bargaining but on agitation by outside forces led to an indelible impression that the general strikes were the work of the OBU. In fact, in Winnipeg, only one of the strike leaders was connected with the new union, which was not established until after the strikes had begun.

Defeat of the general strikes and the counter-reformation by the internationals and the TCL, which involved suspensions of charters of rebellious councils and unions, spelled the end of the OBU, except in the coal fields, where, although the end result was to be the same, the battle raged longer.[65]

The miners had been fighting for a closed shop since before the war and had never been able to secure it. But when they left the UMW for the OBU, the coal companies and the federal government, still running the mines under wartime powers, gave in. The UMW, which had almost no support, was given a closed shop. For the miners, it meant rejoining the UMW, not working, or fighting. Many chose to fight, in a battle that would last for almost two years. The miners were faced with an alliance of the federal government, the coal companies, the courts and their old union, the UMW. The shell of the UMW was being administered by trustees appointed by the international. At one point in the 1919 battle, squads of vigilantes moved into the Drumheller valley, north-east of Calgary, attacked the shacks of striking miners with gunfire, beat up strikers, kidnapped strike leaders, hauled them before kangaroo courts, and kicked them out of the valley. The entire incident occurred with no opposition at all from police. In 1920, the Supreme Court ordered the miners to leave the OBU and rejoin the UMW.

The miners really had no choice: they could stay on strike forever, fighting the awesome array of forces against them, or they could join the UMW, which they did. But the battle had left the union in disarray, a disarray that the unemployment of the 1920s did nothing to dispel.

During the decades of the 1920s, working class militancy reached a low ebb, not just in the Alberta and Kootenay coal fields but across North America. Other than a few major coal strikes, work stoppages tapered off sharply in Alberta from their peak in the immediate post-war period. In 1925, the coal companies ordered a wage cut, following previous cuts in 1922 and 1924, both of which had led to long strikes. Again the UMW resisted. But this time the miners stayed in the pits and left the UMW for local company unions, or "home locals," as they were named. In an attempt to head off the rapid spread of defections and organizations of home locals, the UMW then negotiated a wage cut for the miners they still represented. But the union could not win. Its acceptance of the wage reduction angered the more militant locals in the Drumheller valley and they too left the fold. "In less than one year, UMW district 18 had lost more than four-fifths of its members,"[66] and, as a result, the UMW was placed under international administration for the next 11 years.

The Communist party had built up a large following in the coal fields and it was very disturbed at the drift to company unionism. Recognizing the hostility towards the UMW, the Party tried to weld the home locals into a new union, the Mine Workers' Union of Canada (MWUC). Its early efforts, however, met with only sporadic success.[67] The Mine Workers' Union affiliated in 1928 with the All-Canadian Congress of Labour (ACCL), a militantly nationalist grouping whose largest affiliate was the CBRE. In 1928, seeking to consolidate its position, the MWUC asked Alberta operators to meet with it as a union to negotiate a new agreement. A conciliation board set up to examine the dispute agreed with the owners that they should meet only with the locals. The union rejected the report and called a strike of about 1,200 workers. The walkout lasted from 3 August 1928 to 28 February 1929 and resulted in agreements with all but two operators.

The one bright spot during the decade came in the field of political action. A labour MLA was given a cabinet post in the United Farmers government and workers throughout the province elected aldermen, school trustees, and MLAs under the banner of the Canadian Labour Party. The federated party united Communists and social democrats but the alliance folded by the late 1920s, in large part over internal conflicts.[68]

3. The Great Depression of the 1930s

For the most part, the Depression, which began in 1929, prolonged militancy's ebb tide. Most workers were more concerned about hanging on to their jobs than they were in securing wage increases or, more often, fighting wage cuts. In 1933, the number on relief in Alberta's cities ranged from 13 percent to 15 percent. In Edmonton, the families of 31 percent of the city's children were on relief. Unemployment forced some to abandon their homes and dig out caves in Edmonton's Saskatchewan River valley and countless thousands "rode the rails" in search of work.

Most of the strike activity, and there was not much, involved the unemployed. Often led by communists, they refused to do the work organized by the relief commissions and marched and protested against relief cuts or for increases in allowances. One of the most dramatic protests by the unemployed was the 1932 Hunger March in Edmonton, organized by the Workers' Unity League and the Farmers' Unity League, both communist-led organizations. The Hunger marchers demanded free unemployment insurance, a debt moratorium, adequate relief, protection from foreclosures and eviction, and an end to the labour camps. But the fact that the provincial government was in the hands of the

United Farmers of Alberta, first elected in 1921 as a progressive and reform administration, did nothing to ensure the marchers would receive a sympathetic hearing. A request for a parade permit was turned down and RCMP were stationed at country points to turn back protesters heading to Edmonton. The day before the march, 20 RCMP and 50 city police raided the Labour Temple, looking for guns and ammunition. They did not find any, but arrested one man for obstructing a police officer.

Despite the police and a heavy snowfall, workers, unemployed, and farmers came from all over the province, including Lethbridge, Drumheller, the Coal Branch, Calgary, and smaller centres. Plans called to have the marchers gather at Market Square and proceed from there to the Legislative Buildings where a delegation would meet with Premier Brownlee of the UFA government. On 20 December, about 2,000 marchers and 10,000 spectators gathered at Market Square hoping the UFA government of Premier Brownlee would relent and allow the march. At 2:30 PM, as the parade began, still without a permit, the police moved in. The combined numbers of police included "a reinforcement of 150 RCMP brought in from Regina. Thirty policemen hid inside the market buildings and machine guns bristled from the rooftops of the main Post Office."[69] Club-swinging police were the first to move in on the marchers, and they were followed by RCMP on horseback who came "galloping into the milling crowd, trampling all those who stood in their way. Reinforcements of foot police rushed in after them, their batons cracking against skulls and bones, drawing blood as they went."[70] Some of the demonstrators tore branches from nearby Christmas trees and rushed their attackers but the unarmed crowd could not withstand the police onslaught and the march broke up about 3:05 PM. The next day, the Labour Temple was again raided; this time, 30 persons were arrested and charged with being part of an unlawful assembly. Some of the issues raised by the Hunger marchers were brought to national attention two and a half years later by the Relief Camp Workers strike in British Columbia, a strike that led to the "On to Ottawa Trek."

Of all the industrial strikes in Alberta during the 1930s, the most important was the 1932 strike in the coal fields of the Crow's Nest Pass. The miners were led by the MWUC, which had affiliated to the Workers' Unity League in 1930. The issue was sharing of work among the miners, many of whom were working only one or two days a week. There were also rumours circulating that the companies were planning a wage cut. But a key reason for the six-month strike was management attitudes towards the workers. At one mine, several foremen made a young miner masturbate in front of them after he had talked back to a foreman. The manager of one mine said that he would make Blairmore a "white man's camp," a reference to the large number of eastern European workers employed in the mines. For management, the issue was the union itself; the companies wanted nothing to do with a union led by communists and affiliated to a Communist Labour central. Company officials and local businessmen attempted to divide the strikers, both on the basis of politics and along racial and ethnic lines. The strategy worked at the mine in Coleman where the workers broke away and set up a home local, but strikers at Blairmore and Bellevue held together. In early May, the operator of the Bellevue mine announced he was reopening the mine. On the appointed day, about 75 Mounties led the strike-breakers through a mass picket line which was bolstered by up to 1,200 people from the mining towns. Fighting broke out and continued for two days until the company admitted defeat and kept the mine closed. During the melée, more than a dozen strikers were arrested and two women were badly beaten by the Mounties.

The miners did not get much help from the Brownlee government. The UFA banned all demonstrations in the Pass and ignored pleas from the miners for assistance. In August, six months after the strike began, the government intervened to get the two sides back to the bargaining table. An agreement was signed on Labour Day, 1932. The agreement was a standoff, although victory was claimed by the MWUC. Company officials pledged that a blacklist of militants had been destroyed and that the workers would be free to belong to the union of their choice. However, the wage rates and working conditions under the 1930-32 agreement were renewed and a scab "home local" at Coleman was recognized.

But the real outcome of the strike cannot be measured by examining the contract. The Crow's Nest miners demonstrated to the companies that their fighting spirit prevailed, despite the odds. And in the town of Blairmore, the strike led to the election of a workers' slate in the subsequent municipal election. The council, which earned the town the nickname "Red Blairmore," helped miners fight evictions and established the town's first park. It also uncovered graft and "collected unpaid bills from prominent citizens;...supported the efforts of the unemployed to gain a higher standard of relief from the provincial government;...refused to force those on relief to perform make-work projects such as picking dandelions, etc., for which the Bennett government cut off the town's clothing allowance."[71] It renamed the main street Tim Buck Boulevard (after the leader of the Communist Party) and declared a civic holiday when Buck came to town after his release from jail. Said one observer:

...Blairmore "has gone"—it is a Union Camp...[The miners] are actually "running the town", as far as it is possible under the capitalist system for workers to run any town ...That is why Blairmore is hated, denounced and held up as a terrible example on the one side and hailed, loved and held up as an inspiration on the other....Here it is the businessmen who walk past depressed and sullen, the scabs who won't walk boldly, but slink home to grouch and plot. Even the Mounties who are being stationed in the town lose their habitual arrogance when they walk the streets of Blairmore. There has been no revolution in Blairmore, as is loudly proclaimed by its enemies. All that has happened is that the miners...have won the respect and fear of the exploiters.[72]

In 1936, the Workers' Unity League was disbanded in line with the new "common front against fascism" policy of the Comitern. On the recommendation of their leaders, the miners voted to return to the UMW. The MWUC was dead. The Communists, who were active in most of the mine strikes during the 1930s, also took up the task of organizing agricultural workers and assisted in the formation of a union of sugar beet workers in the Lethbridge-Taber area. The union called strikes in 1935 and 1936.[73]

For the unemployed, probably the most significant protest of the Depression was the "On to Ottawa Trek," organized by the Workers' Unity League to demonstrate opposition to the system of work camps. The relief camps had been established in 1932 by the Conservative government and were originally planned to handle about 2,000 men under military control. By 1933, there were 11,000 in the camps, most in isolated areas. When they were closed in 1936, about 170,000 people had gone through them. In Alberta, about 13,000 men went through the camps, most of which were established in the foothills and mountain areas. The government gave each camp worker a bed in a bunkhouse, three meals a day, and an allowance of 20 cents a day.[74]

In early April 1935, about 1,500 workers in British Columbia went on strike and headed for Vancouver, demanding abolition of the camps and the establishment of a work-and-wages programme. In June, the strikers decided to take their case to Prime Minister Bennett himself and boarded eastbound freights to begin the trek. During a stop at Golden, where they were fed by a group of local residents, a small recruiting contingent left for Edmonton "where we knew there were a few hundred unemployed living on the soup kitchens."[75]

When they arrived in Calgary on 7 June, they were met by police and local sympathizers. The police led them to the exhibition grounds where they camped; the sympathizers gave them coffee and food. The next day, the trekkers marched into downtown Calgary where they blockaded the city relief headquarters until the city and the province agreed to provide three days of relief. When the trek left Calgary, about 400 men from Edmonton joined, bringing the number to about 2,500.

Up to that point, no attempt had been made to stop the trek. Municipal and provincial authorities were quite content to have it move through their jurisdictions as quickly and as peaceably as possible. But the trek was picking up support as it moved across the country and the Bennett government had no desire to see thousands of unemployed workers, led by communists, descend on Ottawa. The decision was made to halt the trek in Regina[76] and orders were given outlawing travel on freight trains. The trek leaders recognized the government and decided to stop the trek in Regina to avoid possible bloodshed.

The protesters planned one final meeting in Regina's Market Square on 1 July "to acquaint the public of our decisions."[77] As the rally began, Mounties and City Police attacked. One city police officer was killed in the bloody riot. In the commons, CCF leader J.S. Woodsworth said:

One of the functions of a government is to maintain law and order, but a government has another function—to see that justice prevails within the country and that every reason for disorder is removed. When a government has removed all the reasons for disorder, then and not until then, is it justified in asking the people to support it. This government has not removed the reasons for discontent, nor has it met the just demands of the people.[78]

Within a year, the relief camps were disbanded and a new government was in Ottawa. The Liberals had won under Mackenzie King with the slogan "King or Chaos," but the country had to wait for the beginning of World War II for the chaos of the Depression to end.

The decline in trade union fortunes after World War I was not due solely to economic conditions. Some of the blame rested with the failure of the craft based unions to come to grips with mass production industries. In the United States, a group of union leaders, including John L. Lewis of the UMW (one of the few industrial unions in the American Federation of Labor), started the Congress of Industrial Organizations (CIO) as a vehicle to bring industrial workers into the labour movement. Organizing drives were started in such industries as auto, meat packing, electrical equipment, steel, and lumber and pulp and paper. These drives spread into Canada. But leaders of the American Federation of Labor, jealous of the growing power of the industrial organizing committees, expelled the CIO in 1937 and forced the Trades and Labour Congress to follow suit in 1939. The CIO unions in Canada then joined with the Canadian Brotherhood of Railway Employees to establish the Canadian Congress of Labour.

In Alberta, the two major CIO affiliates were the UMW and the packing house workers. Conditions in the meat packing plants in Edmonton and Calgary were as miserable as could be found. There had been no organization since the end of the First War, when the companies had broken the first unions established. Sit-down strikes took place in Edmonton and Calgary plants in 1937 and, while they ended in defeat, workers continued to organize. By 1939, the Trades and Labour Congress had organized most into a directly-chartered local. But there was growing dissatisfaction with what many considered the company orientation of Local 78 and, in 1943, the workers began to join the United Packinghouse Workers, the CIO affiliate. But the labour legislation of the Social Credit government of Ernest Manning made the establishment of the CIO in the packing plants a time consuming process. At the big Canada Packers plant in Edmonton, four votes were held before the CIO finally won certification as the bargaining agent. The fly in the ointment was a section in the law that required a majority of all employees in the bargaining unit before certification could be granted. Most other jurisdictions required only a majority of those voting. The law was a constant thorn in the side of organizers in the province.[79] Organization of the packing plants was assisted by a federal regulation (P.C.

1003) approved in 1944 which provided for certification of unions and required employees to bargain with them.

At the same time that packing plant workers were organizing, another of the more exploited groups in Alberta was also turning to the CIO as an answer to their problems. Bush and sawmill workers in Alberta lived in bunk-houses reminiscent of those on railway construction. There were double bunks and mattresses of hay or straw, and the workers carried their own blankets from camp to camp. Early in 1938, workers in camps south-west of Edmonton and in the Hinton-Edson area went on strike under the banner of the International Woodworkers of America (IWA), protesting a cut in minimum wages instituted by the Social Credit government after lobbying by the camp operators. The other main issue was camp conditions. The strikes were successful in winning back the old wage rate but employees in one camp only were able to force their employer to sign a contract with the IWA. By 1949, the union had about 1,000 members and contracts with four companies, but a bitter internal battle in British Columbia forced the IWA to suspend its Alberta operations. It did not re-enter the province until the mid-1950s.[80]

4. World War II and the Cold War

During World War II, the economic pressure was still on labour and was intensified by the wartime experience of rising prices and stricter controls on labour mobility. In 1943, the federal government passed an order-in-council freezing the coal miners to their jobs.

For the UMW and the coal miners, the war marked the high-water point of both militancy and coal production before the decline of the late 1940s and 1950s, a decline caused mainly by competition from cheap oil and gas. In late 1943, the UMW led the first district-wide strike in the coal fields in nearly two decades. A key issue in the strike by almost 10,000 miners was a two-week paid holiday. But even in what was to be its last spectacular gasp, the UMW was unable to run the strike without dissension. The walkout occurred despite a federal government order, approved in October the same year, outlawing coal strikes during the war. The National War Labour Board was unable to settle the dispute, and a special Royal Commission was struck which set an agreement providing a compromise on wage increases but allowing two weeks' vacation with pay.[81] When the government appointed the commission to examine the miners' demands, UMW chief Bob Livett ordered the men back into the pits. More than half ignored him, including miners in the Crow's Nest and Edmonton.[82]

The wave of strikes during the war finally forced the federal government to agree with labour's demands for a Canadian version of US President Roosevelt's "New Deal" Wagner Act (1935). In 1944, order-in-council P.C. 1003 was passed by the federal cabinet. It required employers to bargain in good faith with unions selected by their employees and provided legal machinery for the certification of unions and the determination of an appropriate bargaining unit. After more than 20 years, labour's demand for union recognition had been met. But the regulation, passed out of the government's desire to maintain labour peace during the war, was a compromise that involved a give-and-take between labour and the state. P.C. 1003 also required compulsory conciliation before a strike or lockout and forbade strikes or lockouts during the term of an agreement. The order became the foundation of present day labour legislation.

The decline of coal and coal mining and refining did not result in new trade union organization. There was, first, an attitude problem. Said veteran oil union organizer Neil Reimer: "They'd found a golden egg down here and they weren't going to allow any union representative to spoil it."[84] And there was, second, a problem with the Social Credit government, who, Reimer says, made a deal with the industry that it could operate in Alberta without unions if the province received heavy investment. There were moves to organize drilling workers and refinery employees in 1942 and 1947, both ending in failure. In 1948, the Oil Workers International Union, a CIO affiliate, moved into the Leduc field south of Edmonton. But before the government-supervised vote was taken, the drilling crews were transferred to other locations, and replaced by newly-hired men who voted against the union. In September 1952, however, the union did win certification for the Husky Oil refinery workers in Lloydminster (Local 658).

The most effective tactic employed by the oil companies involved company unions. In Alberta, bona fide unions had to prove that company unions were dominated by the employer, a daunting task. Where the evidence was overwhelming, Social Credit allowed the company unions to register under the Societies Act. According to Reimer:

> Manning sold Alberta on the basis of industrial peace. I think it's our union he wanted to keep out. He wasn't going to have a...situation like British Columbia where the basic industries were organized.[84]

It was not until the mid-1970s that the oil workers' union succeeded in organizing a refinery operated by one of the major international oil companies. The union is shut out of most of the province's gas plants, the tar sands plants, and most of the large refineries despite the fact that the major oil companies have been organized elsewhere in Canada and in the United States.

At the end of World War II, the Cold War began, unleashing a wave of anti-communism and red-baiting that the labour movement would not escape. Communists had been active in the industrial organizing drives that built the CIO but, after the war, they were systematically driven out of the unions they had helped build. Where that was impossible, in unions where communist control was too strong to challenge, the unions themselves were expelled from central labour bodies. Both the craft based Trades and Labour Congress and the Canadian Congress of Labour (CCL) passed constitutional amendments barring communist and "totalitarian" organizations from membership. The UMW did not allow communists to belong and although many in Alberta did, District 18 chief Bob Livett held them closely in check.

The two key communist figures in the Alberta labour movement were Jan Lakeman and Bill Longridge. Lakeman belonged to a small CCL construction affiliate; Longridge was an organizer for the Mine-Mill and Smelter Workers (formerly the Western Federation of Miners) in Calgary. In 1946, when CIO unions in the province established a provincial executive, Lakeman was elected president. But as the Cold War chilled, the leadership of the CCL, which was the central body of the CIO and nationalist unions, decided it was time to get Lakeman and Longridge out. The organizer of the effort was Tom McCloy, Alberta organizer of the CCL and a former UMW member, who worked closely with Pat Conroy, CCL secretary-treasurer and another former mine worker.[85]

The showdown came at the founding meeting in 1949 of the Industrial Federation of Labour. The first defeat for the communists came on the question of political action, whether the federation should endorse the CCF. The CCL had thrown its support behind the CCF, and many union members in the province wanted the industrial federation to follow suit. Obviously, the communists were not anxious to have the federation throw its support exclusively behind another political party. Following that defeat, the communists lost all but one of the elections for the executive; only Longridge managed to hold on.[86]

In the same year, Alberta's Minister of Labour and Industry told the legislature that some employers wanted changes made to the Labour Act to prohibit communists from participating in negotiations. Another indication of the anti-communist mood was the attitude of the *Calgary Herald* towards the Mine Mill local at a Cominco fertilizer plant in that city. Said the *Herald* in an editorial: "The national interest requires that a body under Communist influence should not be allowed to dominate a plant whose operations in wartime would be vital."[87] And the Social Credit minister in charge of civil defence suggested in 1951 that employees should be fingerprinted and tagged to help weed out communist spies; 500 or 600 of them, he claimed, were active in Alberta.[88]

While the Industrial Federation—the CIO unions—were supporting the CCF (mostly without success), the Alberta Federation of Labour found itself growing closer to the Social Credit government. The long journey from sympathy with the Russian Revolution in 1919 to rather open support with a right-wing, business-oriented government was due, in part, to the general rightward drift after World War II. It was also a time of growing prosperity, especially when considered against the Depression. For Alberta, as Reimer said, the oil industry goose was laying its golden egg, changing an agrarian province into an urbanized, industrialized one. Also, the split in labour's ranks had robbed the AFL of its radical heart, the mine workers.

In 1948, Social Credit introduced a new labour act. Several sections proposed severe penalties for unions involved in illegal strikes, including a proposal that a contract could be declared void in the event of an illegal work stoppage. Senior officials of the Alberta Federation of Labour endorsed the bill. And in 1950, the Federation president marked the change with a speech saying that labour and government should work together.[89]

Not all unions belonging to the Federation, of course, supported its relations with Social Credit. Both the Teamsters and Civic Workers unions broke with the federation over its stand on the labour bill. The growing inflation of the 1950s aided several 'young Turks' within AFL unions in organizing a putsch against the old-line leadership. Relations between the two federations were also growing warmer in the 1950s, motivated in large measure by a 1954 hotel worker's strike where the federations cooperated in the face of open union-busting by the hotel owners.

On 23 April 1956, the Canadian Congress of Labour and the Trades and Labour Congress merged to form the Canadian Labour Congress (CLC). (The American Federation of Labour and the CIO had merged as the AFL-CIO in the US in 1955.) Following the Canadian merger, the two Alberta federations merged as the Alberta Federation of Labour on 18 September 1956 at the Masonic Temple in Edmonton. The new president was Charles Gilbert, a member of the International Typographers Union and the secretary of AFL-TLC. The new executive secretary of the united federation was Robert Scott, a Teamster who had been the president of the craft based federation. Jack Hampton of the industrial federation was elected first vice-president. By 1952, the Industrial Federation of Alberta had about 8,000 members, about 3,000 of whom had joined in that year. The craft based TLC federation in 1951 had 18,430 members organized in 121 affiliated locals (almost triple the 1945 membership of 7,551). In 1957, following the merger, the unified federation had a membership of more than 32,000 in 146 locals.

Growth of the labour movement in Alberta was slow in the late 1950s and early 1960s. In 1959, the Federation received a major setback when the Civil Service Association of Alberta left over the issue of "political action." The Canadian Labour Congress had endorsed the formation of a new party, the New Democratic Party (CCF), based on a formal alliance between the CCF and the labour movement. Federation membership dropped from 35,000 to 30,000 at a single stroke; membership did not reach the 35,000 mark again until 1966.

Conclusion
In the formative years of the labour movement, it was unions in the building, coal mining, printing, and railway trades that laid the basis for the labour movement in Alberta, a supremacy that was not seriously challenged until the industrial union organizing drives of the 1930s and 1940s brought packinghouse and oil workers into the movement. During the 1960s, the make-up of the labour movement was undergoing an important change. White collar and

government service workers began to look to the trade union movement as they had never done before. In 1963, two unions of municipal and hospital workers merged to form Canadian Union of Public Employees (CUPE), which is now the largest union in Canada.

Organization in the more traditional blue collar sectors was also continuing and, by 1971, the federation had a membership of 51,000. Two years later, that had jumped to 58,000 and, in 1974, when the Civil Service Association (CSA) reaffiliated, membership stood at almost 90,000. In 1976, the federation claimed more than 100,000 members, about half represented by two unions—the Alberta Union of Provincial Employees (formerly the CSA) with about 30,000 members and CUPE with about 20,000 members.

In 1976, four of the unions among the ten largest organizations affiliated to the Alberta Federation of Labour were building trades organizations representing as a group about 18,000 workers. The sixth largest affiliate was the Public Service Alliance of Canada, representing most federal employees, with 3,800 members. Among the largest unions in the industrial sector in 1976 were the Canadian Food and Allied Workers with about 5,000 members, and the United Steelworkers of America with about 2,800. Outside the AFL, the Alberta Teachers' Association had about 25,000 members, while the Teamsters Union had a membership of about 6,500. The Oil, Chemical and Atomic Workers' International Union (now the Energy and Chemical Workers Union), which had about 2,000 members in Alberta, has been the only country-wide union to have its Canadian headquarters in the province (in Edmonton) and has taken a leading role in the labour movement in Alberta.

With major gains made by the trade union movement since the end of World War II in both wages and working conditions, and social legislation such as pensions, medicare and minimum wages, the labour movement in Canada appeared to some observers to be sinking into self-satisfied lethargy. But in the later 1960s and 1970s growing inflation, unemployment, and government policies gradually eroded much of the complacency that had developed. In late 1975, the federal government confronted Canadian trade unions with one of their greatest battles since the industrial organizing drives of the 1930s. On 13 October of that year, the federal Liberal government announced that it was implementing a system of wage and price controls, the first ever introduced in Canada in peacetime.

To back demands for removal of the wage control programme, which involved the federal government's intervening on behalf of corporations to hold down wage costs, and for implementation of policies to redistribute national income, delegates attending the April 1976 convention of the Alberta Federation of Labour in Edmonton passed a resolution authorizing a general strike if one should be called by the Canadian Labour Congress. A month later, the convention of the CLC in Quebec City gave its executive the authority to call a work stoppage, or stoppages, if necessary to defeat wage controls. In August, CLC President Joe Morris announced a "National Day of Protest" on 14 October

1976 to focus public attention on the inequity of controls. The two million members of the Congress were asked to refuse to work on 14 October, and when the day came about one million across Canada did so. In Alberta, about 48,000 workers joined the work stoppage and rallies and parades were held in Edmonton, Calgary, Lethbridge, Medicine Hat, Hinton, Grande Prairie, Red Deer, and Fort McMurray. About 5,000 trade union members participated in the provincial rallies.

The development of trade unionism in Alberta, as in other areas, followed the development of industry and with it the development of the working class. As industry moved into the province following the railroad, so too did trade union activity. Elements of class conflict were present before the entry of trade unions but organization was able to give workers more power in their dealings with their employers. However, even with the power found through organization, workers still found that the forces arrayed against them by capital and the state were in many cases, too formidable.

The intervention of the state on the side of the employers is a continuing theme, from the early involvement of the Mounted Police in railway construction through the mediation attempts by Mackenzie King, the Industrial Disputes Investigation Act, the War Measures Act, Social Credit labour laws, to the 1976 Anti-Inflation Board. The recognition of the power of the state and its role as an agency of employers has resulted in a political discussion in the labour movement that is still in progress.

The early radicalism of Alberta trade unionism was based on the coal miners, although craft organizations in Edmonton and Calgary also exhibited radical political tendencies, particularly during and after World War I. The political questioning that occasioned that radicalism is ongoing even though the labour movement in the province is today more conservative than it was during the First War and its aftermath. But that political radicalism was the product of the crisis conditions that existed at the time—a heightened awareness of the problems of a capitalist economy. That radicalism died during the 1920s, only to reappear again during the Depression in newer and more potent forms. The boom following World War II and the anti-communism and anti-socialism of the Cold War period forced another retreat of radicalism in trade union ranks. But the inflation and unemployment of the 1960s and 1970s, the wage control programme, and growing attacks on public sector unions and construction unions, such as the elimination of the right to strike and employer lobbying for "right-to-work" legislation (which prohibits all but open shops), have resulted in increased labour militancy and political activity.

There can be no doubt that the nature of the labour movement in Alberta has changed since its beginnings along the lines of rail construction in the 1880s. In large measure, the nature of the movement changed as the nature of work changed and as the attitudes of employers and governments towards unions changed. Workers in the coal camps lived in grimy, small shacks or vermin-infested bunkhouses and laboured for low wages. Their lives were in constant danger and there was no compensation to protect their families and widows. Changes of work were made at whim, with no consultation. The employers had all the power, workers most often had nothing. Attempts to better their lot were met openly by confrontation. When the employers were unable to beat back demands for unionization on their own, the police were called in.

The bitterest strikes in the province's history were over the right to have a trade union. There was no government programme of certification; there was no legal requirement to bargain, let alone a requirement to bargain in good faith. Labour relations battles were played out in far more dramatic, and often violent, fashion, 50 and 100 years ago when labour was often fighting for its very right to exist. But the growing acceptance of labour's right to organize—a battle still not ended[90]—and the growth of mediating institutions have taken the sharp edge off what was frequently open warfare; many negotiations have been reduced to more genteel battles fought with labour lawyers and public relations specialists.

Much has changed in almost 100 years, but none of the changes came without a fight. It took almost 20 years of concerted effort just to win a compensation act. The miners fought more than 10 years just to win the right to have a union and had to keep on fighting to keep it. Legal certification procedures were provided almost 20 years after the 1919 general strikes where collective bargaining rights were a key issue.

But cases remain where some employers show attitudes once expressed by almost all employers. After an organizing attempt at CJOC Television in Lethbridge, the company simply hired strike-breakers and continued operating, ignoring the strike and the strikers. In 1977, more than 60 employees, mainly low-paid women workers, of Parkland Nursing Home in Edmonton walked off the job in a first dispute with the employer. The company, owned by multi-millionaire Edmontonian Dr. Allard, said it would agree to a contract, but only on condition that some of the strikers not come back. Alberta's Conservative labour minister supported the company's position. When picketing impaired the company's operations, the Supreme Court granted an injunction telling the strikers not to sing on the picket line and to picket across the street. At the same time, and all the while claiming neutrality, the provincial government continued payments of several thousands dollars a day to the company.[91]

Alberta's labour development, of course, is not static. The majority of workers remain to be organized. And it remains to be seen whether working people, after an experiment with political conservatism lasting almost 40 years, are prepared to follow the advice of their leadership and look for an alternative.

Notes

[1] This idea is found in the distorted historical picture of Alberta as an exclusively 'agrarian society' made up of small independent farmer households living in conditions

of rough economic and social equality. But the historical picture of Alberta as an agrarian and egalitarian society is, at best, only partly true. The main problem with such a picture is that its misleading view of the homogeneity of Alberta society ignores not only the Native population but the class and sectional divisions and discord among the settler population. There is no denying that in Alberta's development the farmers have been a large and important force, reaching as high as about 45 percent of the gainfully occupied population in the 1920s. However, the absolute number of wage and salary earners in Alberta was roughly the same as the number of farmers in the 1910s and 1920s and larger by increasing amounts in the decades thereafter. By 1951, wage and salary earners were over two and a half times more numerous than farmers. (See D. Leadbeater, "The Development of Capitalism in the Area Currently Called Alberta," M.A. thesis (University of Alberta, 1980), 402,405.)

[2] Canada, *Census of the North-West Territories, 1884-5* (Ottawa, 1886), Tables I and XIX.

[3] R.C. Macleod, "Canadianizing the West: the North-West Mounted Police as Agents of the National Policy, 1873-1905," in L.H. Thomas, ed., *Essays on Western History* (Edmonton, 1976), 104.

[4] Warren Caragata, *Alberta Labour, A Heritage Untold* (Toronto, 1979), 3.

[5] John P. Turner, *The North-West Mounted Police, 1873-1893* (Ottawa, 1950), vol. II, 31, 33.

[6] Caragata, *Alberta Labour*, 4-5.

[7] *Calgary Herald*, 31 December 1886.

[8] See Douglas R. Kennedy, *The Knights of Labour in Canada* (London, Ont. 1956).

[9] Eugene A. Forsey, *The Canadian Labour Movement, 1812-1902*, Canadian Historical Association Booklets, No. 27 (Ottawa, 1974), 8.

[10] Jack Williams, *The Story of Unions in Canada* (Toronto, 1975), 45.

[11] Caragata, *Alberta Labour*, 10-11.

[12] L.G. Thomas, ed., *The Prairie West to 1905: A Canadian Sourcebook* (Toronto, 1975), 209.

[13] Ibid., 207.

[14] Ibid, 208.

[15] Canada, *Commission to Inquire into the Deaths of McDonald and Fraser on the Crow's Nest Pass Railway*, 1899, 40-42. Located in the federal Department of Labour library, Ottawa.

[16] Canada, *Commission to Inquire into Changes of Unjust Treatment of Persons Engaged in the Construction of the Crow's Nest Pass Railway*, 1898, Sessional Papers, 90A-1898, 76-77.

[17] Alberta, *Royal Commission on the Coal Mining Industry in Alberta* (Edmonton, 1907); Alberta, *Report of the Alberta Coal Commission* (Edmonton, 1926).

[18] Caragata, *Alberta Labour*, 18.

[19] An exact date for the formation of the Lethbridge local of the WFM is difficult to establish.

[20] Public Archives of Canada (PAC), RCMP Papers, vol. 141, File 580.

21 In the same year, the union was involved in a strike at the Dunsmuir coal mines at Nanaimo on Vancouver Island; the strike also happened to coincide with the 1903 strike by the United Brotherhood of Railway Employees (UBRE). Both the UBRE and the WFM were affiliated to the American Labour Union, set up as a new trade union centre to counterpose the conservative and craft based AFL.

22 Williams, *The Story of Unions*, 86-87. The report recommended that it be made an offence for any non-British subject "to procure, or incite any employee in Canada to quit the employment without the consent of the employer, or for any person within Canada to exhibit or publish, or in any way communicate to an employee the content of any order, request, suggestion or recommendation...by any person or persons ordinarily resident without Canada, that he quit their employment." See Martin Robin, *Radical Politics and Canadian Labour, 1880-1930* (Kingston, Ont., 1968), 72-73.

23 PAC, RCMP Papers, vol. 141, File 577; Lorne Thompson, "The Rise of Labor Unionism in Alberta," typescript (1965), 19, Provincial Archives of Alberta (PAA), Edmonton.

24 Thompson, "The Rise of Labor Unionism," 28; Williams, *The Story of Unions*, 187.

25 Winnipeg was the main base of shop-craft unions on the prairies. The International Brotherhood of Boilermakers had only one lodge (Lodge 126) on the prairies until 1903, a railway lodge in Winnipeg. On 28 August 1903, a railway lodge (Lodge 392) of the Boilermakers' was chartered in Calgary. (Robert M. MacIntosh, *Boilermakers on the Prairies* [Winnipeg, 1979], 54.)

26 Charles Lipton, *The Trade Union Movement of Canada, 1827-1959* (Toronto, 1973; 1st ed., 1967), 100.

27 Caragata, *Alberta Labour*, 12-13.

28 Ibid., 13.

29 Selig Perlman, *A History of Trade Unionism in the United States* (New York, 1950; first printed, 1922), 214-15. The ALU was a precursor of the Industrial Workers of the World (1905).

30 For accounts of the historic Pullman strike, see: Sidney Lens, *The Labor Wars: From the Molly Maguires to the Sitdowns* (New York, 1973); Ray Ginger, *Eugene V. Debs, A biography* (New York, 1962); Philip S. Foner, *History of the Labor Movement in the United States* (New York, 1955), vol. II, chapter 18.

31 Lipton, *The Trade Union Movement*, 113.

32 Ibid., 102-103.

33 Canada, Department of Labour, *Labour Gazette*, 1906-07, vol. 7, 647, 660.

34 Caragata, *Alberta Labour*, 23.

35 Ibid., 9, 23.

36 Elizabith Taraska, "The Calgary Craft Union Movement, 1900-1920," MA thesis (University of Calgary, 1975), 20.

37 Thompson, "The Rise of Labour Unionism," 56-63.

38 Caragata, *Alberta Labour*, 23-25.

39 Ibid., 20.

40 PAC, King Papers, vol. 16.

41 Caragata, *Alberta Labour*, 21.

42 Stuart Jamieson, *Times of Trouble: Labour Unrest and Industrial Conflict in Canada, 1900-66*, Task Force on Industrial Relations, Study No. 22 (Ottawa, 1968), 128-29.

43 Bradley Rudin, "Mackenzie King and the Writing of Canada's Anti-Labor Laws," *Canadian Dimension*, 8, nos. 4-5 (January 1972).

44 Caragata, *Alberta Labour*, 37-38.

45 Ibid., 58-60.

46 Ibid., 37. As for Mackenzie King, in 1915, he went to work for the Rockefeller family in the United States as a labour relations consultant. It was during this time that he began promoting the concept of company councils, or company-dominated "unions," which are still the norm in several Rockefeller-controlled companies, such as Exxon (Imperial Oil).

47 Thompson, "The Rise of Labour Unionism, 96-99.

48 *Bound of Brotherhood*, (Calgary, 1903-04). PAA; Edmonton Trades and Labour Council Minutes, 7 December 1914, PAA: *Canadian Parliamentary Guide*, 1909-1910.

49 John Blue, *Alberta Past and Present* (Chicago, 1924), vol. I, 370.

50 Andrew Ross McCormack, "The Origin and Extent of Western Labour Radicalism, 1896-1919," PhD thesis (University of Western Ontario, 1973), 197-98. Later published as *Reformers, Rebels, and Revolutionaires: The Western Canadian Radical Movement, 1899-1919* (Toronto, 1977).

51 Alberta Federation of Labour, Proceedings of the 1912 (Founding) Convention, Department of Labour Library, Ottawa. In the first year, more than 60 percent of membership dues were from the miners.

52 Caragata, *Alberta Labour*, 35-36.

53 Records of the Department of Labour, vol. 3009, file 151, Department of Labour Library.

54 See McCormack, *Reformers, Rebels, and Revolutionaries*, 121-22, 138.

55 Blue, *Alberta, Past and Present* 381, 391-92.

56 Taraska, "The Calgary Craft Union Movement," 53.

57 Ibid., 69.

58 Alberta Federation of Labour, Proceedings of the 1919 Convention, Resolution no. 27.

59 Caragata, *Alberta Labour*, 71-72.

60 Williams, *The Story of Unions*, 117.

61 For further discussion of the Edmonton situation, see W.R. Askin, "Labour Unrest in Edmonton and District and Its Coverage by the Edmonton Press: 1918-1919," MA thesis, University of Alberta, 1973).

62 Taraska, "The Calgary Craft Union Movement," 79.

63 D.C. Masters, *The Winnipeg General Strike* (Toronto, 1950); PAC, R.G. 27, vol. 313, files 151A-B, 153.

64 PAC, R.G. 27, vol. 313, file 153.

65 For more on the OBU, see Lipton, *The Trade Union Movement*, chapter 12: David J. Bercuson, *Fools and Wise Men: The Rise and Fall of the One Big Union*, (Toronto, 1978).

66 Jamieson, *Times of Trouble*, 205.

67 Ibid., 204-205; Alberta, *Report of the Alberta Coal Commission*, 1925, 198-201; Allan Seager, "A History of the Mine Workers Union of Canada, 1925-36," MA thesis (McGill University, 1977).

68 See Caragata, *Alberta Labour*, 93, 95; Lipton, *The Trade Union Movement*, 234-36.

69 Anne B. Woywitka, "Recollections of a Union Man," *Alberta History* , vol. 23, no. 4 (Autumn 1975), 19.

70 Ibid., 19.

71 Allan Seager, "The Pass Strike of 1932," *Alberta History* vol, 25, no. 1 (Winter 1977), 10.

72 Seager, "A History," 10.

73 See John Herd Thompson and A. Seager, "Workers, Growers, and Monopolists: The 'Labour Problem' in the Alberta Beet Sugar Industry During the 1930s," *Labour/Le Travailleur*, vol. 3 (1978), 153-74.

74 Ronald Liversedge, *Recollection of the On to Ottawa Trek*, edited and with an introduction by Victor Hoar (Toronto, 1973), viii-ix.

75 Ibid., 93.

76 According to Victor Hoar (ibid., vii-viii), Calgary was not the place to stop the trek as the the city was the Prime Minister's home constituency. Regina was a small, isolated city with the presence of a strong RCMP detachment. Regina was also located in a Liberal province, and relations between the Liberal provincial governments and the Conservative federal government were strained.

77 Ibid., 112.

78 Ibid., 253.

79 Caragata, *Alberta Labour*, 130-31.

80 Ibid., 126-27.

81 Jamieson, *Times of Trouble*, 200.

82 Caragata, *Alberta Labour*, 132.

83 W. Caragata, Interview with Neil Reimer, 1978, PAA.

84 Caragata, *Alberta Labour*, 136.

85 Ibid., 139-40.

86 Thus, the CCL chartered the Industrial Federation of Labour of Alberta, three years after the first provincial council of CCL unions had been formed. (The CCL had been established in 1940 as a merger between the ACCL and the CIO unions expelled from the TLC). The new federation of labour for industrial unions included the UMW, the Packinghouse Workers, the IWA, the CBRE, "Mine-Mill," and others. The miners had returned to the UMW after the WUL was disbanded, and although they were not allowed to hold union offices, the communists had many members working in the coal fields. Mine-Mill, the new name of the Western Federation of Miners, had started organizing in the late years of the war and had contracts with Calgary metal shops and glass and brick plants in Medicine Hat. It was, with the United Packinghouse Workers (now the Canadian Food and Allied Workers) and the UMW, one of the largest CIO unions in Alberta.

87 PAC, CLC Papers, vol. 154; *Calgary Herald*, 14 July, 1951.

88 *Calgary Herald*, 17 February 1951 and 3 March 1951.

89 Caragata, *Alberta Labour*, 141.

90 The largest group of unorganized industrial workers remains the oil workers. They are kept isolated from the labour movement not so much by brute pressure and raw intimidation as by a large measure of paternalism combined with wages and benefits packages that either equal or better those of their union brothers and sisters.

91 Caragata, *Alberta Labour*, 146.

The Municipal Government Reform Movement and Alberta*

Jim Anderson

And what else, day by day, imperils and slays cities, countries and single persons so much as the new amassing of wealth by anyone? Which amassing reveals new longings, the goal of which may not be reached without wrong to someone.

Dante Alighieri

1. Introduction

Municipal governments, particularly those of large cities, have considerable power over a broad range of policy, and the way this power is wielded makes a great deal of difference to the lives of urban residents. Local governments share the public power with federal and provincial institutions of the state and are therefore the objects of political struggle. "It is for the state's attention, or for its control that men compete; and it is against the state that beat the waves of social conflict."[1]

During the period of rapid urban growth and industrialization around the turn of the century, the public functions of the city became increasingly important to various urban groups in Canada. Local governmental institutions were called upon to provide essential services to a rapidly expanding population and burgeoning industry. Regulation of business and labour; provision of subsidies to industry; supply of water, gas and electricity; health and sanitation services and taxation were a few of the activities of local governments that had an increasing material effect on groups within the city.

The early importance of urban government in the Canadian political economy can be indicated in various ways. One such measure is the rate and extent of urbanization. By 1912, an estimated 45 percent of Canadians were concentrated in urban centres of 4,000 or more in population.[2] Even in western Canada, often depicted as an agricultural frontier, the urban population increase exceeded the rural. Between 1901 and 1911, for example, Winnipeg's population tripled; Edmonton's increased sevenfold, and Calgary's rose tenfold.[3] At the end of the first decade of the twentieth century, the population of Alberta was 38 percent urban.[4] Like other western cities Alberta's urban centres were pivotal in relation to the total population of the province. For example, Edmonton's population of 31,000 in 1911

---

*This is a revised version of an essay that appeared in Alan F.J. Artibise and Gilbert A. Stelter, eds., *The Usable Urban Past: Planning and Politics in the Modern Canadian City* (Toronto: Macmillan, 1979).

formed a higher proportion of the provincial total than Toronto's share of Ontario's population in 1867.[5]

The public expenditures of large urban centres reflect the role of the city as a significant unit of the Canadian state. At the turn of the century, for example, the budgets of Winnipeg, Toronto, and Montreal exceeded those of the respective provinces in which they were situated.[6] Large cities also have had a considerable degree of local autonomy with respect to taxation and expenditure.[7] But even to the degree that local jurisdictions act as agencies of senior governments, the way in which they carry out these duties has a differential impact on socio-economic groups in the city. There has always been a strong element of 'politics' in the 'administration' of programmes at the local level. Moreover, the local councils, which are charged with carrying out, or working within the scope of, provincial policies, are themselves elective and, in this sense, political bodies.

The era of the rise of the modern city in Canada between 1880 and 1920 was characterized by a heightened struggle over the role and function of local government. A logical connection was often made between the importance of local government to a particular class and the need to take steps to make certain that it serve that class interest. This argument was perceived and acted upon by both business and labour groups. For example, a member of the Chamber of Commerce of London, Ontario, made this point in his address to the Ontario Municipal Association in 1919:

If the mercantile and other business interests of a community are to progress there must be a close relationship between the Chamber of Commerce and the city government. Legislation to protect the community merchant and the money he invests annually in taxes from the transient cannot be effected without co-operation between the two forces. Fire, police, health and the necessary protection for every business cannot be secured without close relationship between the two.[8]

Labour groups slowly began to contest business hegemony in local government. In the second decade of the century, organized labour sought a measure of power at city hall. They did so in Winnipeg, for example, "… because local bodies controlled housing, sanitation, public health, charity and other departments of public effort."[9]

The purpose of this essay is to examine the class character of the key changes that occurred in municipal government during the era of the municipal "reform" movement between 1880 and 1920. My analysis is focused on the prairie region of western Canada with particular attention to Alberta. The West, as historian Paul Rutherford has pointed out "… was a veritable laboratory for reform"[10] and municipal reform was perhaps most fully worked out in Alberta cities. Yet, little has been written on urban government reform in the West.

2. The Canadian Urban Reform Movement

The urban reform movement that swept across Canada around the beginning of the twentieth century originated in the latter decades of the nineteenth century and culminated in the aftershock of World War I. It coincided, not accidentally, with the initial period of rapid urbanization and industrialization in Canada. The movement stemmed from a variety of causes, but can be viewed as a campaign by which identifiable classes and sections of classes sought to ensure that their respective interests and values would dominate in the local political economy and that the benefits and sanctions emanating from local institutions would conform to their different conceptions of the public interest.

A principal objective of the reform movement was the alteration of the structure and function of civic government itself. Reformers did not stop at campaigns to change the personnel of local government. The local "constitutions" or civic charters, they found, were relatively easy to change by the dominant forces within the community. And when new cities arose in western Canada, particularly in Alberta, it was possible to model the form of government on the latest reform schemes because the inertia of an older organizational framework was relatively insignificant compared to that of central Canadian eastern cities, or even the older cities of Saskatchewan and Manitoba.

The reform era around the turn of the century was the time of the "great barbecue"—a time of burgeoning capitalism when the successful businessman was the folk hero. It was a period in which "...there was general agreement that the chief duty of government was to produce material prosperity by supporting business enterprise."[11] It was also a period in which organized labour was weak and its official legitimacy dubious, as the reaction to the Winnipeg General Strike of 1919 (and early actions by labour) suggests.[12]

Business found it necessary to use the instrument of local government to promote growth, to help in establishing economic dominance over the rural hinterland, to compete with rival urban centres, to control wages and working conditions, and to confer public legitimacy on corporate objectives. A related and important factor in local government reform was the desire by business to keep input costs low through municipal ownership of utilities such as gas, electricity, and waterworks.[13]

The incentive to bring municipal utilities under sound public management was compelling. A University of Toronto political economist calculated that municipally-owned waterworks systems in Canada charged 50 percent less than private waterworks for the same service.[14] Similar results were claimed for other utilities which were taken under municipal ownership. For example, *The Canadian Municipal Journal* reported in 1911 that over the five years the city of Calgary had been operating its electric lighting plant, the rates had been reduced by 45 percent relative to those charged previously by a private concern.[15] When Winnipeg ended its reliance on a private electrical franchise in 1911, the new public hydro-electric facility reduced the cost of power in Winnipeg from 9 cents to 3 cents per kilowatt hour. The *Manitoba Free Press* credited the availability of inexpensive power for an influx of new manufacturing concerns to the city and, not incidentally, a real estate boom: "[public] power is the force which has carried real estate upwards in phenomenal bounds, and which has created many fortunes for the holders of property."[16]

In Albertan and other prairie cities, plans for restructuring local government often were linked expressly to the need for efficient operation of municipal utilities. It was seen as essential that these vital services be operated on principles of businesslike efficiency and economy. Therefore, it was of crucial importance to "reform" the inefficient council-committee form of local government by introducing features characteristic of the private business corporation. For example, the city charter of Edmonton, which incorporated the latest reform principles, "was designed with special regard to the question of municipal ownership."[17]

The conception of "local government as business" relegated the notion of representation of non-business interests to a position of little or no importance. As prominent Toronto reformer, academic, and businessman Samuel Morley Wickett wrote in 1902, "throughout Canada the Municipality is regarded more as a species of joint stock company, only those contributing to the capital being allowed to share in the direction of its affairs."[18] According to the prevailing ideology, the only segment of the community that contributed to the civic coffers were those who paid business or property taxes. Tenants and other urban residents with little income or property were denied the right to vote in civic elections and plebiscites long after universal manhood suffrage had been won at federal and provincial levels.[19]

Other urban groups saw benefits in an expansion of the public role of the municipality and control over its operation. Organized labour concentrated its attack, however, on the restrictive franchise provisions in local elections and the high property qualifications necessary to run for civic office. Often, labour's preoccupation was with the immediate concerns of wages, working conditions, public transportation costs, housing, and social services.[20]

The structural forms and the accompanying ideology of local government formulated during the municipal reform era are largely still with us. In many cities, the form of government (for example, Edmonton's Board of Commissioners plan) instituted at the turn of the century remains intact or in slightly modified form today. The city-wide or at-large local electoral system has persisted until very recently in many cities and the "non-partisan" sentiment is still a potent force in urban politics. The ideology of the urban reform movement appears to have congealed as an important component of the Canadian political culture. It clearly affects present day civic decision-making—defining in crucial ways what are legitimate topics for local consideration and, just as importantly, excluding an equal number from the arena of legitimate and public debate at the civic level.

In recent years there has been a noticeable reaction against the ideology and institutions implanted by turn-of-the-century municipal government reformers. Ironically, in some respects municipal government "reform" has come full circle. In the early years of the century, for example, a typical municipal reformer was opposed to ward elections, against open party politics in municipal matters, and in favour of strengthening the civic executive or bureaucracy. The present day urban reformer, however, is in favour of ward elections, often advocates a form of local partisanship, and supports measures designed to shift power away from the civic bureaucracy or executive to the elected council. Yet, the recent reaction to the earlier conception of municipal reform cannot be understood adequately without some knowledge of the class character of reforms popularized by an earlier generation.

In order to determine the nature and extent of the class bias of local government reform in Alberta, as in the rest of Canada, it is necessary to make some analytical distinctions concerning urban reform in general and urban government reform in particular. Distinctions must be made among groups advocating various reforms as well as among the reform proposals themselves. The rhetoric of reform very often masked the reality. In the following section, there is a brief analysis of the core features of the movement for municipal government reform in Canada generally. Local government reform in Alberta will then be analyzed in terms of these key planks in the bourgeois reformers' platform. The alternate reform package of labour will be contrasted to the elite conception of reform later on in this essay.

3. Municipal Government Reform Defined and Delimited

Since this study deals with the municipal reform "package" as it relates to the attempt by urban elites to change the structure and function of urban political institutions, it is useful at the outset to distinguish between the social reform element of the movement and the campaign for structural reform. As Paul Rutherford points out:

Clearly there were different concerns sheltered under the umbrella of urban reform—the elimination of vice and crime, social justice, the creation of a healthy environment, the regulation of utility corporations, the beautification of the industrial city, town planning, and the remodelling of the municipal government.[21]

While there was some overlap of membership between groups advocating moral, humanitarian, and social reform on the one hand, and good government advocates on the other, the emphasis of social reformers like J.S. Woodsworth was not directed primarily to revamping the structure of civic government. Woodsworth, for example, was perhaps the greatest crusader of his time for measures such as improving the conditions of the slum, civic charity, and health and sanitation. He was not, however, a central figure in any campaigns for civic charter reform. It appears that urban reform groups pressing for moral and humanitarian reforms usually were made up of clergymen, women's groups, temperance advocates, and academics. However, the typical leader of campaigns for local government reform, particularly in Alberta, were leading businessmen, usually members of the boards of trade.[22] An analytical distinction, therefore, must be made between the structural and humanitarian elements of the movement.

The interrelated group of reform measures which I examine below includes measures designed to 'reform' civic elections and revamp the structure of the city council and civic bureaucracy. These proposals made up the core of the elite model of municipal government reform. These measures were motivated by an underlying political ideology; they were often linked to each other in reform campaigns in particular cities; and were frequently bound together in specific city charter reforms. Usually, they were instituted by a distinct economic segment of the population.

Specifically, the core features of municipal reform consisted of:

(1) *Abolition of ward elections:* At-large elections—or elections based on large, socially heterogeneous wards—were to replace the prevailing practice of electing councillors from relatively small wards.

(2) *Civic executive and bureaucratic reform:* In order to separate policy-making from administration and to strengthen the bureaucracy and/or executive relative to the city council a number of civic charter reforms were recommended. The most common forms adopted in Canada included variations of the following: (a) the Board of Control; (b) the Commission Plan; (c) the Board of Commissioners; and (d) the City Manager Plan.[23]

(3) *Non-partisanship:* In Canada, non-partisanship was held to be a consequence largely of civic executive reform and at-large elections. Nevertheless, it can be considered an institutional reform because it implied the absence of political parties from municipal elections. Non-partisanship did not involve legal changes as it did in the United States, where the removal of the political party designation from the ballot and measures such as primary elections were designed to insulate local elections from political party activity.[24] This phenomenon was no less significant in Canada, however, as the campaign against the parties of labour in Calgary and Edmonton reveal.

(4) *The municipal reform ideology:* This political ideology provided the rationale for municipal institutional reform and thus embodied the attitudinal counterpart of structural reform. Some of its key tenets can be stated as follows:

   (a) City government is primarily business, not politics.[25] It should therefore be run by administrative experts, particularly successful businessmen,[26] on businesslike principles of efficiency and economy.

   (b) A clear distinction between policy and administration in civic government is necessary.[27] City Council should function in the same fashion as a board of directors of a private corporation, giving board policy direction only. The administration (implementation) of policy should be left entirely to the civic administrations or a small executive elected at-large, the duties of which are to correspond to that of the manager of a private business firm.

(c)   The public power of the civic corporation must be centralized by (i) shifting power from the council to a strengthened city bureaucracy or a small elected executive and (ii) abolishing ward elections so that councillors elected from the city at-large can safely ignore the parochial interests based on class, ethnicity, or geographic location within the city.[28]

(d)   Party politics must be kept out of municipal 'business' since local government is largely technical and administrative in nature. In the absence of political parties in local elections, however, it is appropriate for the most prominent ratepayers (i.e., those who have the greatest interest in the municipal corporation) to guide the voters in order to elect the right kind of candidates to civic office.[29]

While at-large elections, commission or manager-style forms of administration along with non-partisanship constituted the institutional core of the municipal reform movement, the attitudinal counterpart of these related structural measures was the pervasive municipal reform ideology. There was a great measure of unanimity among the elite Canadian municipal reformers on these features. Together, municipal reformers would take city government out of the hands of parochial politicians whose loyalties were to individual wards and would instill the principles of efficiency and economy in a businesslike local government. Moreover, the scuttling of wards and the removal of important policy matters from the council to either a small executive elected at-large or a professional civic administration would both decrease the potential for petty patronage available to councillors and wipe out the electoral base of the "logroller" or ward-heeler at the same time. Thus, these measures would eliminate the chief incentive for political party activity at the local level. Most importantly, by changing the basis of representation, municipal reform would "...prevent the candidature of inconspicuous men."[30]

There were a number of other important proposals for change in municipal government current during the reform era that cannot be considered part of the core of bourgeois reform. The extension of the franchise is one such example. Leading 'reformers,' as well as the schemes they devised, often reflected a general reluctance to broaden the franchise, though an expanded franchise was a key demand of civic labour groups. A related factor, the property qualification for holding municipal office, was similarly regarded. Reform schemes often provided for a higher rather than a lower property or income qualification, despite the outcry of urban labour spokesmen. A host of examples could be given: the Montreal reformers' campaign for a board of control retained provisions for a restrictive franchise and a very high property qualification for civic office;[31] Edmonton's 'reform' charter of 1904 contained a provision that in plebiscites on referred (money) by-laws allowed as many as four votes to burgesses according to the amount of property each owned.[32] The effect of this latter provision was significant. For example, the City of Edmonton's voters' list for 1914 contains a high proportion of names of persons and corporations with two, three, or four votes each. Of the 52 such names on the first page of the list (which appears to be representative of the entire list), 28 burgesses were allowed more than one vote each.[34] Thus, in this instance not only were non-property owners excluded entirely from plebiscites on money by-laws, but also large property owners wielded about twice as much voting power as those who held little property.

In Regina, where the Edmonton Charter was adopted virtually intact, a cumulative voting clause was incorporated into the draft charter that would have permitted large property owners as many as sixteen votes (four votes in each of four wards). This provision, however, was modified by the rural-dominated Saskatchewan legislature such that a property holder could vote only four times—once in each ward in which he owned property.[34] Yet, leading reformers across the nation heralded the Edmonton city charter of 1904 and imitations of it adopted in other western cities as the latest innovations in progressive civic reform.[35]

The restrictions with respect to voting for municipal candidates during the reform era were little better than the provisions for plebiscites on money by-laws. In early Calgary, for example, the *Herald* estimated that 50 percent of property owners did not have a sufficiently high assessment to qualify for the vote.[36] At the peak of municipal reform activity in Winnipeg in 1906, that city's population was 101,057 but only 7,784 were qualified to vote in the civic election.[37] In Montreal, at the turn of the century, an estimated 30 percent of otherwise qualified electors were disenfranchised for failure to pay the municipal water tax and other municipal rates.[38] The franchise was further weighted in favour of the substantial owners of property in almost all cities by the provision that electors could vote in each ward in which they held property. Alan Artibise noted that this provision enabled wealthy electors in Winnipeg to cast up to seven ballots each. In the 1910 election in Winnipeg, for example, there were an estimated 6,000 repeaters on the voters' list.[39]

The failure of reformers to press for an extension of the franchise to the non-property owning segment of the population was not a mere oversight. A noted Canadian reformer, S. Morley Wickett, for example, proclaimed in an article published in 1907 that Canada's conservative municipal franchise was a positive feature of the Canadian municipal system in that it gave tax-paying corporations the vote and that it excluded from the voters' lists those with little or no income or property, thereby operating "chiefly against newcomers of various classes and nationalities who have little ground for interest in civic affairs."[40]

The property or income qualifications for municipal office were usually left intact in the elite reformer campaigns to restructure government in prairie cities. In some cases, reformers actually succeeded in raising the qualifications so that leading businessmen could be persuaded to seek election to these newly created municipal positions. Thus, when the board of control scheme was adopted in Winnipeg in 1906, an accompanying "reform" raised the property qualification for the mayoralty candidate from $500 to $2,000—a fourfold increase. The candidates for the Board of Control were also required to own at least $2,000 worth of property in order to qualify.[41] When Calgary civic leaders devised a city charter in 1893, they included a provision by which councillors were required to meet a property qualification of $1,000. This factor prevented over 65 percent of Calgary ratepayers from qualifying for municipal office in 1889.[42] In 1906, the City of Medicine Hat set a property qualification of $1,000 for the offices of both mayor and alderman.[43]

Not surprisingly, during the reform period city councils and, in particular, mayoralty offices were usually beyond the reach of even skilled workers. Max Foran's study of Calgary during the period 1884-95 reveals that "on no occasion did artisans or labourers run for [civic] office."[44] And in Winnipeg, Henry Huber's research demonstrates that all of the successful mayoralty candidates were members of the Board of Trade and of the Liberal or Conservative parties.[45]

Even direct legislation provisions—initiative, referendum, and recall—cannot be considered core features of the dominant model of municipal government reform. Only a minority of reform campaigns resulted in the adoption of these measures and they were soon diluted by reform councils. The direct legislation features were more noticeable in southern Alberta's cities where American immigration was significant. But even here the percentage of voters required to initiate policies or recall errant legislators was high. For example, when Lethbridge adopted the American-style commission form of civic government in 1913, it incorporated the direct legislation provisions of initiative, referendum, and recall which formed part of the populist crusade of the progressive era. These three key features of direct democracy provided the means by which a stated number of qualified voters, by signing a petition, could: (a) initiate legislative proposals which the elected Commission would be required to consider, (b) force the Commission to submit matters to a referendum, or (c) "recall" one or more Commissioners by petitioning that the offending local legislator(s) again submit to a special election in order to be confirmed in, or removed from, office. However, the proportion of electors required to petition in order to exercise these democratic provisions was high. In order to force the Commissioners to submit a by-law to a referendum, 20 percent of the number of voters polled in the preceding election were required to sign a petition to this effect. An identical number of voters were required to initiate proposed local legislation, which the Commission could either ratify or submit to a referendum. And the recall petition required the signatures of 15 percent of the number of voters in the preceding election.[46]

To ensure that these democratic mechanisms would be used sparingly, if at all, the Lethbridge Commission petitioned the Alberta legislature in 1914 to raise the number of signatures required to bring into play the referendum and recall provisions.[47] By 1916, the Commissioners were successful in securing a charter amendment which increased the number of voters required to set in motion the initiative, referendum, and recall procedures to the virtually prohibitive level of 35 percent, 25 percent, and 25 percent respectively.[48] The Lethbridge charter contained other provisions that also fell short of the populist ideals supposedly embodied in direct legislation. In order to exercise the franchise, for example, a resident required a property or income qualification of $200; in addition, representatives of private companies were allowed to vote.[49]

These examples illustrate the point that it is crucial to determine what democratic measures reformers usually *excluded* from the dominant schemes for restructuring civic government. While extension of the franchise, reduction in property qualifications for office, and direct legislation were well known devices designed to give the average citizen a greater voice in civic affairs, most successful reform campaigns in Canadian cities seem to have excluded them or included them only reluctantly. Yet this alternate reform package was often advocated by labour and other non-elite segments of the community at the time. For example, the Edmonton Trades and Labour Council constantly campaigned for an extended local franchise during the first two decades of this century.[50] Not surprisingly, reforms favouring labour in the municipal arena were consistently resisted by "reform" councils and what little ground was gained resulted as a rule from lobbying the Alberta legislature.

4. The Roots of Reform

A study of the historical roots of reform in the Canadian context allows one to identify some of the most significant indigenous factors that gave rise to the movement in Canada. Social scientists have assumed too often that the Canadian municipal reform movement was simply an imitation of the great American crusade against the corrupt urban political party machine. In a recent study, for example, it is declared that Canada was "...a country lacking in the social conditions that gave rise to the movement."[51] This statement could not be more misleading. The influence of the American movement must be acknowledged, but local government reform in Canada was unique in some respects and differed in degree if not in kind from its American counterpart in other ways.[52] Nor was reform in prairie cities entirely derivative of Ontario adaptations of American reform models. While the West was indeed a 'laboratory' in which the reform formulae of central Canadians were applied, it is not at all clear that the application of these experiments conformed to the prescriptions of the self-proclaimed spokesmen of the new "civic science" living in Toronto or Westmount. More importantly, it is possible to conclude from the evidence now available that the *results* of these experiments in revamping civic government and politics in the West were not nearly as benign as leading central Canadian reform advocates had predicted.

During the reform period, the form and style of civic political institutions in the rapidly growing cities of Alberta were closely patterned after the Ontario model. The Baldwin Act, passed in 1849, often called the "magna Carta" of Canadian local government, was virtually replicated in the municipal legislation of the North-West Territories and, later, the prairie provinces.[53] The Ontario municipal system was copied in the West in part because it was the "nearest established system" and because many western settlers came from Ontario.[55] For example, Bob Edwards (later the editor of the *Calgary Eye Opener*) wrote that homes in Edmonton contained "...nothing but the pictures of deceased Ontario relatives."[55] Moreover, Ontario born men in large part formed the elite in western centres, including those in Alberta. As Wickett observed at the turn of the century with respect to the West,

Owing largely to the fact that so many Ontario men have accepted municipal appointments or entered into the practice of law in its leading cities, the municipal system of Ontario has in many respects served as a model.[56]

An Ontario boyhood was also a distinguishing characteristic of many members of western boards of trade and city councils. And these two civic bodies, characterized by a great degree of overlapping membership, cooperated in spearheading most campaigns for local government reform in the West. For example, four of the six mayors of Winnipeg who held office between 1901 and 1914 were from Ontario and all six were members of the Board of Trade.[57] Both the original act of incorporation of Winnipeg and the subsequent adoption of the Board of Control in 1906 were based closely on the form of government prevailing in Toronto at each point in time.[58]

When Edmonton obtained its reform charter in 1904, the former solicitor of the City of Toronto and editor of *The Municipal Manual of Ontario*, W.H. Biggar, was called in to assist in the formulation of the local charter which subsequently served as the basis for similar reforms in Calgary, Regina, Saskatoon, and other western cities, and which was also the first general act governing cities in Alberta. Due to the provision for the innovative board of commissioners form of administration and other reform features, the Edmonton charter was widely imitated in the West—Edmonton became the quintessential 'reform' city of western Canada. The Edmonton charter was a virtually perfect institutional realization of the ideology of the leading central Canadian reform advocates who were prevented from imposing their ideal model so completely upon the cities of their own region because of the inertia inherent in the strength of tradition in these older urban centres.

The Edmonton charter included provisions for a small council; an explicit allocation of significant powers to an appointed board of commissioners; a distinct separation of legislative and administrative functions; virtually complete municipal ownership of utilities; a cumulative voting clause that allowed holders of property to cast up to four votes on referred money by-laws; and a high property qualification for municipal voters.[59]

Both the pre-reform and reform models of local government in the West were based on Ontario precedents. The Ontario reform schemes themselves, however, had been influenced by American models. Ontario cities during the reform era often modified their traditional form of government, characterized by political decentralization and legislative dominance, by grafting on to the civic body politic the latest American reform structures. American 'good government' influence also penetrated the West through the media of periodicals, newspaper reports, and books as well as more directly through attendance by leading western reformers at American municipal conventions. Some civic leaders in the West had even spent some part of their lives in the United States and were very likely influenced by American ideas concerning local government. Mayor W.D.L. Hardie of Lethbridge, for example, had emigrated to the United States when he was 20 years of age and later returned to Canada and became the 'mayor' of the American-style commission government instituted in that city in 1914.[60]

Municipal government reform in Alberta was also influenced by social and economic forces that differed from central Canadian patterns in crucial respects. A massive influx of "unassimilable" non-English-speaking immigrants was a particular western Canadian phenomenon during the reform era, and the fear of immigrant voting strength was a factor in the development of western municipal reform. Labour militancy, based on the industrial union tradition of working class British immigrants, was greater in the West than in central Canada before 1919. The desire to harness the instrument of the local unit of the state to attract railways became a virtual obsession with western business leaders who, unlike their central Canadian counterparts, could not rely on water transportation and nearby markets. The municipal borrowing power was also particularly important to business in the West where capital was scarce and the need for economic infrastructure (roads, bridges, utilities) was pronounced. As well, municipal non-partisanship was reinforced by the strong antipathy of westerners to the established parties controlled in central Canada, and in Alberta the non-partisan tradition was most firmly rooted, as C.B. Macpherson documents in his classic, *Democracy in Alberta*.[61]

5. The Class Character of Municipal Government Reform in Alberta

The most direct way to discover which groups benefitted or suffered from reform measures adopted in urban centres in Alberta and the prairie west generally is to examine the circumstances surrounding the introduction of key features of reform in specific cities and the changes these reforms brought about. Because existing research on individual prairie cities is not very extensive, conclusions about the manner in which core features of civic reform affected different economic groups in these jurisdictions must be based on incomplete evidence. Enough is known, though, to provide considerable support to the contention that the thrust of the dominant local government reform model tended to reduce or make more difficult the *representation* of the working class, lower status ethnic groups, and the electoral organizations they supported in the civic political arena. A related bias apparently introduced by 'reform' structures and ideas was a reduction in the degree of *responsiveness* of local government to the needs and demands of workers and non-English speaking immigrants, particularly Slavs and Jews. These immigrant groups, however, were almost entirely working class during the reform period, and the electoral organizations attempting to represent labour drew their support from working class and immigrant districts. Local government reform had the effect of reducing the power of immigrant groups and labour based slates in civic politics. Thus, it is possible to treat such ethnic and partisan bias as another form of class bias.

The central contention of this study is that civic government 'reform' in western centres was detrimental to working class interests. This does not imply that reform was in all respects or in every instance disadvantageous to the interests of lower class or lower status ethnic groups.[62] It can be argued, for example, that civic non-partisanship (supported by labour as a rule) was a device that served to lure workers away from the bosoms of traditional parties and to enlist them in the ranks of the "independent" parties of labour. However, the cry of non-partisanship was (and continues to be) also a signal for the coalition of anti-labour and anti-socialist Liberals and Conservatives in the local political arena.[63] The political affiliations of local councillors during the reform period suggest that the 'non-partisan' features of reform were, on balance, not in the interest of labour.[64]

I shall now employ the analytical distinctions set out earlier in this study to determine, in a tentative way at least, the class interests reform measures appear to have served.

(a) *The Attack on the Ward System.* A major feature of the municipal government reform movement in Alberta cities was the campaign to abolish wards. For example, Edmonton's at-large system dates back to its origin as a city in 1904. Calgary changed to an at-large electoral system in 1913 as a result of a narrow victory by an anti-ward lobby in a plebiscite in that city.[65] Wards were abolished in Victoria in 1912 and eight years later the number of wards in Winnipeg was reduced from seven to three.

In addition to the strong attack on the ward system under the influence of central Canada and the United States,[66] the system of apportionment of municipal expenditures by wards and the control of expenditures by individual councillors were widely criticized by civic leaders as being parochial, corrupt, and inefficient. The alleged extravagance and favoritism practised by the city councillors of Winnipeg was one of the key factors that prompted the Board of Trade to mount a reform campaign in that city in 1885. With the victory of the reform group, power over divisional expenditures was withdrawn from individual aldermen and vested in council.[67] With respect to the prairie region in general, the official journal of most municipal associations in the prairie provinces, *The Western Municipal News*, campaigned ceaselessly against the ward apportionment tradition during the reform period, in part because under such decentralized administration, "…work is very often placed with the friends of the councillor of the division."[68]

The main motivation behind the campaign to abolish the ward system, however, was the desire to change the basis of representation. J.M.S. Careless has pointed out that, at a very early stage in their growth, urban centres on the prairies developed segregated districts based on sharp differences in income levels, quality of housing, and ethnic make-up.[69] Working class and eastern European groups, concentrated in particular wards, were occasionally able to elect 'one of their own' to urban councils.[70]

Organized labour also was able to mount a challenge of sorts to the dominance of business interests on civic councils with the aid of ward elections. Of the 515 councillors elected in Winnipeg between 1874 and 1914, a total of 21 have been identified as "artisans and workingmen." At least several of these had strong links with organized labour, who actively supported their election.[71] Winnipeg's ward system was evidently still an important factor later in the reform period when economic conditions associated with World War I and its aftermath increased both union strength and militancy. By the end of the second decade of the twentieth century, labour had almost gained control of Winnipeg city council, but then lost ground rapidly when the basis of representation was changed through the reduction in the number of wards.

The abolition or enlargement of wards was perceived by reformers as a way to prevent the election of representatives of non-elite groups to city councils. At-large or large-ward elections would have the added effect of inducing prominent businessmen to run for office by reducing the necessity for candidates to engage in personal canvassing and otherwise mending political fences.[72]

Urban electoral reforms also greatly increased the costs of campaigning. Very little has been discovered to date on financing of early municipal elections in the West but it is possible to get an indication of the effect of the at-large system on election expenses by examining evidence from eastern cities with populations similar to that of growing western centres. In 1913, for example, the mayor of Halifax noted that it cost candidates for the Board of Control from $5,000 to $10,000 to run in a city-wide contest. Therefore, he declared, "if you abolished the ward system they [the incumbent ward representatives] would not be liable to run."[73]

In the West, at-large contests for civic office also increased the power of those groups able to finance a city-wide campaign, as Edmonton's labour groups repeatedly pointed out.[74] Consequently it was more difficult for low income segments of the community to win local office. As a noted authority on Canadian local politics observed, "experience shows that many of those who retain office under the ward system fail to return to council when a change is made to the general vote basis."[75] A comparison of cities with ward and at-large elections respectively seems to support this view. For example, in the absence of a ward system in Edmonton, labour and immigrant groups concentrated in the eastern section of the city were largely unsuccessful in obtaining representation on city council despite organized attempts to do so.[76] In Winnipeg, however, labour groups and Jewish and Slavic immigrant communities elected several spokesmen to council early in the century.[77]

In the twin cities of Port Arthur and Fort William (now Thunder Bay), a similar effect of the two different forms of local electoral system is suggested, although other factors cannot be discounted. During the reform period, labour-affiliated local candidates often won election in Ward I in Port Arthur but suffered defeat in Fort William which had city-wide elections.[78] The ward system of the latter city was seen as a threat by the civic establishment, as the remarks of Port Arthur's Mayor Oliver at a municipal convention suggest:

In Port Arthur, we have one ward in which there are about 7,000 people of whom about 5,500 are foreigners,who have not been long enough in Canada to any more than know how they are to vote. They do not know anything about government, nor do they try to study it, and by voting at-large we try to get the aldermen elected who have the best interests at heart.[79]

Since an at-large system was part of the reform-inspired "business government," it was more credible to businessmen. The mayor of Red Deer, for example, quoted the words of President Elliot of Harvard University: "to the performance of business functions in an honest and intelligent manner, the notion of representation by districts of population has no sensible applications."[80] When wards were abolished, businessmen could, however, run for office with reasonable confidence that they would be insulated from popular pressures.[81] "The would-be Cincinnatus in the business community would only put down his tools to govern, not to engage in politics."[82]

Electoral reform in Calgary is a case in point. When an at-large system was adopted there in 1913, it appears to have affected the recruitment of candidates for local office as well as the results of the election itself. The Conservative *Calgary Herald*, pleased with the first election campaign under the at-large system, commented in an editorial on 2 December 1913: "we cannot say that the abolition of the ward system is responsible but it is a fact that some first class businessmen have permitted their names to go before the people." The *Herald* was equally pleased with the results of the election, expressing mock surprise that no labour-supported candidates had won. It suggested that labour's fate may have been due to the candidacy of the unusually prestigious candidates that had run for the business faction.[83]

(b) *Civic Executive and Bureaucratic reform.* The US-style commission form, the board of commissioners, the city manager forms, and a variation of the board of control were all adopted in Alberta cities. As with local electoral reform, revamping the civic executive and bureaucracy was designed to reduce the representation of "lesser men" and to enshrine the principles of business efficiency in the municipal corporation. Four schemes were adopted, with some variations, in prairie cities. The board of control scheme, first adopted in Toronto, spread to Winnipeg, Montreal, Hamilton, Ottawa, and, by another name, to Calgary. In its typical form, it removed considerable power from the common council and transferred it to a group of approximately five controllers elected at-large who formed an executive body superior to the council. The board of control itself usually assumed particular responsibility for finance and the awarding of civic contracts.[84]

A similar centralization of power in fewer and more expert hands was accomplished by the elected commission form of local government, adopted in Lethbridge in 1913. Three to five commissioners were to be elected at-large, each of whom would have responsibility for a particular department of civic administration.[85]

The elected commission form, an American scheme, is not to be confused with the appointive board of commissioners form that flourished in prairie cities in Canada. The board of commissioners plan implied not only the concentration of authority but an explicit removal of administration from the inexpert hands of elected councillors. Edmonton's council-board of commissioners charter, adopted in 1904, expressly placed administration in the domain of several chief appointed civic officials. While the mayor was an *ex-officio* member of the board, his role was largely that of liaison between council and the board. The scheme soon spread to Regina, Saskatoon, Red Deer, and other cities. In Saskatoon, there was for some time a single commissioner—in effect, a city manager.

Finally, the well known city-manager plan, first adopted by Westmount in 1913, placed much of the power of policy initiation and implementation in the hands of a single appointed official.

While it has been pointed out that Canadian civic executive/bureaucratic reform schemes often retained the council committee system and ward elections, it is nevertheless the case that these structural changes weakened the elective component of city government. In Red Deer the board of commissioners replaced council committees, which formerly functioned as quasi-administrative units of city hall.[86] Commissioners in Edmonton and other cities could be fired only by a vote of two-thirds of council. Hence, the public power in Alberta cities shifted either towards the appointed arm of government or towards an elite executive body elected from the city at-large. As John Weaver points out:

Reformers often blurred the distinction between an executive and a civil service; in simple terms they wanted strong men on top. The blinking owls and vultures on Council (a reform analogy too often close to the mark) were to be cut down to size by "big men."[87]

Not only were reformed civic structures generally adopted as the result of campaigns by local boards of trade and the press, but the recruitment of candidates and campaigning for the newly restructured government was often more assiduously pursued by elites. Lethbridge provides a striking example. When the first election for the three-member Commission took place in 1913, "the citizens' slate, composed of three candidates selected by a body of seventeen prominent businessmen and representatives of the two political parties triumphed."[88]

Again, Alberta cities were in the vanguard in revamping the structure of local administration. The commission board form was pioneered in Edmonton and set the pattern for the most common bureaucratic structure in prairie cities. Calgary initiated a system of elected commissioners along with mayor and council that was very similar to the board of control form. Red Deer followed Edmonton's lead in erecting a powerful commission board during the reform period and Lethbridge abolished city council entirely in 1913 in favour of a three member elected commission closely modelled after the American city commission plan.

(c) *Non-partisanship.* The proposition that there has been an inherent class bias to local non-partisanship has been given very little attention by Canadian scholars.[89] One of the untested assumptions of Canadian social science research on municipal non-partisanship is that the anti-party sentiment in Canadian local politics was largely imported from the United States. According to the conventional academic view, the importation by Canadian reformers of the American municipal non-partisan sentiment and institutional devices designed to eliminate local party politics was both inappropriate and ironic—after all, Canadian cities at the turn of the century were not bastions of machine politics and urban party bosses.[90] This argument is wrong on two counts. First, the impetus for the movement for non-partisanship in municipal politics was often a product of indigenous conditions; second, there was a distinct partisan dimension to Canadian municipal politics of the reform era.

Party politics have long been present in local elections and council deliberations in Canadian cities, and though partisan groupings have not been as organized and powerful as American civic machines led by the local party boss, in at least one of the senses in which "machine politics" is used[91]—that is, corrupt politics—Canadian cities during (and since) the reform era have had spectacular cases of local graft and patronage. The Cannon Commission established by the province of Quebec reported in 1909 that Montreal politics had been "saturated with corruption" since 1892. Eight aldermen were found guilty by the inquiry.[92] In Toronto and Winnipeg, provincial inquiries discovered similar, if less sensational, examples of local corruption.[93] In all three cases these revelations were used by 'non-partisan' reformers as a springboard to power at city hall. Calgary, too, was the scene of civic scandals involving land deals by aldermen in 1904. Two aldermen were thrown out of office by the Chief Justice and three city officials resigned in disgrace.[94] Frequent scandals such as these led J.S. Woods-worth to declare in 1909, "already we have had revelations of municipal corruption, of the party machine in our civic elections and the 'handling' of the foreign vote."[95]

Another indigenous factor in the development of local non-partisan sentiment in Canada was the widespread practice of political party competition for local office. Rival political party activists in municipal contests often denounced their opponents for bringing "irrelevant" party considerations into the local political arena.[96] In the West in particular local coalitions of Conservatives and Liberals cooperated on civic councils to 'save the City from socialism.' Organized labour also formed parties such as the Independent Labour Party and the Dominion Labour Party, both of which were active in Alberta, to challenge Liberal-Conservative hegemony in city councils.

The strong non-partisan tradition of western Canada was related to the domination of political parties based in central Canada and was apparently a reinforcing factor in local non-partisanship. While this anti-party feeling was strongest among rural groups, it easily penetrated the cities in the West. One linkage was apparently through rural migration to the urban centres; a second was through farmer-labour political exchange within organizations like the Alberta Non-Partisan League in which William Irvine played a leading role.

A brief examination of the activities of the Alberta Non-Partisan League is instructive in terms of the interaction of farmer and labour elements in the West in a common crusade against the established party system. The Non-Partisan League, born of agrarian discontent in North Dakota, penetrated Saskatchewan and Alberta where it made some impact during the period between 1916 and 1922. The Alberta Non-Partisan League, of which Irvine was secretary, originated in Calgary in 1916 and adopted a platform attacking the established party system and calling for extensive public ownership. The first objective of the League was "to overcome partisanship by the election of a truly people's government and the establishment of a business administration instead of a party administration."[97] By "business administration" Irvine and his associates clearly meant honest and efficient administration in the interest of the masses, rather than government by and in the interests of business. In fact, the League's activities were directed at reducing, not increasing, the degree to which business interests dominated all levels of government.

In addition to the League's strong ties to the United Farmers of Alberta, Irvine and other League members were involved in setting up the Labour Representation League in Calgary in 1917 in cooperation with the Calgary Trades and Labour Council. By 1919 the Labour Representation League had evolved into the Independent Labour Party and later in the same year it became the Calgary branch of the Dominion Labour Party. These parties of labour succeeded in electing a few candidates to municipal, provincial, and, finally, federal legislatures with the victory of William Irvine in East Calgary in 1921.[98]

The philosophical and electoral challenge to established traditions at the local level was not confined to Calgary. At the urging of the Labour Representation League of Calgary,[99] an organization with the same name was set up in Edmonton by leading members of the Trades and Labour Council of Alberta's capital city. It, too, was transformed into the Independent Labour Party and then the Dominion Labour Party by 1919 and achieved a measure of success in Edmonton civic elections in the post-war years. In the 1919 Edmonton local election, for example, three aldermanic candidates nominated by the Dominion Labour Party were successful. In addition, the winning mayoralty candidate, Joe Clarke, had the endorsement of the DLP.[100]

It is important to note that urban labour groups, influenced by the persuasive anti-party tradition of prairie farmers as well as by the experiences of workers themselves with the established parties, evolved from a position outside the party system to active participation in third parties. This process was particularly noticeable at the municipal level towards the end of the reform era when almost every western city developed a local organization centred on organized labour which supported candidates for civic office. Because local government was generally perceived as a matter of administration, local labour groups could contest municipal elections and still claim to be unsullied by party politics. The edict of Samuel Gompers forbidding union involvement in party politics which was enshrined in some union constitutions was not interpreted as applying to municipal elections. And since the urban trades and labour councils were set up explicitly to deal with the common concerns of various unions within the city, it was natural that such organizations would attempt to secure workers' representation on urban councils.[101]

If non-partisanship served as a rationale for labour and socialist forces to act as a party in civic affairs without suffering the full force of hostility to the established party system, it also served as a convenient cover for local wings of established parties to coalesce in civic politics disguised as citizens' committees or good government groups of various designations. Covert partisan coalitions of Liberals and Conservatives in such organizations as the Winnipeg Citizens' League could generally be counted on to prevent 'socialists' and labour representatives from capturing city hall.[102] The anti-party rhetoric of such local party coalitions was a highly effective if dishonest way of discrediting electoral organizations of labour which were often accused of representing narrow class interests rather than the general good of the city population. Mayor William Short of Edmonton, for example, warned delegates to a 1907 municipal convention in Alberta that "the trade union's political party may place a man in the council irrespective of his fitness."[103]

Local coalitions of Liberals and Conservatives were motivated by more than the threat of political activity by labour, however. The need for leading business figures to cooperate politically at the local level was usually stronger than the partisan differences that might exist among them. This was so particularly in the precarious economic climate of the prairies where such cooperation was obviously in their joint pecuniary interest. As long as their "economic tutelage"[104] existed, open competition between Liberals and Conservatives in Alberta civic politics was a luxury neither group could afford.

On balance, the non-partisan camouflage appeared to have benefitted Liberal and Conservative business-oriented interests in Alberta cities during the reform era. Labour was apparently disadvantaged in several related ways by non-partisanship. First, pervasive anti-party sentiments of the voters in general evidently prejudiced them against any civic group that made a point of calling itself a party—as did the Independent Labour Party and the Dominion Labour Party. Second, to counter the charges of radicalism and narrow class motivations in civic contests, labour usually nominated the most 'respectable,' hence most moderate, members of its leadership.[105] For example, J.A. Kinney, a labour alderman in Edmonton during the period of the First World War, drew the fire of some of his labour colleagues for his moderate position on civic issues.[106]

Third, because party lines in civic elections were not as clearly drawn as in senior-level contests, voters were forced to cast about for other ways of choosing candidates. Likely, they were influenced to some degree by the partisan biases of influential community institutions. Chief among these agencies offering political advice was undoubtedly the local newspaper. The success rate of newspaper-endorsed candidates has not been systematically studied in western cities, but fragmentary evidence suggests that it was significant. For example, in the Calgary civic election of 1913, seven of the eight candidates endorsed by the *Calgary Herald* were successful.[107]

The examples listed above are some of the more obvious ways the non-partisan ideology operating in local politics manifested a class bias. On balance, it was apparently easier for labour to elect representatives to the provincial level than to civic office.[108] The effect of the franchise provisions, which were more liberal in provincial elections than in local contests, must also be considered a contributing factor. There is little doubt, however, that by openly engaging in party-like activity rather than making a vague claim to represent all interests in the city, labour suffered a backlash from many voters who believed that such obvious partisanship was inappropriate for the management of the civic business.

(d) *The Ideology of the Local Government Reform Movement.* It is important to bear in mind the close relationship between structure and ideology, for the legacy of reform is as much an attitude as it is a particular set of institutional arrangements. It is possible to expand upon two general themes in reform thought, both of which were decidedly anti-democratic in their implications. First, advocates of the dominant reform package had a very restrictive notion of what municipal matters were political in nature and therefore subject to a

measure of popular participation if not control. Second, their views were dominated by a profound sense of *noblesse oblige*—a belief that those who were best
suited to the task of governing the city had a civic duty to accept local office
and, because of their superior virtue, would rule in the best interests of all urban
residents.

Reformers sought to expand the domain of administration in local politics
and narrow the realm of legislation of 'politics.' For example, reformers persistently argued that,

City government is mostly, almost entirely administrative. What laws are enacted in the
city hall have mostly the nature of by-laws which any board of directors of a large
company would pass for the expedition of ordinary business.[109]

Since municipal matters were held to be essentially administrative, almost any
challenge to the status quo could be dismissed as political meddling. Thus, at a
1917 convention of the Union of Alberta Municipalities, "a resolution asking
for conscription of wealth was ruled out as politics."[110] Yet, there was nothing
political about the invitation by the Calgary City Commissioners to a committee
of the Board of Trade to sit in and offer advice when the 1915 civic estimates
were being considered. The *Calgary Herald* editors described the commissioners'
invitation as "an exhibition of good sense" since the Board of Trade was made
up of a "body of recognized representative citizens."[111] Less than two weeks
later, however, the *Herald* editors described the board of trade as a body whose
"membership includes most of the wealthy and well-to-do people of the city"
and whose principal objective was "furthering the interests of merchants and
manufacturers."[112]

Second, structural reformers consistently claimed that municipal government was primarily a technical task, to be operated to the maximum feasible
extent by experts on the basis of 'scientific' principles.[113] By their invocation of a
civic science and by raising the expert to the pinnacle of the municipal corporation, reformers forged a weapon with which they could effectively beat down
competing claims regarding structural reform based on value premises they did
not share.

The fact that the reform model of local government was anti-democratic in
the extreme was rarely mentioned by leading reform spokesmen. Even the well
known view of municipal government as the school of democracy was not held
to be inconsistent with municipal reform philosophy. Democratic traditions and
practices (for example, parliamentary procedure) could be *learned* in local
councils, to be applied when councillors graduated to senior levels of government. To a leading thinker in the municipal reform movement, municipal councils were "schools of democracy" because "they train the crowd for public life in
wider fields."[114] The anti-democratic strain in reform did not go completely
unnoticed. The director of the Toronto Bureau of Municipal Research, H.L.

Brittain, warned in 1917 that because local government was perceived as a technical matter, "impatient people have been able to accept frankly some form of benevolent despotism."[115]

6. The Policy Impact of Municipal Government Reform

The self-proclaimed 'benevolence' of reformers must be qualified in light of the policies they pursued or chose to ignore in practical situations. If they were able to admit on occasion that the schemes they proposed involved government by an elite, they were nevertheless adamant in their view that reform regimes would govern only in the interests of all the people of the city. Some modern writers on municipal history have kept alive this rosy interpretation of reform, claiming that while the movement was elitist and anti-democratic in that it reduced the power of lower status groups to influence urban public decision-making, it nonetheless contributed to rationalizing and modernizing urban life. It was, in this view, an exercise in "saving the Canadian city." Significantly, the chief proponents of this interpretation of reform examine almost exclusively the ideas, not the actions, of municipal reformers and focus heavily on central Canada.[116]

The class character of reform can be seen clearly in the responsiveness of reform councils to various groups in the community. In Edmonton, the city council eagerly financed the expansion of street railway lines and other municipal services to land situated far beyond the populated area of the city, thereby increasing the value of the property held by real estate interests. When the economic boom collapsed after 1913, the council tried to solve the problem of a heavy debt and a dwindling tax base by dismissing some civic employees and reducing the salaries of others.[117] In Alberta, as in the United States, the reduction of civic expenditures by reform councils "was often made at labor's expense."[118]

Copp's study of the conditions of the working class in Montreal is another case in point. In a wave of protest over the 1909 revelations of civic corruption, a Board of Control was adopted in Montreal and a reform regime was swept into office. Yet, "throughout the four years of the 'regime of honest men' nothing significant was accomplished. The Committee of Citizens and its candidates were fascinated with new boulevards and city beautification."[119]

Similarly, the first reform regime elected in Winnipeg in 1884 with solid backing of the Board of Trade quickly ended the extravagance and graft of the previous council by instituting tighter accounting procedures. But it also reduced substantially the wages of civic employees and cut relief expenditures by 58 percent over the preceding year, despite the fact that unemployment was high and the need for relief was great.[120]

Reform regimes were also less responsive to the needs of the districts of the city inhabited by working class families and lower status ethnic groups. It was clearly this type of inequity that the Edmonton Trades and Labour Council sought to correct when, in 1907, it decided to endorse those candidates who would fight for "the equal expenditures of the city in its different sections."[121] The policy bias of reform councils with respect to the poorer segments of the urban population took yet another form. The hiring practices of "honest" reform regimes were evidently decidedly discriminatory. For example, in 1921, when Winnipeg's population was 33 percent non-Anglo-Saxon (comprised largely of Jewish and Slavic residents of the North End), only 6 percent of civic employees were drawn from this minority group.[121]

Civic reformers did little to stop another practice that involved the expenditure of municipal funds for private gain. During the reform era, western cities followed the example of their eastern counterparts in offering manufacturing firms, agri-business, railways, and other industries bonuses in the form of cash grants, free land, tax exemptions, bond guarantees, and low utility rates. In this way, revenue raised from the less well off urban residents by means of the regressive municipal tax system was spent in an attempt to attract and retain industries or railways. Despite the official rhetoric of reform spokemen, which was strongly against bonusing, Alberta civic elites were driven by their booster ambitions to continue to compete with rival centres by offering bonuses.

In the early phase of the reform era, spectacular concessions offered in industry and railways encountered little opposition from reform leaders.[123] In 1906, Edmonton granted the Grand Trunk Pacific Railway a cash bonus of $100,000 and free land estimated at $60,000 to encourage the company to locate its line in the city.[124] In addition, Edmonton followed a policy of granting free light and water to firms for a period of five years after their establishment in the city.[125] In 1905, Calgary exempted the Alberta Portland Cement Company from payment of property taxes for a period of 20 years.[126] By 1911, Calgary was offering entrepreneurs industrial sites at cost, a low assessment rate, and a seven-year tax holiday on buildings and stock.[127] In 1905, a by-law was passed by the Lethbridge council granting tax exemptions and rebates on water rates to the CPR.[128] A year later the Lethbridge city fathers guaranteed $40,000 in debenture bonds of the Medicine Hat Woolen Mills Company.[129]

The reform elements themselves recognized some of the harmful effects of the system of competitive bonusing and a great outcry began against the practice, led by boards of trade and civic officials. Yet, their opposition was usually based on the unfair advantage bonusing provided to competing firms not already established in the community.[130]

If the bonusing craze did not slacken during the latter period of the reform era, it became more subtle and refined in form. A great deal was spent on promotion schemes, including advertising, the employment of professional civic boosters, and sending civic representatives on missions to other cities to attract industries. For example, in 1905, the Edmonton City Council granted the Board of Trade $3,500 for publicity purposes; in 1911, it gave the Board $15,000 to promote the city as a haven for private investment. In 1910, Edmonton's industrial committee sent a former member of the Board of Trade to central Canadian and American cities to lure manufacturing firms to the Alberta capital. Upon his return, he recommended that rather than bonusing specific industries, the city should provide "at minimum cost suitable sites and adequate power, light and water at low rates."[131]

Restrictions on bonusing placed in city charters did not stop the practice. Despite these limitations, Alberta cities, for example, regularly sought and obtained amendments that permitted them to offer substantial concessions to individual firms. Significantly, it was the rural-dominated Alberta legislature that legislated against municipal bonusing in 1913. Even this stipulation, however, did not put an end to municipal concessions to private industry. Calgary obtained an amendment to the legislation in 1914 which permitted the expenditure of up to $15,000 on civic promotion and incentives to enterprises to establish in the city.[132] For a number of years after the provincial anti-bonusing legislation was passed, Edmonton continued to tax land only, thereby exempting industrial or other establishments from rates on improvements.

There was a close relationship between the policy of municipal ownership and the practice of bonusing industries. In fact, the former was often perceived by reformers simply as a more sophisticated form of the latter. The mayor of Medicine Hat explained the connection lucidly: "the town with something to offer which is equivalent to a bonus, frequently escapes being required to put up a cash bonus. Municipal ownership and industrial progress go hand in hand."[133] Time and again, members of reform councils stressed the point that municipally-owned utilities would serve to entice industry. In 1910, it was argued in the Edmonton Council debates that "cheap power is essential in order to induce manufacturing establishments to locate in the City of Edmonton."[134]

Yet, municipal ownership was not an ideological matter among reformers. As John Weaver has pointed out, municipal ownership often came about by default, frequently after a private franchise had been granted to a firm that could not fulfil the terms of the agreement with the city, or when a private concern could not be found to provide the service. Public power came to Edmonton in 1902, for example, when a frustrated town council bought out the private power company because it refused to upgrade its plant.[135] Similarly, when Edmonton's growth created a need for an improved water system, city officials found they could not interest private capital in providing the service because "we were a mere village, with comparatively little but high expectations to justify our ambitions."[136]

Municipal ownership or, as it was sometimes called, 'municipal socialism,' was not justified by reformers in terms of the benefits it would bring to the urban residents as such. Alan Artibise demonstrates that in the campaign for a municipally-owned power system in Winnipeg, "public good was simply a dividend; it was not the operating principle."[137] The gas and water socialists were not opposed to a society dominated by private ownership; rather, they sought to make it more viable. One of the founders of the Union of Canadian Municipalities and a leading reform spokesman made this point well in 1909:

It seems to be necessary to constantly rebut a notion...that we are the enemies of private enterprise, of lighting and power companies and street railway companies and of all capital. On the contrary, we are the true friends of capital and all private enterprises.[138]

The above discussion indicates that reformers sought to ensure that civic policy-making favoured their class interests. In the current writing on municipal reform in Canada, this point is usually conceded. However, two historians have recently made the very valid point that the reformers' victories were seldom complete. They point out that other forces in the community were able to assert themselves either through modifying the reform structures to make them more democratic or by electing representatives to council.[139] It is true that men of modest means, including workers, did get elected to city council during the reform era, despite the reformers' preference for leading businessmen. At best, however, this argument provides a useful qualification to the interpretation of the reform movement as a victory of an entrenched urban elite. Even though structural reforms were not always implemented in the 'pure' form (for example, the ward system was never abolished in Winnipeg), the ideological crusade that invariably accompanied institutional reform was itself a potent factor in directing policy-making along certain lines. In Alberta, for example, reformers were able to exercise a virtual ideological hegemony with respect to the ends local government should serve.

Moreover, many leading businessmen, especially in western cities, did accept elective civic office.[140] Equally important, in many cases where business leaders themselves did not run for office, they often were instrumental in recruiting and supporting lesser business figures in local elections. A striking example of this phenomenon was the 1884 civic election in Winnipeg, in which leaders of the Board of Trade were accused by a Winnipeg newspaper of nominating their 'clerks' for local office. This criticism was something of an overstatement (the Board's mayoralty nominee was a law partner of the CRP's legal counsel in the West); yet it was also appropriate since the council of 'clerks' proceeded to implement to the letter the anti-labour policy of economic retrenchment that their more prestigious backers had advocated.[141] A study of the Winnipeg elections at the end of the reform period revealed a similar pattern. The fifty-six-member executive of the Citizens' League which sponsored a majority of successful candidates in the 1919 election was made up almost entirely of leading business and professional men who resided in the more exclusive sections of the city.[142] As Ralph Miliband puts it in *The State in Capitalist Society*,

...members of the upper classes do not necessarily or even very often take a direct part in local and state government. But this does not mean that they do not run these units of government. In the light of the real economic power which business enjoys, and of the prevailing culture which legitimizes this power, the question whether top executives or middle ones actually run for election and serve in state and local government appears grotesquely irrelevant.[142]

The impact of reform on the lives of urban residents cannot, however, be assessed adequately unless the role of non-elites in the movement is examined. Current research concentrates almost exclusively on the prominent business elements that led campaigns for local government reform in the west. Yet workers and the non-English-speaking immigrants were lukewarm or actively opposed to reform. Future research might well focus on the role of organized labour and immigrants in reform campaigns. Particularly in the West, labour was more militant than in central Canada, at least until 1920, and local trades councils were active participants in civic politics. In the West, too, labour was led by British immigrants who brought with them a tradition of civic involvement associated with the British Labour Party and the Fabian socialists. Moreover, the reform movement coincided with the great influx of European immigrants. Since there is reason to believe that reform in the West was in part a response to the perceived threat posed by these newcomers, the role of immigrants in reform should be of more than passing interest.

7. Conclusion

The movement for municipal government reform between 1880 and 1920 coincided with the rise of important urban centres on the prairies. Western cities eagerly adopted the most up-to-date reform structures. The ideology of municipal reform was readily accepted by the disciples of the philosophy of rapid urban growth who formed the business and governmental elite of these centres. The central question for students of the reform movement—the class character of reform—is, therefore, most fruitfully examined in the context of urban development in the prairie region. The research that has been published to date on municipal reform in the West has tended to confirm the view that the core features of reform had the effect of making it much more difficult for working class elements of the population to elect representatives to civic government. It also indicates that reform measures made city government less responsive to the needs of the lower status urban groups who were segregated into distinct areas of prairie cities.

Like other social movements, the crusade for municipal government reform was directed *against* something. The petty politician, the saloon-keeper, the self-conscious representative of an ethnic block, or the nominee of organized labour was seen by the urban elite that spearheaded the drive for structural reform as the chief obstacle to civic progress. Progress, in turn, was defined by reformers almost exclusively in terms of the role of municipal corporation in supporting the aims of business. This class bias is most clearly evident in the campaign for local governmental or structural reform. Too often, researchers have confused the goals of the structural reformer with those of reformers like J.S. Woodsworth whose primary goals were the social and humanitarian reform of the city. Local *government* reform is perhaps of greater significance since it structured the role of the municipal corporation in the local political economy.

Finally, the reform legacy is still clearly evident in Alberta today. The recent history of Alberta cities, for example, proves that both the structures and the ideology of the movement for municipal government reform have had an important influence on civic decision-making ever since. The reform structures have persisted with little or no alternation. Both Calgary and Edmonton, for instance, retain the council-board of commissioner system that was pioneered in Edmonton in 1904. In Edmonton, in 1982, the four members of the appointed commission board are full-time employees, earning approximately $76,000 per year while the 12 members of council spend only part of their time on civic matters and earn about $24,000 each. The relative power of the elected and appointed arm of this 'reform' administration can be inferred from this comparison. Similarly, the ward systems, which were abolished in Calgary and Edmonton in the early years of the century, were not reinstated until the 1960s, and even then the large wards that were adopted did little to improve representation of lower income groups. For example, in the 1971 Edmonton election based on four large strip wards, two-thirds of the aldermen who were elected came from the higher income areas of the south side of the city while the south side as a whole contained only one-third of the city's population.[144]

The ideology of reform is still a potent force in present day civic politics. A recent sample of Edmonton voters revealed, for example, that only 13 percent favored party politics in civic elections. A province-wide opinion survey in 1971 also indicated that only 25 percent favored the involvement of "party type organizations" in local elections.[145] The class character of the reform ideology can also be clearly detected in recent municipal election campaigns. An observer of a recent Edmonton election, for example, noted that business experience was the most advertised virtue of successful candidates.[146] The reform belief that a "local government is business" was more provocatively stated by a recent mayor of Edmonton who denounced his potential rival for the chief magistrate's position in these words:

But he has had no business experience. He's been a school teacher. I've worked in business all my life, and we're running a business.[147]

Jim Anderson: The Municipal Government Reform Movement and the Prairie West

Notes

[1] Ralph Miliband, *The State in Capitalist Society* (London, 1973), 3.

2 S. Morley Wickett, "City Government by Commission," address delivered to the Canadian Club of Hamilton, November 1912 (n.p., n.d.), 3.

3 J.M.S. Careless, "Somewhat Narrow Horizons," *Historical Papers*, Canadian Historical Association (1968), 4.

4 J.M.S. Careless, "Aspects of Urban Life in the West, 1870-1914," in A.W. Rasporich and H.C.Klassen, eds., *Prairie Perspectives 2* (Toronto, 1973), 25.

5 Ibid., 26.

6 S. Morley Wickett, "Present Conditions," in S. Morley Wickett, ed., *Municipal Government in Canada*, University of Toronto Studies in History and Economics, II (Toronto, 1907), 149.

7 Ibid., loc. cit.

8 J.H. Laughton, "Chambers of Commerce and City Government," *The Municipal World*, XXIX (December 1919), 176.

9 Lionel G. Orlikow, "A Survey of the Reform Movement in Manitoba, 1910-1920," MA thesis (University of Manitoba, 1955), 85-86. See also A. Ross McCormack, "The Origin and Extent of Western Labour Radicalism: 1896-1919," PhD thesis (University of Western Ontario, 1973), 256.

10 Paul Rutherford, ed., *Saving the Canadian City: The First Phase, 1880-1920* (Toronto, 1974), xiii.

11 Frank Underhill, *In Search of Canadian Liberalism* (Toronto, 1960), 197.

12 For example, troops were used against strikers in Winnipeg in 1906. The state was not prepared to tolerate militant action by unions. See W.L. Morton, *Manitoba: A History* (Toronto, 1955), 304-305.

13 A.H. Sinclair, "Municipal Monopolies and their Management," in Rutherford, ed., *Saving the Canadian City*, 35-36.

14 Ibid., 36.

15 "Municipal Ownership in Calgary, Alberta," *The Canadian Municipal Journal*, VII (March 1911), 95.

16 Quoted in Alan Artibise, *Winnipeg: A Social History of Urban Growth, 1874-1914* (Montreal and London, 1975), 99-100.

17 Alderman Wilfrid Gariepy, "A Daring Experiment in City Government," *The Municipal World*, XX (November 1910), 289. See also the article by William Short, "Municipal Government by Commission," *The Canadian Municipal Journal*, III (April 1907), 143-46.

18 "City Government in Canada," in Wickett, ed., *Municipal Government in Canada*, 10.

19 By 1889, manhood suffrage applied to all federal and provincial elections in the provinces and territories in the West and Ontario. W.L. Morton, "The Extension of the Franchise in Canada: A Study of Democratic Nationalism," *Report*, Canadian Historical Association (1943), 78.

20 These 'bread and butter' concerns are clearly highlighted in the references to municipal government in the Minutes of the Edmonton Trades and Labour Council between 1905 and 1920. Alberta Provincial Archives (Edmonton).

21 "Introduction," in Rutherford, ed., *Saving the Canadian City*, xiii. A number of

students of municipal reform distinguish governmental reform as a separate aspect of the movement. See, for example, John Weaver, "Elitism and the Corporate Ideal: Businessmen and Boosters in Canadian Civic Reform, 1880-1920," in A.R. McCormack and Ian MacPherson, eds., *Cities in the West*, Papers of the Western Canada Urban History Conference, University of Winnipeg, October 1974 (Ottawa, 1975), 48-73. Students of local politics have concentrated on structural reforms and the ethos that is alleged to accompany the 'package' of urban government reforms. See Edward C. Banfield and James Q. Wilson, *City Politics* (Cambridge, Mass., 1963), chapters 11-13.

[22] John Weaver, "Framing an Executive: The Western Cities, 1904-1912," unpublished paper, Institute of Local Government, Queen's University (Kingston, Ont., n.d.). Some prominent advocates of moral and humanitarian reform of the city were also involved in civic government reform, as in the case of businessman H.B. Ames of Montreal. His proposals with respect to local government reform, however, included a high property qualification for local office and a restricted franchise. See Michael Gauvin, "The Municipal Reform Movement in Montreal, 1886-1914," MA thesis (University of Ottawa, 1972).

[23] Each of these forms of civic administration can be described briefly as follows: (a) The board of control consisted of an executive body of several controllers, usually elected at-large, with executive and administrative powers superior to those of the council; (b) The commission plan implied the elimination of the city council, to be replaced by three to five commissioners elected at-large, each of whom would be responsible for a particular aspect of civic administration; (c) The board of commissioners scheme included a strengthened bureaucracy consisting of several appointed officials (with the mayor an *ex-officio* member) designed to take over all of the "administrative" duties, leaving council the power of legislation only; (d) The manager plan was very similar to the board of commissioners, except that all administrative matters were to be handled by a single appointed manager whose role was held to be analagous to that of a manager of a business corporation. The city council was to continue to perform the restricted legislative function.

[24] Even though Party labels were not printed on the local ballot in Canada, an exception to this general pattern was the charter setting up a US-style commission form of local government in Lethbridge in 1913, which contained a clause expressly forbidding the printing of a political party label on the local ballot. See *Statutes of Alberta*, 1913, chapter 22, section 24. The wording of this clause was identical to the ballot restrictions in the charters of Spokane, Washington, and Grand Junction, Colorado. See Carl D. Thompson, "The Vital Points in Charter Making from a Socialist Point of View," *National Municipal Review*, II, no. 3 (July 1913), 421.

[25] Thus the former mayor of Red Deer, Alberta, in a speech to the Alberta Union of Municipalities in 1909, quoted approvingly the words of President Elliot of Harvard University that "municipal government is pure business and nothing else—absolutely nothing else...." H.H. Gaetz, "Municipal Legislation," *Western Municipal News*, 4 (March 1909), 1078-81. Also, a leading municipal reformer, businessman, academic, and

Toronto Alderman, Samuel Morley Wickett, for example, stated in 1902 that "...municipal administration is, after all, mainly a technical task." In Wickett, ed., *Municipal Government in Canada*, 22.

[26] Businessman and civic reformer Herbert Ames of the Volunteer Electoral League of Montreal proudly announced the victory of one of the League's candidates over a corrupt ward politician in 1892. The reform candidate was chosen because he was "...a businessman of recognized ability and sterling integrity." Herbert B. Ames, "The 'Machine' in Honest Hands," in Rutherford, ed., *Saving the Canadian City*, 308.

[27] See, for example, remarks by the city commissioner of Saskatoon, C.J. Yorath, "Municipal Finance and Administration," *Report* of the Conference on Rural and Urban Development in Canada, Winnipeg, 1917, Commission of Conservation, 32.

[28] Gaetz, "Municipal Legislation;" Ontario Commission on Municipal Institutions, *First Report* (1888), 31; James Bryce, *The American Commonwealth*, vol. I (London, 1928), 651.

[29] The anti-party view of reformers in both Canada and the United States did not prevent them from advocating electoral involvement by "a committee of citizens...whose ability and selflessness are widely recognized." Richard S. Childs, cited in Eugene C. Lee, *The Politics of Non-Partisanship* (Berkeley, Calif., 1960), 3. In Canada many cities had such blue ribbon "citizens' committees" which functioned as quasi-parties in recruiting, endorsing, and financing civic candidates who were then expected to represent the "citizens'" class interests.

[30] S. Morley Wickett, "Municipal Government in Toronto," in Wickett, ed., *Municipal Government in Canada*, 38.

[31] In 1893 the Montreal Volunteer Electoral League of which reformer Herbert Ames was president submitted a proposed amendment to Montreal civic electoral law that "...provided for the disfranchisement of mere boarders and lodgers." Ames, "The 'Machine' in Honest Hands," 309. This provision was passed.

[32] Gariepy, "A Daring Experiment in City Government."

[33] City of Edmonton, *Voters' List*, 1914.

[34] Earl G. Drake, *Regina: The Queen City* (Toronto, 1955), 122.

[35] Wickett, "Present Conditions," 166-67.

[36] *Calgary Herald*, 5 August 1887. Cited in Max Foran, "The Calgary Town Council, 1884-1895: A Study of Local Government in a Frontier Environment," MA thesis (University of Calgary, 1970), 45.

[37] Henry Huber, "Winnipeg's Age of Plutocracy, 1901-1914," unpublished paper, Department of History, University of Manitoba (1971), 30.

[38] R. Stanley Weir, "Some Notes on the Charters of Montreal and Related Statutes," in Wickett, ed., *Municipal Government in Canada*, 295.

[39] Artibise, *Winnipeg*, 40.

[40] S.M. Wickett, "City Government in Canada," in Wickett, ed., *Municipal Government in Canada*, 22; see also Wickett, "Municipal Government in Toronto," 55; and his "Present Conditions," 166-67, 170.

41 Wickett, "Present Conditions." See also J.S. Woodsworth, *My Neighbor* (Toronto, 1972), 116.

42 Foran, "The Calgary Town Council," 44.

43 *Statutes of Alberta*, 1906, chapter 63.

44 Foran, "The Calgary Town Council," 46.

45 Huber, "Winnipeg's Age of Plutocracy," 32.

46 See *Statutes of Alberta*, 1913, chapter 22; and Mayor W.D.L. Hardie, "Straight Commission Government," *The Canadian Municipal Journal*, XII (October 1914), 475.

47 "Municipal Affairs in Alberta," *The Canadian Municipal Journal*, X (December 1914), 475.

48 *Statutes of Alberta*, 1916, chapter 33, sections 7, 13, 14.

49 *Statutes of Alberta*, 1913, chapter 22, title III, section 2.

50 *Minutes of the Edmonton Trades and Labour Council*, Public Archives of Alberta (Edmonton).

51 J.G.Joyce and H.A. Hosse, *Civic Parties in Canada* (Toronto, 1970), 15.

52 The class bias of municipal government reform in Canada and the US was similar, however. On this point, see Samuel P. Hayes, "The Politics of Reform in Municipal Government in the Progressive Era," *Pacific Northwest Quarterly*, LV (October 1964), 157-69.

53 C.W. Biggar, "Some Notes on the Growth of Municipal Institutions of Ontario," *Canadian Law Journal* (January 1897).

54 Kenneth Grant Crawford, *Canadian Municipal Government* (Toronto, 1954), 19-20.

55 Quoted in J.G. MacGregor, *Edmonton: A History* (Edmonton, 1967), 130. For an example of the pressure from prairie settlers for the Ontario Municipal form, see Jane McCracken, "Yorkton during the Territorial Period, 1882-1905," *Saskatchewan History*, XXVIII (Autumn 1975), 105-106. J.E. Rea has adapted a useful theoretical perspective to the early development of the West as a "fragment" of Ontario political culture. See his article, "The Roots of Prairie Society," in David P. Gagan, ed., *Prairie Perspectives* (Toronto, 1970), 46-55.

56 Wickett, "City Government in Canada," 7.

57 Huber, "Winnipeg's Age of Plutocracy," Table II, 39.

58 Artibise, *Winnipeg*.

59 The Edmonton Civic Charter was embodied in the ordinance of the North-West Territories, chapter 19, third session, fifth legislative assembly, 1904. The features of the Edmonton city charter outlined in this paragraph are enthusiastically explained by Alderman Wilfrid Gariepy in his article "A Daring Experiment in City Government." Edmonton continued to set the pace in urban reforms in such areas as the adoption of the single tax, that is, taxation based on land values with no tax on improvements (buildings). The fame of its charter extended far beyond Canada, as an article in an American journal attests. See Fred Bates Johnson, "A City that Taxes Things as They Are," *The World's Work* (August 1910), 13292-94. The editor of *The Canadian Municipal Journal*, Harry Bragg, noted in 1913 that Edmonton had for some time been well known for its "up to date" legislation because it had adopted at-large elections, the single tax,

and the (appointed) commission board form of administration (IX [1913], 443).

60 *The Canadian Municipal Journal*, XII (1916), 54. Sanford Evans, Mayor of Winnipeg, had also spent some time south of the border, obtaining his MA degree at Columbia University (*Western Municipal News*, IV [1909], 1105). For a more detailed account of the American influence on municipal reform in Canada, see my article "Nonpartisan Urban Politics in Canadian Cities," in Jack K. Masson and James D. Anderson, eds., *Emerging Party Politics in Urban Canada* (Toronto, 1972), 5-21.

61 C.B. Macpherson, *Democracy in Alberta: Social Credit and the Party System* (Toronto, 1962; 1st ed., 1953).

62 See Gregory S. Kealey and Peter Warrian, "Introduction," in Gregory S. Kealey and Peter Warrian, eds., *Essays in Working Class History* (Toronto, 1976), 9-10.

63 For example, the Citizens' League of Winnipeg and the Non-Partisan Association of Vancouver are local coalitions of political party activists. The former originated at the end of the reform era.

64 Non-partisanship is treated more fully further on in this essay.

65 See, for example, Gaetz, "Municipal Legislation."

66 Also, wards were abolished in Victoria in 1912 and eight years later the number of wards in Winnipeg were reduced from seven to three.

67 David Spector, "The 1884 Financial Scandal and the Establishment of Business Government in Winnipeg," unpublished paper (May 1976).

68 *Western Municipal News*, XI (1916), 35.

69 "Aspects of Urban Life in the West," in Rasporich and Klassen, eds., *Prairie Perspectives 2*, 35.

70 During the first two decades of the century, Jewish and Ukrainian groups concentrated in ward 5 in Winnipeg's distinctive north end elected several representatives to city council. The first successful Jewish candidate, Moses Finkelstein, elected to council in 1904, wrote later that an organized effort by the Jewish community to obtain representation on council began in the first few years of the century. By 1912, the Ukrainian community of ward 5 was able to celebrate the success of T. Stefanik in the Winnipeg civic election with an enthusiastic parade down Main Street. Murray S. Donnelly, "Ethnic Participation in Municipal Government: Winnipeg, St. Boniface and the Metropolitan Corporation of Greater Winnipeg," *Report* of the Royal Commission on Bilingualism and Biculturalism (1965), 21-22.

71 Artibise, *Winnipeg*, 26-27.

72 The latter sentiment was expressed by Thomas Sharpe, the mayor of Winnipeg, as one of the arguments for adopting the board of control form of government. See Weaver, "Elitism and the Corporate Ideal," 4.

73 However, the mayor of London responded to this concern by describing the procedure in his city where a "Citizens' Committee" dominated by representatives of business organizations recruited and nominated a group of candidates and provided the campaign expenses of this approved slate. *The Canadian Municipal Journal*, IX (October 1913), 404.

74 The substantial financing provided by the anti-labour Citizens' Committee of Winnipeg

is a case in point. See Paul Barber, "Class Conflict in Winnipeg Civic Politics: The Role of the Citizens' and Civic Election Organizations," unpublished paper, University of Manitoba (12 March 1970).

[75] Crawford, *Canadian Municipal Government*, 84-85.

[76] See, for example, *Minutes of the Edmonton Trades and Labour Council*, 21 October 1907, 117, and 6 November 1916.

[77] In Winnipeg, however, lower status populations were more concentrated in distinct districts than in Edmonton. Organized labour was also a stronger force in Winnipeg than in Edmonton.

[78] Jean Morrison, "Community in Conflict: A Study of the Working Class and its Relationships at the Canadian Lakehead, 1903-1913," MA thesis (Lakehead University, 1974).

[79] *The Canadian Municipal Journal*, IX (October 1913), 403.

[80] Gaetz, "Municipal Legislation," 1080.

[81] Ontario Commission on Municipal Institutions, *Report* (1888), 31.

[82] Michael Bliss, *A Living Profit: Studies in the Social History of Canadian Business, 1883-1911* (Toronto, 1974), 127.

[83] *Calgary Herald*, 15 December 1914.

[84] In Ottawa, for example, the finance committee of council was abolished when the board of control was adopted.

[85] St. John, New Brunswick, also adopted such an elected commission form of government, 1912.

[86] Commissioner A.T. Stephanson, "Red Deer's System of Government by Commission," *Western Municipal News*, VI (January 1911), 15-16.

[87] John C. Weaver, "The Modern City Realized: Toronto Civic Affairs, 1880-1915," in Alan F.J. Artibise and Gilbert A. Stelter, eds., *The Usable Urban Past: Planning and Politics in the Modern Canadian City* (Toronto, 1979), 49.

[88] *Calgary Herald*, 9 December 1913, 1.

[89] Most studies of the implications of local non-partisanship focus on Canadian cities during the last decade. See, for example, Masson and Anderson, eds., *Emerging Party Politics*.

[90] Crawford, *Canadian Municipal Government*, 55, 57; Harold Kaplan, *The Regional City* (Toronto, 1965), 30.

[91] Raymond E. Wolfinger, "Why Political Machines have not Withered Away and other Revisionist Thoughts," *Journal of Politics*, XXXIV (May 1972), 365-98.

[92] Gauvin, "The Municipal Reform Movement in Montreal."

[93] Dennis Carter-Edwards, "Toronto in the 1890's: A Decade of Challenge and Response," MA thesis (University of British Columbia, 1973). See also Spector, "The 1884 Financial Scandal."

[94] Grant MacEwan, *Calgary Cavalcade: From Fort to Fortune* (Edmonton, 1958), 123-27.

[95] Woodsworth, *My Neighbor*, 127.

96 Partisan and factional rivalry even characterized early township politics in Upper Canada. John McEvoy, *The Ontario Township*, University of Toronto Studies in Political Science, no. 1 (Toronto, 1899), 30. The first election in the City of Toronto was an open contest between Reformers and Tories. F.H. Armstrong, "William Lyon Mackenzie, First Mayor of Toronto: A Study of a Critic in Power," *Canadian Historical Review*, XLVIII, no. 4 (December 1967), 309-331.

97 *The Alberta Non-Partisan*, III, 12, 9. Cited by A.M. Mardiros, *William Irvine: The Life of a Prairie Radical* (Toronto, 1979), 57.

98 Ibid.

99 In a letter, the Calgary Labour Representation League urged the Edmonton Trades and Labour Council to form a labour party in Edmonton. The Edmonton Labour Representation League was founded after the TLC in Edmonton had discussed "the platform and principles" of the Calgary League. *Minutes of the Edmonton Trades and Labour Council*, 3 January, 16 April, 7 May, and 4 June 1917.

100 William Askin, "Labour Unrest in Edmonton and District and its Coverage by the Edmonton Press, 1918-1919," MA thesis (University of Alberta, 1973), 39.

101 W.J.C. Cherwinski, "Organized Labour in Saskatchewan: The TLC Years, 1905-1945," PhD thesis (University of Alberta, 1971), 255-56.

102 Barber, "Class Conflict in Winnipeg Civic Politics."

103 "Municipal Government by Commission," paper presented to the Second Annual Convention of the Union of Alberta Municipalities, Red Deer, Alberta, 8-10 January 1907; published in *The Canadian Municipal Journal*, III (April 1907), 144.

104 The phrase is used by Evelyn Eager, "The Conservatism of the Saskatchewan Electorate," in Norman Ward and Duff Spafford, eds., *Politics in Saskatchewan* (Don Mills, Ont., 1968), 4.

105 Winnipeg alderman and Mayor S.J. Farmer, for example, was a 'gas and water socialist' who later in his political career as CCF leader in the Manitoba legislature accepted a cabinet post in the "non-partisan" government of John Bracken. Paul Phillips, " 'Power Politics': Municipal Affairs and Seymour James Farmer, 1909-1924," in McCormack and MacPherson, eds., *Cities in the West*, 159-80. Bracken, who became national leader of the Conservative party in 1942, gave as one of the chief qualifications for the post his ability to check the growth of the CCF.

106 Askin, "Labour Unrest in Edmonton," 58.

107 See *Calgary Herald*, 6 and 9 December 1913.

108 Artibise, *Winnipeg*, 38.

109 Frank Underhill, "Commission Government in Cities," in Rutherford, ed., *Saving the Canadian City*, 332.

110 *Western Municipal News*, XII (1917), 285.

111 15 October 1914, 6.

112 27 October 1914, 6.

113 See, for example, J.O. Miller, "The Better Government of our Cities," in Rutherford, ed., *Saving the Canadian City*, 352.

172   *Essays on the Political Economy of Alberta*

114 S. Morley Wickett, "A Toronto Viewpoint," Papers and Proceedings of the First Annual Meeting of the Canadian Political Science Association, Ottawa, 4-6 September 1913, 136.

115 "Municipal Finance and Administration," *Report* of the Conference on Rural and Urban Development in Canada, Commission of Conservation, 28-30 May 1917, 20.

116 See, for example, Paul Rutherford, "Tomorrow's Metropolis: The Urban Reform Movement in Canada, 1880-1920," *Historical Papers*, Canadian Historical Association (1971), 203-224. See also Rutherford, ed., *Saving the Canadian City*.

117 The remarkable success of real estate interests in obtaining the extension of street railway and other municipal services to their far-flung property holdings is analyzed by several writers. See John C. Weaver, "Tomorrow's Metropolis Revisited: A Critical Assessment of Urban Reform in Canada, 1890-1920," paper presented at the annual meeting of the Canadian Historical Association, June 1976; Alan F.J. Artibise, "Boosterism and the Development of Prairie Cities: 1871-1913," paper presented at the Canadian Urban History Conference, University of Guelph, May 1977; and Edmund H. Dale, "The Role of Successive Town and City Councils in the Evolution of Edmonton, Alberta," PhD thesis (University of Alberta, 1969).

118 James Weinstein, "Organized Business and the City Commission and Manager Movements," *Journal of Southern History*, XXVIII (May 1962), 178.

119 Terry Copp, *Anatomy of Poverty: The Condition of the Working Class in Montreal, 1897-1929* (Toronto, 1974), 147.

120 Spector, "The 1884 Financial Scandal," 14-17.

121 *Minutes of the Edmonton Trades and Labour Council*, 4 November 1907, 121.

122 Donnelly, "Ethnic Participation in Municipal Government," 50-51.

123 An example often cited is the $200,000 cash bonus granted the CPR by the City of Winnipeg in 1882, to which was added an exemption from civic taxation in perpetuity. By 1909, Winnipeg had forgone more than $900,000 in tax revenue because of these bonuses. Theodore A. Hunt, "How Municipalities should Deal with Corporations," *Western Municipal News*, V (1910), 12.

124 *Western Municipal News*, I (1906), 198.

125 The Canadian Municipal Journal, VIII (August 1912), 315.

126 Statutes of Alberta, 1906, chapter 55. For a number of other bonuses granted by Calgary city council, see Max Foran, "Early Calgary 1875-1895: The Controversy Surrounding the Townsite Location and the Direction of Townsite Expansion," in McCormack and MacPherson, eds., *Cities in the West*, 38-39.

127 "Calgary, Alberta," *The Canadian Municipal Journal*, VII (1911), 341.

128 *Statutes of Alberta*, 1906, chapter 24.

129 Ibid., 108, chapter 23.

130 For example, the Winnipeg City Solicitor explained in 1910, "Very often a person who has been a citizen in town or city for a number of years and has established a moderately-sized plant of an industrial character, never asks for any concessions, and never gets any; but five men, perhaps four of them straw, will form themselves into a joint stock company, come along and establish a rival concern, get concessions by way of

bonus or exemption or free sites, and set up in opposition to the other man who has been paying taxes for a large number of years to the municipality and [has] helped in this way to build up the municipality. If you grant concessions to industrial concerns, it should apply generally." Hunt, "How Municipalities should Deal," 11.

131 Dale, "The Role of Successive Town and City Councils," 32-33.

132 *Statutes of Alberta*, 1914, chapter 14.

133 Mayor F.G. Forster, "Development of Natural Resources under Municipal Ownership," *The Canadian Municipal Journal*, II (April 1906), 134. Forster noted that the yearly benefit to a single firm using his city's cheap gas was equivalent to a bonus of $2,500. Ibid., 135.

134 Cited in Weaver, "Tomorrow's Metropolis Revisited," 14.

135 Ibid., 14-15.

136 William Short, "Municipal Ownership in Edmonton," *Western Municipal News*, IX (1914), 192.

137 Artibise, *Winnipeg*, 101.

138 W.D. Lighthall, Annual Report to the Union of Canadian Municipalities, *Western Municipal News*, IV (1909), 1267.

139 H.V. Nelles and Christopher Armstrong, "The Great Fight for Clean Government," *Urban History Review*, no. 2-76 (October 1976), 50-66.

140 See, for example, Artibise, *Winnipeg*, and J.M.S. Careless, "The Development of the Winnipeg Business Community, 1870-1890," *Transactions* of the Royal Society of Canada, VIII (1970), 239-54.

141 Spector, "The 1884 Financial Scandal."

142 This information first appears in Barber, "Class Conflict in Winnipeg Civic Politics," 2-3. It then appears in J.E. Rea, "The Politics of Conscience: Winnipeg After the Strike," *Historical Papers*, Canadian Historical Association (1971), 278.

143 Miliband, *The State in Capitalist Society*, 154-55.

144 *Edmonton Journal*, 3 January 1972.

145 Robert Gilsdorf, "The Popular Basis of Urban Political Institutions: Reformed Institutions and Centralization in Edmonton," paper presented at the Annual Meetings of the Canadian Political Science Association, Toronto, 4 June 1974, 9-10; and Robert Gilsdorf, "Cognitive and Motivational Sources of Voter Susceptibility to Influence," *Canadian Journal of Political Science*, VI (December 1973), 626n. In the Edmonton survey, voters were asked if they favored involvement of the three major parties in local politics. In the provincial survey, the question referred to "party-type organizations."

146 James Lightbody, "Edmonton Politics: Business as Usual," *Canadian Forum*, LII (December 1972), 8-9.

147 *Edmonton Journal*, 22 November 1976.

The Political Economy
of Oil in Alberta

Ed Shaffer

The best- laid schemes o'mice an'men
Gang aft agley,
An lea'e us nought but grief an' pain,
For promis'd joy!

Robert Burns

1. Introduction

Oil has been Alberta's leading staple export since the early 1950s. Before the discovery of oil at Leduc in 1947, wheat had been the province's chief staple. In that era Alberta's economy differed little from the economies of Canada's other two wheat exporting provinces, Saskatchewan and Manitoba.

After the ascendancy of oil in Alberta, the economy of Alberta began to differ markedly from those of its two sister prairie provinces. Among the more significant changes were: (1) the much more rapid growth in Alberta's population and labour force and (2) the much more rapid rise of the relative importance of Alberta's non-agricultural labour force.

Between 1941, the last census year before the Leduc discovery, and 1951, Alberta's population grew by 18 per cent. By contrast, the population of its two sister provinces decreased by one percent. In the 20 years preceding 1941, Alberta's population expanded at a rate of 1.5 percent per year; in the 20 years after 1951, at a rate of 2.8 percent. Hence the population growth rate almost doubled during the 'oil boom' years. In the other prairie provinces the growth rate remained static at 0.9 percent in both the pre-1941 and the post-1951 years.[1] Labour force growth rates followed a similar pattern.

Perhaps more significant than this quantitative change in growth rates was the qualitative change in the labour force structure. The non-agricultural labour force became far more important in Alberta than in the other two provinces. In 1941, for example, 49 percent of Alberta's labour force was engaged in agriculture. In the other two provinces, agriculture's share was 48 percent. By 1971, agriculture accounted for only 13 percent of Alberta's labour force but almost one-fifth of the force in the rest of the prairies.[2]

This rise in the relative importance of the non-agriculture labour force was, however, not accompanied by a rise in the relative importance of manufacturing employment. Between 1961, when Statistics Canada first started compiling data on employment by industry on a provincial basis, and 1980, employment in Alberta's non-agricultural industries rose by more than 500,000. Of this total, only 10 percent represented jobs in manufacturing. Approximately 80 percent of the newly created jobs were in the transportation, distribution, and service industries. Manufacturing's share actually fell from 13 percent of non-agricultural employment in 1961 to 11 percent in 1980.[3]

This change in the composition of non-agricultural employment has increased the dependence of the province on the oil industry. By their nature, the transportation, distribution, and service industries are incapable of generating an independent economic base. Their activities must be ancillary to industries such as agriculture, mining, and manufacturing, which are the bases of economic activity.

In the non-agricultural, non-mining sector only manufacturing can create an independent economic base. Only through such a base can Alberta acquire the "capacity to transform." Should a decline occur in the demand for or supply of Alberta's oil and natural gas resources, then the manufacturing industries can provide the exports to pay for the imports to maintain living standards or, alternatively, reduce the manufactured imports necessary to maintain those standards.

Within the manufacturing sector itself, a great deal of the newly formed jobs have been created not in 'independent' industries, that is, in industries capable of existing independently of the oil industry, but in what Hirschman calls "satellite" industries.[4] These industries are composed largely of small-scale enterprises clustered around the "master" industry and whose very existence is dependent on the "master" industry. Among these industries in Alberta are primary metal industries, metal fabricating industries, machinery except electrical, and electrical products. That the average size of their enterprise is small can be seen from Table V-1 below.

Table V-1		
Average Number of Employees Per Establishment in Selected Industries-Alberta and Canada Ex-Alberta, 1978		
Industry	Alberta	Canada Excluding Alberta
Primary Metal	139	325
Metal Fabricating	27	35
Machinery	45	72
Electrical Products	53	121

Calculated from: Statistics Canada, *Manufacturing Industries of Canada: National and Provincial Areas, 1978*, cat. no. 31-203 (Dec. 1980).

Only in the primary metal industries is the average size of establishment above 100 employees. But this industry employed only 2,000 people in 1978 or only 3 percent of the 77,000 manufacturing workers in Alberta.[5] Furthermore, the average size of establishment in this industry was considerably smaller than the average size in the rest of Canada. In each of the other three industries the average size of establishment was also significantly smaller than in the rest of Canada. These particular manufacturing industries appear to have all the characteristics of "satellite" industries.

Satellite industries do little to spur economic development. In fact, they may hinder development by making the economy more dependent on the master industry through inducing investment flows into their industries and away from other, non-dependent industries.

The growing dependence of the Alberta work force on the oil industry poses two serious problems. First, it increases the vulnerability of the province to the repercussions of fluctuations in the demand and supply of crude. Second, it reduces the bargaining power of the province in its dealings with the multinational companies, who control almost all of Alberta's oil. This dependence places the companies in a better position to obtain concessions by threatening to reduce their expenditures in the province, thereby affecting the level of employment and rate of development in Alberta.

2. Three Theories of Development
I am going to discuss this particular impact of oil on Alberta's economic development in the context of three theories of economic development: Innis's staple export theory, Levin's theory of foreign factors, and Lenin's theory of imperialism. Of the three, the staple theory has had the greatest influence in Canadian and other North American universities.

Harold Innis explained the economic development of Canada through this country's exports of staple products, a staple being a raw material that is exported in an essentially unprocessed form. From its colonial beginnings in the sixteenth to eighteenth centuries Canada exported fish and furs. Early in the nineteenth century timber and lumber replaced fish and furs, which declined in relative importance. From the opening of the present century until the 1920s, wheat became the export staple. Since the 1950s fuels and metallic minerals have become the major staples.

As enunciated by Innis, W.A. Mackintosh, and others, a staple export generates economic development in the following manner. The expansion of the export industry raises incomes, creating a demand for consumer goods in the economy. Local enterprises spring up to meet this demand. In addition, the export industry creates demand for material inputs, some of which are met by local industries. Finally, the output of the export industry can serve as an input for processing industries that desire to locate close to the supply of raw materials. Over time, these local enterprises become more important and tend to develop independently of the export industry. This independence gives the economy the ability to shift to new activities should the export industry decline.[6] Roemer calls this "capacity to transform...one of the most important by-products of development."[7]

Canada apparently acquired this "capacity to transform." As the demand for one of its staples, for example, furs, declined, it was able to shift to other staples and to other forms of economic activity. However, the staple model has not worked in most other parts of the world.

Economists have offered various explanations why staple exports have led to development in Canada but not in most other countries. Most explanations revolve around differences in production functions, that is, the relationship between inputs and outputs, transportation costs, and other such technical variables. While some of these explanations are valid as far as they go, they largely ignore the social relationships that govern every system of production.

One economist who took some of these relationships into account was J. Levin. In his book, *The Export Economies*,[8] Levin cited the importance of the "foreign factors" of production in the export sectors of many countries. These "foreign factors," that is, labour, enterprise, and capital, migrated to under-developed areas in order to extract the raw materials. Some of these factors like skilled labour and capital, did not exist at all or existed in insufficient quantities within the exporting country. Their importation, therefore, was necessary in order to produce the staple.

Implicit in Levin's thesis is an element of racism. The corollary of the "necessity" to import foreign skilled labour, essentially white labour from Europe and North America, is the assumption of either the impossibility or undesirability of training the indigenous population. The force for development can thus come only from the outside, from the more developed areas, rather than from within the region itself. This racism also applies to the staple theory, which largely ignored the role of Indian labour in the production of furs.[9]

In any event Levin argues that the presence of these "foreign factors" inhibited the development process because these factors remitted their earnings abroad. Levin thus differed sharply from those staple theorists who assumed that the increased earnings from the export industry would be spent in the domestic economy. According to neoclassical theory, the factors' earnings are rents, wages, interest, and profits. They are the earnings that accrue to the factors of production, land, labour, capital and enterprise. When these earnings are spent in an area, they create demand for consumer and investment goods and foster economic activity within that area. If they are spent abroad, they foster economic activity abroad.

The key to economic development is the reinvestment of profits in new factories, buildings, machinery, and equipment. If profits are not reinvested, development will not take place. In many underdeveloped areas these profits, representing the return on capital, are largely remitted abroad. As a result, very little of the earnings of the export industry is invested in the domestic sector. As Levin puts it:

...a thriving export industry could operate for decades alongside a stagnating, poverty stricken domestic sector. Where the structure of an export industry was characterized by foreign factors and luxury importers, high export earnings contributed little to domestic growth. In this process lies a large part of the explanation for the slow development of any export economies.[10]

Levin showed why, given the presence of "foreign factors," the ordinary market forces cannot lead to economic development. His analysis in this respect is superior to that of those market-oriented staple theorists who have an uncritical faith in the capitalist market. Nevertheless, couched as it was in the framework of neoclassical economic theory, it never gave explicit recognition to the role of imperialism in inhibiting development—in fact, Levin never even mentioned the word.

Yet Levin's analysis can make sense only in a context that recognizes the existence of economic imperialism. More than four decades earlier, in the midst of World War I, V.I. Lenin provided just such an analysis in his *Imperialism: The Highest Stage of Capitalism.*

Lenin pointed out that modern imperialism is a particular stage of capitalist development arising from the growth of monopoly. "This transformation of competition into monopoly," he wrote, "is one of the most important—if not the most important—phenomena of modern capitalist economy...."[11] Following Marx's reasoning, Lenin argued that "free competition gives rise to the concentration of production, which, in turn, at a certain stage of development, leads to monopoly."[12] This new stage of capitalism, according to Lenin, was definitely established in Europe and North America by the beginning of the twentieth century.[13]

Lenin attributed several characteristics to imperialism. One was the export of capital. "Under the old capitalism, when free competition prevailed," he said, "the export of *goods* was the most typical feature. Under modern capitalism, when monopolies prevail, the export of *capital* has become the typical feature."[14] The export of capital stems from its vast accumulation of a few monopolies in a small number of developed countries. As Lenin stated:

On the threshold of the twentieth century we see a new type of monopoly coming into existence. Firstly, there are monopolist capitalist combines in all advanced capitalist countries; secondly, a few rich countries, in which the accumulation of capital reaches gigantic proportions, occupy a monopolist position. An enormous "superabundance of capital" becomes accumulated in the advanced countries.[15]

This "surplus capital...will be used for the purpose of increasing profits by exporting abroad to the backward countries. There the profits are usually high, for capital is scarce, the price of land is relatively low, wages are low, raw materials are cheap."[16] Thus, the anticipation of greater profits in the underdeveloped countries leads to an export of capital from the developed ones. This export of capital furthermore serves to counteract the long run tendency of the rate of profit to fall as capitalism advances.[17]

Lenin coupled the export of capital with the power relationship under monopoly. He berated the establishment economists of his day for ignoring these relationships, a criticism that can be levelled against many of today's neoclassical economists, including Levin. He spoke of "the monoplies throttling those which do not submit to them, to their yoke, to their dictation"[18] and the dominant position of the leading monopolies. "Domination, and violence that is associated with it, such are the relationships that are most typical of the 'latest phase of capitalist development'; this is what must inevitably result, and has resulted, from the formation of all-powerful economic monoplies."[19]

The export of capital thus implies not merely the presence of "foreign factors" in raw materials-exporting areas but also a power relationship in which these "foreign factors" dominate the political, economic, and social life of these areas. This dominance is important to the foreign monopolies because it is the only way they can guarantee that these areas will remain profitable to them. Therefore, they deliberately institute policies to arrest independent development, to preserve the archaic social orders found in many of these areas, and to keep these areas in a general state of backwardness. Such policies are enforced not merely by the monopolies themselves but also by the government of the monopolies' home countries through economic, diplomatic, and military pressure. This is an observable political reality that accompanies the export of capital.

However, Lenin noted that the intentions of the foreign monopolists may not be realized. "The export of capital," he wrote, "greatly affects and accelerates the development of capitalism in those countries to which it is exported."[20] This acceleration of the development of capitalism gives rise to new capitalistic classes, to new forces, which may challenge the dominance of the old.

Thus we see a 'dialectical' process taking place. The advanced capitalist states, in order to solve their own internal contradictions, export capital to less developed areas. Though they try to keep these less developed areas in a state of relative backwardness, they can only succeed partially. The introduction of capitalism to these areas gives rise to an indigenous capitalist class and to an incipient working class, which will attempt to extricate itself from the dominance of the foreign monopolists. This continuous struggle—in which today the working class, the peasantry, and the intellectuals also play a significant role—changes the alignment of politico-economic forces both in the less developed areas and in the capitalist world as a whole.

3. The Case of Oil in Alberta
With this brief discussion of the three theories—staples, "foreign factors," and imperialism—we now turn to the question of their relevance to the political economy of oil in Alberta.

First, oil has not brought about the linkages suggested by the staple theory. As we already noted, most of the increased employment went into trade and services rather than into manufacturing. Second, even in manufacturing, most of the growth occurred in "satellite" rather than in "independent" industries. In sum, dependence on the staple has increased rather than decreased.

A key explanation of the failure of the province to develop along the lines suggested by the staple theory is the role played by the multinational oil corporations in exploiting Alberta's resources. These multinational oil corporations are Levin's "foreign factors." A relatively small number of them control Alberta's oil production. A provincial paper, issued in 1972, revealed that "thirty oil companies accounted for about 95 percent of total crude oil royalties paid to the Province of Alberta in 1970" and "about 50 percent of net acreage holdings in the Province."[21] They are also the same corporations that, by and large, control the bulk of oil production in the rest of the capitalist world.

That these investments by the "foreign factors" turned out to be highly profitable can be inferred from the share of gross domestic product accruing to corporate profits. Table V-2, which compares the profits' share in Alberta with the share in the rest of Canada from 1961[22] to 1979, shows that the share in Alberta has been higher, and often considerably higher, than in the rest of Canada in each year. The table also reveals that this share rose significantly in Alberta during the 1970s. The lowest figure for this period occurred during 1971, when corporate profits claimed 15.2 percent of provincial GDP. This figure was only 0.2 percentage points below the 1960s high of 15.4 percent, reached in 1968. For the rest of Canada, the lowest share of the 1970s, 8.4 percent in 1971, was considerably below the high of the 1960s, 11 percent in 1964. The portion of the GDP accruing to profits in Alberta for the years 1964-70 averaged 14 percent. This portion rose to 19.7 percent for the years 1971-79.[23] For the rest of Canada this portion averaged 10 percent in both periods.

Another way of examining this qualitative shift towards corporate profits in Alberta is to compare these profits with those in all of Canada. Alberta's share of total corporate profits has steadily increased, rising from 8.7 percent in 1964 to 21.9 percent in 1979. In the latter year Alberta accounted for over one-fifth of all corporate profits in Canada even though its share of national GDP was less than 13 percent. During the years of 1964-70, Alberta's share of national corporate profits averaged 11 percent. This share rose to 18.9 percent during the years 1971-79. Alberta's share of GDP rose at a much slower rate, from 8 to 10.5 percent. [24]

This marked shift towards profits in Alberta in the 1970s was the result of (1) the escalation in oil prices and (2) the election in 1971 of a government that found it to its interests to ally itself with the international oil companies in its disputes with the federal government. The implications of these disputes will be analyzed later in this article. What is significant at this point is that most of the corporations in Alberta are foreign owned oil companies. A disproportionately high share of domestic product thus went to these "foreign factors."

	Table V-2	
	Corporate Profits' Share of Gross Domestic Product, Alberta and Canada Ex-Alberta 1961-1979 (Percent)	
Year	Alberta	Canada Excluding Alberta
1961	11.7	9.7
1962	10.8	10.0
1963*	11.7	10.4
1964*	12.4	11.0
1965	13.5	10.9
1966	13.9	10.3
1967	14.9	9.7
1968	15.4	10.0
1969	14.3	9.6
1970	13.6	8.2
1971	15.2	8.4
1972	16.7	9.4
1973	19.5	11.4
1974	19.9	12.4
1975	21.7	10.2
1976	19.8	9.1
1977	20.8	8.5
1978	21.1	9.3
1979	22.6	11.6

*The figures before 1964 are not strictly comparable with those of later years.
Calculated from: Statistics Canada, *Provincial Economic Accounts, 1961-1974, Experimental Data* (Ottawa, n.d.), and *Provincial Economic Accounts, Experimental Data, 1964-1979*, cat. no. 13-213 (Ottawa, 1981), 2-3, 20-21. Gross Domestic Product (GDP) is the market value of the output of an area, regardless of the owners of the factors of production. Gross Provincial Product (GPP), on the other hand, is the market value of the output of a province plus receipts by owners of factors resident in the province of income generated outside the province minus payments to owners of factors of production, located in the province, who are not residents of the province. In other words, the GDP of Alberta is higher than the GPP because investments by non-residents in Alberta are higher than investments by Albertans in other areas.

Given the development pattern of Alberta we can also infer that these profits, to the extent that they were reinvested in Alberta, were either reinvested in the oil industry directly or in industries dependent on the oil industry. Very little was invested in "independent" manufacturing industries. All this conforms to Levin's thesis.

Levin's thesis, however, does not explain the shifts in Alberta's labour force and, especially, the significant growth in the non-agricultural sector. His theory of economic 'dualism,' (as exemplified in the quote on page 177), in which he argues that "a thriving export industry could operate for decades alongside a stagnating, poverty stricken domestic sector," does not apply to Alberta. While the domestic sector in Alberta may be relatively underdeveloped, it can by no stretch of the imagination be called either "stagnating" or "poverty stricken." If the Levin thesis really applied, the non-agricultural labour force would not have grown to the extent it has.

Economic dualism did not arise in Alberta because of the specific role played by the state, a role largely ignored by both the staple and Levin theories. In Alberta, the state, as exemplified by the province, was forced to play a role because it owned directly most of the sub-surface mineral rights since 1930. The oil royalties were therefore 'socialized' in that they did not go directly to private interests. The inflow of these royalties confronted the old Social Credit government, which ruled the province from 1935 to 1971, with the problem of what to do with these funds.

The Social Credit Government could have used the funds to lessen income inequalities and to reduce poverty. But this was not done because such a redistribution would undermine the incentives of the market system—income inequality is essential for the survival and the efficient operation of capitalism. Therefore, they decided to spend the funds on social services in such a way as to minimize the redistributional effects.

The Socreds greatly expanded the health care system, providing free medical services to all segments of the population. This expansion unquestionably benefited the working class, the farmers, and the poor much more than the upper class. It represented a limited redistribution of income with a minimum impact on incentives.

The Socreds also expanded post-secondary educational facilities. The chief beneficiaries of this policy were the middle and upper classes, who provided the bulk of the students in the universities, although some of the benefits also extended to the farmers and working class, in the sense that more children of farm and working class families were able to receive a post-secondary education.

This policy of rapidly expanding the social services resulted in a great increase in employment in the public sector. As can be seen in Table V-3 below, more jobs were created in non-commercial services than in any other industry during the years 1961-71. Statistics Canada defines non-commercial services as "hospitals, education and related services, welfare organizations, religious organizations and private households."[25] The bulk of these services are provided by the public sector.

The role of the state in converting the surplus of the export industry into jobs in other industries is what I call 'discretionary' linkage. 'Discretionary' linkages are distinct from the linkages envisioned in the staple and Levin models in that they do not 'automatically' result from the normal workings of the market mechanism. They result only from state policy.

The use of 'discretionary' linkage to develop the public sector prevented the rise of a 'dual economy' in Alberta during the Socred years. Along with the expansion of the export sector came an expansion of the domestic sector and, especially, the public portion of that sector.

Table V-3				
Changes in Employment in Alberta's Non-Agricultural Industries, 1961-71, 1971-80				
	1961-1971		**1971-1980**	
	(000)	**(percent)**	**(000)**	**(percent)**
Manufacturing	16.3	9.1	33.2	9.9
Construction	16.9	9.5	42.2	12.6
Transportation	11.5	6.4	32.8	9.8
Trade	32.2	18.1	63.8	19.0
Finance	9.7	5.4	29.3	8.7
Commercial Services	31.9	17.9	81.7	24.3
Non-Commercial Services	48.1	27.0	28.2	8.4
Public Administration	11.7	6.6	25.0	7.4
TOTAL	178.3	100.0	336.2	100.00

Calculated From: Statistics Canada, *Estimates of Employees by Province and Industry*, May 1978, pp. 68-70 and May 1981, p. 22. Excludes forestry and mining.

This expansion played a key role in transforming the labour force from one that was agricultural to one that was non-agricultural in character. It also undermined the rural political base of the Socreds. Because of their base the Socreds did not welcome rapid industrialization, which would undermine the dominant role of the rural sector. Nevertheless, their policies—their "best-laid plans"—helped achieve a result that they wanted to avoid.

The Socred policies created a large urban based interest group that looked upon industrialization as a panacea rather than as an anathema. This group, which centred itself around the Progressive Conservative Party, came to power in 1971. With the Conservative rise to power there came a change of emphasis in 'discretionary' linkage. For instance, as Table V-3 indicates, the rate of expansion of non-commercial services was significantly lowered.

Though the coffers of the Provincial Treasury swelled from the effects of both increased oil prices and the higher royalty rates instituted by the Tories, the Tories did not permit social services in general, and education in particular, to expand as rapidly as in the past. Instead they concentrated on building up a huge surplus, which will be used to spur industrialization. The full thrust of this Tory policy can be seen in Tables V-4 and V-5 below.

Table V-4 shows both the dollar receipts and expenditures and their distribution in selected years from the fiscal year ending 31 March 1946 to that ending 31 March 1980. As can be seen readily in the top part of the table, there has been a great expansion in both receipts and expenditures in that time span. Accompanying this expansion was a growth in the relative importance of social service expenditures—education, health, and welfare—between 1946, one year before the Leduc discovery, and 1971, the last year of the Social Credit era.

Table V-4

Province of Alberta's Cash Receipts and Selected Expenditures, Selected Fiscal Years Ending 31 March ($ Millions)

	1980	1975	1971	1966	1956	1946
Receipts						
1. Total[1]	9,340.0	3,009.8	1,130.6	603.9	247.6	43.3
2. Minerals[2]	4,592.6	1,372.0	235.6	250.1	128.1	3.4
3. Deficit	—	—	100.8	—	—	—
Expenditures[3]						
4. Education[4]	1,127.6	516.7	379.4	123.2	37.5	4.8
5. Health and Welfare[5]	1,745.4	578.0	322.1	159.7	40.1	8.7
6. Lines 4 + 5	2,874.0	1,094.7	701.5	282.9	77.6	13.5
7. Industry and Manpower[6]	194.5	67.4	7.3	6.2	1.2	0.3
8. Surplus	4,186.3	772.3	—	78.5	15.9	11.6
(PERCENT OF RECEIPTS)						
Receipts						
9. Total	100.0	100.0	100.0	100.0	100.0	100.0
10. Minerals	49.2	45.6	20.8	41.4	51.7	7.9
11. Deficit	—	—	8.9	—	—	—
Expenditures						
12. Education	12.1	17.2	33.4	20.4	15.1	11.1
13. Health and Welfare	18.7	19.2	28.5	26.5	16.2	20.1
14. Lines 12 + 13	30.8	36.4	62.0	46.9	31.3	31.2
15. Industry and Manpower	2.1	2.3	0.7	0.9	0.5	0.7
16. Surplus	44.8	25.7	—	13.0	6.4	26.8

[1] All cash receipts including taxes, royalties, bonuses, lease rentals, fees, fines, subsidies and other transfer payments from other governments, borrowings, loan repayments, and proceeds from sales of securities. Excludes receipts from Alberta Government Telephones and income from debt reorganization funds in 1946. The 1980 receipts include allocations by the Province of $1,348 million to the Alberta Heritage Savings Trust Fund (AHSTF) and of $99 million to oil companies as incentive grants for exploration drilling and geophysical work. The Government of Alberta, instead of treating these allocations as expenditures, deducts them from its total receipts. The official budget figures therefore understate the revenues accruing to the Provincial Treasury. The receipt figures in Table V-4 also include the investment income of the AHSTF, which amounted to $476 million in the fiscal year ending 31 March 1980.

[2] Receipts of the Department of Mines and Minerals. In 1946 the department was called the Lands and Mines Department. In the 1970s its name was changed to the Department of Energy and Natural Resources. The receipts for 1980 encompass income from all non-renewable resources, which consist of royalties, bonuses and sales of crown leases, rentals, and fees.

[3] Includes both income and capital expenditures.

[4] Includes the combined expenditures of the Department of Advanced Education and the Department of Education in 1975 and the expenditures of the Department of Education in previous years. The 1980 expenditures on education include the outlays of the Department of Advanced Education and Manpower and the Department of Education minus the former Department's spending on Manpower Development and Training Assistance. They also include the $10 million spent by the Capital Projects Division of the AHSTF on developing Canadian content educational resources and on the improvement of libraries in colleges and universities.

[5] Includes the expenditures of both the Health Commission and the Department of Health and Social Development in 1975; the Health Department and the Social Development Department in 1971; and the Public Health Department and the Public Welfare Department in the other years. Because the expenditures of Health and Social Development were combined by the government in 1975, they were combined in this table to ensure historical comparability. The 1980 expenditures on health and welfare include the outlays of the Department of Hospitals and

Medical Care and the Department of Social Services and Community Health. They also include a $436 million grant by the Capital Projects Division of the AHSTF for health care facilities and for the Alberta Heritage Foundation for Medical Research. The funds for the latter came to $300 million.

6 Includes the expenditures of both the Department of Industry and Commerce and the Department of Manpower and Labour in 1975; the Department of Industry and Tourism and the Labour Department in 1971; the Industry and Development Department and the Labour Department in 1966; the Industries and Labour Department in 1956; and the Trade and Industry Department in 1946. Because the Industries and Labour Department figures were combined by the government in 1956, they were combined in this table to ensure historical comparability. The 1980 expenditures on industry and manpower include the outlays of the Department of Development, the Department of Tourism and Small Business, and the Department of Labour. They also encompass the expenditures on Manpower Development and Training Assistance by the Department of Advanced Education and Manpower, the incentives given to oil companies for exploratory drilling and geophysical work, and contribution of $38 million by the Capital Projects Division of the AHSTF for research in oil sands technology.

Source: Alberta, *Public Accounts of the Province of Alberta.*

Table V-5

Province of Alberta
A Comparison of Annual Growth Rates
Total Receipts and Selected Expenditures
(Percent Per Year)

	1971-1980	1946-1971
Receipts		
1. Total Receipts	26.4	13.9
Expenditures		
2. Education	12.9	19.1
3. Health and Welfare	20.7	15.5
4. Education, Health and Welfare	17.0	17.1
5. Industry and Manpower	44.0	13.6
$\text{RATIO} - \dfrac{\text{PERCENT CHANGE IN EXPENDITURES}}{\text{PERCENT CHANGE IN RECEIPTS}}$		
6. Education	0.5	1.4
7. Health and Welfare	0.8	1.1
8. Education, Health and Welfare	0.6	1.0
9. Industry and Manpower	1.7	1.0

Source: Table V-4.

As the bottom part of Table V-4 shows, expenditures on education (line 12) rose from 11 percent of receipts in 1946 to 33 percent in 1971; those on health and welfare (line 13) from 20 percent to 29 percent; and those on social services as a whole (line 14), from 31 percent to 62 percent. This rise was continuous and even occurred between 1966 and 1971 when oil revenues actually declined (line 2). In addition, the portion of funds going to industry and manpower did not rise significantly during the Socred years (line 15).

Since 1971 the pattern of expenditures has changed significantly. The share going to education has fallen to 12 percent; that going to health and welfare, to 19 percent; and that going to social services as a whole, to 31 percent. In contrast the share accruing to industry and manpower has risen from 0.7 percent in 1971 to 2.1 percent in 1980. The counterpart to the decline in social services has been the generation of a surplus, amounting to 45 percent of total receipts (line 16). In contrast to the surplus of 1946, which was used to retire debt, this surplus will be invested, as is discussed below, in the Alberta Heritage Savings Trust Fund and in other instruments of industrialization.

Table V-5 contrasts the growth rates in receipts and expenditures in the Tory years (1971-80) to the last 25 years of Socred rule (1946-71). The top part (lines 1-5) shows the annual percentage growth rates. Thus, as line 1 demonstrates, receipts in the Tory years rose at a much faster rate, 26 percent per year, than in the Socred ones, 14 percent. In contrast, the growth rates of expenditures on education (line 2) fell significantly in the Tory era. The 1971-80 rate, 13 percent, was well below the 19 percent rate of the Socred period. Furthermore, it was insufficient to meet the needs of a school system burdened by a rapidly growing enrolment caused by the influx of population during the oil boom. The crisis in the educational system brought about a series of teacher strikes in Edmonton, Calgary, and other centres during the late 1970s and the early 1980s.

A similar situation prevailed in health and welfare. Though their rate (line 3) rose under the Tories, from 16 to 21 percent, the rise was inadequate to cope with social problems caused by the heavy immigration. Alberta's social service agencies have been plagued with scandals flowing from their inability to meet basic needs and, in some instances, to prevent deaths. The *Edmonton Journal,* in particular, carried a number of stories exposing the glaring inadequacies of the government's social service programmes.

The bottom part of Table V-5 shows the ratios of the growth rates of expenditures to those of receipts. A value greater than 1 indicates that the expenditures were growing at a faster rate than receipts. A value less than 1 indicates a slower growth rate. The values (lines 6, 7, 8) were equal to or above 1 in the Socred years, indicating that these expenditures were rising more rapidly than receipts. In the Tory years, they were all significantly below 1. In contrast, those on industry and manpower (line 9) were significantly above 1 under the Tories but equal to 1 under the Socreds. These figures show the extent to which the Tories are pushing industrialization at the expense of social services.

4. The Industrialization Drive in Alberta

The industrialization drive, if successful, will come about not in the way suggested by the staple theory, that is, by the "automatic" linkages of the market mechanism. It will come about despite the presence of "foreign factors" in the Levin model. It will come about because 'socialization' of the economic rents[26] opens the possibility for a new, indigenous industrial class to arise through the use of the state mechanism and it is this possibility that is consistent with Lenin's view that the export of capital gives rise to new capitalist classes. I shall discuss the implications of this development later. At this point I want to focus on the methods by which this relatively 'new bourgeoisie' in Alberta is attempting to achieve industrialization.

Though the industrialization will be financed mainly by public funds, by the economic rents collected from the oil and gas industry, it will be carried out by private enterprise through a system of government joint ventures with multinational corporations. The Tories have established two principal instruments to promote this industrialization policy, the Alberta Energy Company and the Alberta Heritage Savings Trust Fund.

Set up in 1973, the Alberta Energy Company has the authority to issue 100,000,000 shares of stock.[27] In 1974, the legislature passed the Alberta Energy Company Act, which defined the Company's powers and the conditions of ownership of its shares. Among the AEC's stated objectives were:[28] (1) the granting of opportunities to "Albertans and other Canadians" to "participate in the development of Alberta's industrial and resource potential" and (2) the strengthening of "the industrial and resource bases of the Canadian economy, particularly in Alberta." The AEC intends to achieve these objectives through investment policies that "presently emphasize new, large, long-range, capital-investment projects." The company plans to participate in these projects on its own and "through affiliated companies and joint ventures."

The initial capital for these projects is to be raised through the sale of its 100,000,000 shares. Though these shares have no par value, they can be sold for no more than $500,000,000.

Half the shares are to be sold first to residents of Alberta and then, if Albertans fail to purchase the entire offering, the "residents and citizens of Canada." Thus the government intends to use the AEC as a vehicle of channelling private savings into industrial development.

The remaining shares are to be purchased by the province.[29] The funds for these purchases will come from the Alberta Heritage Savings Trust Fund. Established by the legislature in 1976, the AHSTF immediately received $1,500,000,000 from the Treasury and is to receive 30 percent of all future revenues from non-renewable resources.[30] By 1981 this fund had assets of approximately $9 billion. The bulk of these funds, at least 65 percent, are to be invested in projects that "will yield a reasonable return or profit to the Trust Fund and will tend to strengthen and diversify the economy of Alberta."[31] These particular funds will be used to purchase shares in the AEC, to pay for the province's equity in Syncrude, and to buy into private companies. Their use will be determined by the Cabinet and will not require approval of the legislature.[32]

Through both the AEC and the AHSTF the Tories are mobilizing capital to spur industrialization. In the AEC they are tapping both private and public capital for this purpose. By making AEC's shares available to the middle class, they are broadening their political base and trying to give this class a vested interest in the industrialization programme. By concentrating both the AEC and the AHSTF funds on joint ventures, they have resolved the dilemma of how to use public funds without expanding public ownership.

The one apparent exception to this policy, the purchase of Pacific Western Airlines (PWA), actually dovetails with it. This airline, which serves the growing northern regions of Alberta and the Northwest Territories, enables Alberta businessmen to penetrate those areas. It provides the necessary infrastructure for this expansion. Through controlling the rates on air freight, the province can also control the pace at which Alberta businesses can move into these areas. PWA is just another vehicle through which public funds can be used to help private enterprise.

5. The Changing Alignment of Power

Alberta's 'new bourgeoisie' is using its newly found economic power as a means of strengthening its position *vis-à-vis* the older national bourgeoisie of eastern Canada. Because the national bourgeoisie is relatively weak, hemmed in as it is by the US bourgeoisie, it has always relied on the West as a means of bolstering its position *vis-à-vis* the Americans. The West, to a large extent, has 'subsidized' the East. The new bourgeoisie in Alberta want to change this internal 'colonial' relationship. The oil funds, for the first time, give them the potential to do so.

They have therefore formed an alliance with the multinational oil companies against the established bourgeoisie in central Canada. The oil companies, for their part, are encouraging the local bourgeoisie. In general, the oil companies would prefer to deal with a host of relatively weak provincial or regional governments than with a strong federal government. In this way they can play one province against the other and the provinces against the federal government. Through such a policy they can prevent the various governments from extracting the maximum possible economic rents.

In the United States, for example, the oil companies have always been strong advocates of state control and opponents of federal control. By erecting a system of state controls, the oil companies are able to keep all the states in line by shifting production, exploration, and development expenditures from the 'tough' states to the 'moderate' ones. Such tactics were used recently in Canada. When Saskatchewan raised its royalty rates above those of Alberta, the companies greatly reduced their activity in Saskatchewan and increased it in Alberta. Saskatchewan 'got the message' and changed its royalty policies. The companies forced British Columbia to change its natural gas policies. The companies also benefitted from a dispute during the 1970s between the federal government and the provinces over the sharing of oil revenues. When that dispute was finally settled, the companies received concessions from both sides.

In the early 1980s a bitter controversy arose between the Alberta and the federal governments over oil pricing and the shares of oil revenues. The province wanted oil prices to approach world levels, with economic rents from this increase being divided between the province and the oil companies. The federal government rejected world prices, calling instead for a "made-in-Canada" oil price. This price was to be based on the replacement cost of crude oil, presumably the cost of producing a barrel of synthetic oil. The federal government, representing the national bourgeoisie, also wanted a much larger share of the economic rents created by a price increase.

The federal election of 1980 was fought over the issue of oil prices. The Liberals won on a promise to keep the prices from rising as fast as the Progressive Conservative government of Joe Clark had proposed. Following their victory, the Liberals introduced the National Energy Program (NEP), which provided for both an increase in oil prices, though at a lower rate than proposed by the Clark government, and an increase in the federal government share of oil and natural gas revenues from 12 percent in 1979 to an estimated 27 percent in 1983. This increase in the federal share was to come mainly at the expense of the provincial and industry shares. The provincial share was to decline from 49 to 41 percent and that of the industry from 39 to 32 percent.[33]

Not surprisingly, the Alberta government vigorously objected to this proposed decline in its share. Premier Lougheed ordered a phased reduction of oil production to force Ottawa to change the NEP. Coupled with his attack on the reduction in the province's share was one on the decline in the industry's share. The NEP, he claimed, destroyed incentives for exploration and development of Alberta's oil resources. The industry backed him by going on a 'capital strike' against the NEP. It significantly reduced investment and sent rigs from Alberta to the United States. The industry also got the US government to bring pressure against Ottawa and especially against the Canadianization provisions of the NEP, which favored Canadian companies over foreign ones.

After much wrangling, the Alberta and federal governments reached an agreement in September 1981. Under this agreement oil prices are scheduled to rise more rapidly than under the NEP. What is more important is that the share going to the oil companies has significantly increased, mainly at the expense of Alberta. The comparative shares are shown in Table V-6 below:

Table V-6

Estimated Distribution of Revenues from Oil and Gas Production (Percent)

	Actual 1979	NEP 1983	Oil Agreement 1981-86
Federal Government	12.1	27.4	25.5
Industry	39.4	31.6	44.3
Alberta	48.5	41.0	30.2

Calculated from: Energy, Mines and Resources Canada, *The National Energy Program, 1980* (Ottawa, 1980), 108, and "Memorandum of Agreement between the Government of Canada and the Government of Alberta relating to Energy Pricing and Taxation" (1 September 1981), 22.

Thus, as in the past, the companies have turned out to be the real winners in this dispute between the federal and provincial governments. They have received both higher prices and a higher share of the increased revenues. The companies nevertheless have expressed disappointment at the energy agreement, contending that their cash flow will be insufficient to meet their future needs. In the latter part of 1981 they threatened to postpone indefinitely the tar sands and heavy oil projects unless they received concessions from both governments. This stance could provoke another dispute between Alberta and Ottawa, which might reap further benefits for the companies.

Despite their protestations, the multinational oil companies cannot be unhappy about the energy agreement. Furthermore, they cannot be unhappy that the present policy of industrialization in Alberta is oil-related. Petrochemicals are the prime example. The Alberta bourgeoisie, at least up to now, has not revealed any serious intention of developing an independent manufacturing base. They are thus making the province even more dependent on oil and weakening its future bargaining position *vis-à-vis* the oil companies.

But this may well change. Elements of the new bourgeoisie may decide to 'sow their wild oats,' to seek their independence, and go off in their own direction. The present alliance between the oil companies and the new bourgeoisie may therefore come to an end. The best laid schemes of the oil companies may "gang aft agley."

Whichever way the struggle goes, it is doubtful that Alberta's oil resources will be developed in such a way as to maximize benefits to the people of Alberta. This can be done only if: (1) the province maximizes its rent collections from the industry and (2) disburses them according to a rational plan. Professors Gainer and Powrie have suggested that "full nationalization may be the only way government can be sure to get all of its rents."[34]

Given their ideological outlook and their present alliance with the oil companies, the local bourgeoisie are not willing to nationalize the industry. They are also unwilling to establish a planning agency that would expend the funds in a rational manner. They would prefer to have full flexibility to make deals with individual corporations for joint ventures. Thus, the development that will occur will have all the evils associated with capitalist development: boom-and-bust, over-expansion in some sectors accompanied by under-expansion in others, urban blight, and the degradation of the environment. The benefits will accrue mainly to the new bourgeoisie. The working class, the farmers, and large sections of the middle class will receive, at the very most, a few crumbs. As can be seen in Table V-7, their relative shares of gross domestic product have declined since the advent of the Tories. These few crumbs will have to be matched against the decline in the quality of life, which will inevitably occur. In the jargon of the orthodox neo-classical economists, the development is bound to be "suboptimal."

In summary, the rising bourgeoisie in Alberta is engaged in a struggle to strengthen their position against both the older, more established national bourgeoisie of Canada and the bourgeoisie of the United States. While the staple and foreign factor approaches offer significant insights into the process of development in Alberta, Lenin's theory may be more appropriate because it

Table V-7

Relative Shares of Alberta's Gross Domestic Product, 1971-77 (Percent)

	Corporate Profits	Wages and Salaries	Farm Income	Small Business Income
1971	15.2	46.5	3.2	5.9
1972	16.7	45.6	3.6	5.3
1973	19.5	42.4	5.5	4.8
1974	19.9	37.3	5.2	3.6
1975	21.7	39.2	3.8	3.5
1976	19.8	41.5	2.4	3.6
1977	20.8	41.9	1.4	3.5
1978	21.1	40.2	2.3	3.2
1979	22.6	39.4	2.9	2.9

Calculated from: Statistics Canada, *Provincial Economic Accounts, Experimental Data, 1964-1979,* cat. no. 13-213 (1981) 20-21.

deals with these dynamic power relationships. In the present era of monopoly capitalism—of multinational corporations—understanding modern imperialism is the key to understanding the political economy of oil in Alberta.

Notes

[1] Calculated from: Statistics Canada, *Population, 1921-1971*, cat. no. 91-512 (Ottawa, 1973).

[2] Calculated from: Statistics Canada, *Census of Canada, Labour Force and Individual Income, Historical Labour-Force for Canada and Provinces, 1911-1971*, cat. no. 94-702 (Ottawa, November 1974), 1.1-1.4.

[3] Calculated from: Statistics Canada, *Estimates of Employees by Province and Industry,* (May 1978), 68-70; (May 1981), 22.

[4] R.O. Hirschman, *The Strategy of Economic Development* (New Haven, Conn., 1958), 102.

[5] Calculated from: Statistics Canada, *Manufacturing Industries of Canada: National and Provincial Areas, 1978*, cat. no. 31-203 (December 1980).

[6] This summary admittedly does an injustice to many of the staple theorists. As Watkins points out, Innis had some reservations about the efficacy of the staple process. (See "The Staple Theory Revisited," *Journal of Canadian Studies* [Winter 1977], 83-84 and 85-86.) The above is merely an amalgam of the views of the market-oriented staple theorists, who believe that the free market mechanism will both allocate resources optimally and bring about economic development. For further readings on the staple theory see: H.A. Innis, *The Fur Trade in Canada: An Introduction to Canadian Economic History* (Toronto, 1930) and *The Cod Fisheries: The History of an International Economy* (Toronto, 1940); W.T. Easterbrook and M.H. Watkins, eds., *Approaches to Canadian*

Economic History (Toronto, 1967), Introduction and Part 1; R. Caves, "'Vent for Surplus' Models of Trade and Growth," in R. Caves, H. Johnson, and P. Kenen, eds., *Trade, Growth and the Balance of Payments* (Chicago, 1965), 95-115 and "Export-Led Growth and the New Economic History," in J. Bhagwati et al., eds., *Trade, Balance of Payments and Growth* (Amsterdam, 1971), 403-442; and M. Roemer, *Fishing for Growth: Export-Led Development in Peru, 1950-1970* (Cambridge, Mass., 1970), 5-23.

[7]   Roemer, *Fishing for Growth*, 10.

[8]   J. Levin, *The Export Economies* (Cambridge, Mass., 1960).

[9]   Note, for example, the assumption of the "empty" land with its distinctive characteristics of a "favourable man/land ratio" and an "absence of inhibiting traditions" as discussed in M.H. Watkins, "A Staple Theory of Economic Growth," in Easterbrook and Watkins, eds., *Approaches to Canadian Economic History*, 53. See also Watkins, "The Staple Theory Revisited," 89-90.

[10]   J. Levin, "The Export Economies," in J. Theberge, ed., *Economics of Trade and Development* (New York, 1968), 24.

[11]   V.I. Lenin, *Imperialism: The Highest Stage of Capitalism* (New York, 1969), 17.

[12]   Ibid., 20.

[13]   Ibid., loc. cit.

[14]   Ibid., 62.

[15]   Ibid., loc. cit.

[16]   Ibid., 63.

[17]   In Vol. III of *Capital* Marx formulated "the law of the tendency of the rate of profit to fall" as capital accumulated. He pointed out, however, that this "tendency" can be offset by a number of influences, one of them being foreign trade. He did not mention the export of capital since that was relatively unimportant in his time. (See *Capital* [Moscow, 1959], III, chapters XIII and XIV.) Joseph Moses Gillman, in a more contemporary study of the fall rate of profit, does mention the export of capital as a counteracting influence. See *The Falling Rate of Profit: Marx's Law and Its Significance to Twentieth-Century Capitalism* (New York, 1958), 133-35.

[18]   Lenin, *Imperialism*, 26.

[19]   Ibid., 27.

[20]   Ibid., 65.

[21]   Province of Alberta, Position Paper: Tentative "Natural Resource Revenue Plan" for the Government of the Province of Alberta (April 1972), 13.

[22]   Statistics Canada has not compiled data on provincial gross domestic product for the years before 1961. Therefore, we cannot make any comparison on profits' shares before that year. We should also note that the profits are before income tax payments but after royalty payments, i.e., even after paying royalties the corporations of Alberta garnished a higher share of domestic product than corporations in the rest of Canada.

[23]   Calculated from: Statistics Canada, *Provincial Economic Accounts, Experimental Data, 1964-1979*, cat. no. 13-213 (Ottawa, 1981), 2-2, 20-21.

[24]   Ibid.

[25] Statistics Canada, *Estimates of Employees by Province and Industry*, 6, no. 12 (December 1970), cat. no. 72-008.

[26] 'Rent' in this context is understood as the residual between the cost of production of oil (including a 'normal' profit paid to capital) and the market value of oil.

[27] Alberta Energy Company, *Preliminary Prospectus Dated October 30, 1974* (Edmonton), 5.

[28] Ibid., especially 5.

[29] In January 1975, the Government of Alberta purchased 7,500,000 shares for $75,000,000 (see ibid., 22). It remained the sole stockholder until November 1975, when the AEC sold 7,500,000 shares in Alberta at $10 a share. Approximately 60,000 Albertans purchased shares.

[30] This percentage may be changed in the fiscal years after the end of the fiscal year 1976-77. See *The Alberta Heritage Savings Trust Fund Act*, sec. 5(1)(b) and (c).

[31] Ibid., sec. 6(1)(c)(i) and (ii). See also sec. 6(2)(b) and 6(3)(c).

[32] Ibid., sec. 6(4)(a) and (b).

[33] Calculated from: Energy, Mines and Resources Canada, *The National Energy Program, 1980* (Ottawa, 1980), 108.

[34] W. Gainer and T. Powrie, "Public Revenue from Canadian Crude Petroleum Production," *Canadian Public Policy*, 1 (January 1975), 8.

The Political Economy of Province-Building: Alberta's Development Strategy, 1971-1981*

Larry Pratt

If you ask them what is the meaning of their restless activity, why they are never satisfied with what they have, thus appearing so senseless to any purely worldly view of life, they would perhaps give the answer, if they know any at all: "to provide for my children and grandchildren". But more often and, since that motive is not peculiar to them, but was just as effective for the traditionalist, more correctly, simply: that business with its continuous work has become a necessary part of their lives. That is in fact the only possible motivation, but it at the same time expresses what is, seen from the view-point of personal happiness, so irrational about this sort of life, where a man exists for the sake of his business, instead of the reverse.

Max Weber

1. Introduction

This is an interpretative essay on the private purposes of public government. Its themes are the role of the state in planning and promoting Alberta's economic development since the advent to power of the Conservative government in 1971, and the synthesis of business and politics in the new West.

In what follows, the proposition is advanced that the powers and resources of an interventionist, 'positive' government are being employed to nurture the development, and to defend the province-building¹ interests of an ascendant class of indigenous businessmen, urban professionals, and state administrators. The objectives of this nascent class are to strengthen its control over the Albertan economy, to reduce Alberta's dependence on outside economic and political forces, and to diversify the provincial economy before oil and natural gas reserves are exhausted.

Driven by the dual fear of economic stagnation and encroachments by a federal government dominated by central Canadian interests, Alberta's business-state alliance supports a strong, interventionist provincial government which can perform the following functions: first, intervene in the marketplace to secure higher prices and returns for oil and gas producers, thereby creating room for the province to capture part of the windfall through higher royalties—which can in turn be used to

---

*This is a revised version of an essay which appeared in Leo Panitch, ed., *The Canadian State: Political Economy and Political Power* (Toronto: University of Toronto Press, 1977). The argument is developed in John Richards and Larry Pratt, *Prairie Capitalism: Power and Influence in the New West* (Toronto: McClelland and Stewart, 1979).

subsidize industrial diversification; second, increase its control over the supply and pricing of natural resource feedstocks, so as to gain leverage for the promotion of "forward linkage" effects; third, stand as a bulwark of 'provincial rights,' intervening where necessary to block incursions by the federal government into Alberta's economy, especially into its resource base; fourth, secure local control over transportation routes and systems as part of an effort 'to correct the mistakes of history' and to overcome the disadvantages of geography; and fifth, use the resources of the state to arrange joint ventures between multinational corporations and Alberta based businesses, thereby increasing local ownership of the economy and giving Alberta companies an entry into high growth industries such as petrochemicals and access to know-how, new markets, and technologies. It is essentially the province-building imperatives of business that lie behind the expansion of state activities in Alberta since 1971.

The leading role of the state in support of indigenous business, professional, and administrative elites has manifested itself in a variety of policy areas since about 1972. I will be discussing several of these later. Here, in the interest of avoiding misunderstanding about the argument, I want to make three important generalizations about the methods and purposes of state intervention in Alberta. First, except in circumstances of last resort, Alberta has eschewed public ownership as a mode of intervention, preferring to intervene through its unique quasi-state corporations and through joint ventures with the private sector. With this has come an ideological emphasis on the development of 'peoples' capitalism' and more local participation by Albertans in province-building. Nonetheless, the activism of the state has occasionally given rise to conservative anxieties in a community where property rights and fear of socialism are virtually a secular religion.

Second, underlying the specific instances of state intervention in Alberta, we can discern a coherent strategy of development which I would describe as the provincial equivalent of economic nationalism—the ideological emblem of a rising middle class. Closely resembling Ontario's nineteenth-century "manufacturing condition," Alberta's development strategy is to encourage local industrial processing of its energy resources and to negotiate a transfer of secondary industry, high income jobs, and decision-making from central Canada to the West. The cornerstone of this strategy is the province's attempt to foster an Albertan world-scale petrochemical complex.

Third, it must be stressed (and the case of petrochemicals well illustrates the point) that the primary target of this development strategy is central Canada. That Alberta's ascendant class perceives its development struggle as being essentially an intra-confederation affair, and that its main quarrel is with what Premier Lougheed calls "the Toronto-Montreal establishment" and "its" federal government—these are obviously true. But (and this seems to be a good deal less apparent to some observers) *within* the province the old alliance of interests and outlook between the major petroleum companies and the government of

Alberta has also been yielding to a much more fluid and ambivalent relationship. In part this is the predictable consequence of Alberta's declining potential as an oil producing region; in part it results from the province's aggressive pursuit of its own development plans. To argue that the Lougheed government is merely the instrument of outside capital is a serious error.

2. Antecedents: The Law of the Jungle and the Positive State

It is well to begin by noting that although the Crown has a strong ownership position with respect to minerals in Alberta, historically the province has rejected the option of developing its resources through government departments or Crown corporations. The norm has been public regulation of private development. When the province has seen the need to create new corporations to fulfill some social purposes, in the area of mineral resources it has invariably placed control of such enterprises in private hands. In spite of the fact that the province owns 80 percent of minerals in Alberta, "in many respects the Crown has been the passive partner of private enterprise in the development of these resources."[2]

Oil and gas are resources whose peculiar characteristics in many ways compel state intervention and regulation, and even Social Credit proved to be no exception to this rule. In the struggle for conservation of resources, in the need to regulate markets, and in the fear of encroachments by outside monopoly or the federal government Social Credit found sufficient rationale for intervention. Here it is useful to explore the origins of two of Alberta's most important economic institutions—the Energy Resources Conservation Board (ERCB, formerly the Oil and Gas Conservation Board) and Alberta Gas Trunk Line Company Ltd. (AGTL), each of which continues to play an important role in shaping the province's development.

Conservation came to Alberta in the 1930s when the oil and gas industries were still in their infancy and struggling in chaotic conditions of overproduction, inadequate markets, and unstable prices. In the Turner valley natural gas field, where a host of small producers and royalty owners had for years waged a hopeless fight against Imperial Oil and its entrenched subsidiaries, unregulated drilling and production and the flaring of natural gas resulted in a disastrous rate of depletion and a scandalous waste of energy:

The fearful flares burned night and day and turned the country into what was referred to as "hell's Half Acre", a yawning chasm that spouted flames for 14 years until Alberta established a conservation board in 1938, with enough legal powers to force operators to produce naptha and then crude oil in an orderly fashion. Until that time it proved very difficult to persuade numerous small independent operators to adopt the scientific methods of production urged by the large companies and their personnel. The latter had difficulties in applying such methods to their own properties since oil and gas are migratory and come to the surface in whatever holes are drilled in a field; the independent operators were anxious to get their investments back in as short a time as possible and drilled wells accordingly.[3]

   This situation, combined with a perverse legal tradition ascribing ownership of oil and gas only when reduced to possession (that is, the so-called "rule of capture" which, by giving ownership rights to the person who can first bring the oil and gas to surface, gives every leaseholder a legal incentive to rob his neighbour before his neighbour robs him—thus sanctioning the kind of resource development that is both profoundly anticonservationist and the antithesis of Adam Smith's maxim about each man working for the common good by working for his own gain[4]), had made the Turner valley field by the 1930s into what a disapproving provincial Royal Commission later described as "a law of the jungle."[5] Problems in the field were exacerbated in June 1936 with Alberta's first major crude oil discovery, the Turner Valley Royalties well. Two years later, following bitter public outcry against Imperial Oil's monopolistic practices in the field, the Aberhart government created the Petroleum and Natural Gas Conservation Board[6] to fix production quotas and to prevent waste, but also to stabilize an industry that seemed on the verge of open war.

   Populist pressures and a widespread demand in Alberta for a takeover of part of the industry resulted in October 1938 in the setting up of a Royal Commission charged to investigate the entire oil industry; but when the commissioners reported in April 1940, they seemed far more concerned to press home the need to eliminate "the evils of over-production" through state regulation. They commented in their report, *Alberta's Oil Industry*, "that free competition and the so-called law of supply and demand would not have served, without government interventions, to prevent shameful waste of a natural resource and to keep the industry itself from complete demoralization." While rejecting the idea of a government takeover of the industry, the commissioners argued that unrestricted competition in the oil industry "is an economic absurdity which must every so often lead to chaos and to a cry for government intervention by those who are the first to decry government intervention in normal times. We believe in unrestricted competition but not at the price of economic stability, waste of a great natural resource and a disregard for reserves in nature's reservoir."[7] Here, in a convenient conjunction of society's interest in conservation and the industry's interest in stabilization, was a classic liberal rationale for positive government.

   Greatly influenced by American ideas and legislation concerning petroleum conservation—much of which had been evolved by the major United States companies[8]—the Alberta Board was thus in position to regulate production and to stabilize relations within the Canadian industry in the wake of the great discoveries that commenced at Leduc in February 1947. Once again, the industry's oldest bogey—the spectre of over-production, falling prices, and cut-throat competition—reared its ugly head; and, when a voluntary system of market sharing broke down following the discovery of the giant Redwater field northeast of Edmonton, in December 1950, acting upon the urgent request of the industry the Conservation Board introduced the controversial practice of prorationing oil according to market demand. Market demand prorationing, first begun in Texas and Oklahoma in the 1930s, is designed to keep prices high and to promote equitable sharing of markets; in Alberta it is buttressed by the Conservation Board's legislative mandate to prevent not only the physical waste of resources but also 'economic waste' defined as "the production of oil, gas or crude bitumen in excess of proper storage facilities or of transportation and marketing facilities or of market demand."[9]

Viewed from a broad political perspective, Alberta's Conservation Board performs several important functions. First, it stands as an administrative buffer between the oil and gas industries and the Alberta cabinet, thereby permitting potentially difficult political issues to be resolved in the sheltered environment of the regulatory tribunal. Second, it performs the role of a cartel secretariat, supervising the output and allocation of production according to the industries' own rough definition of "equity." Third, it provides a forum (the National Energy Board is another) within which conflicts and grievances inside the oil and gas industries, notably those dividing independent and integrated producers, can be aired and legally resolved. The latter role is particularly significant. One of the central functions the state performs in capitalist society is to mediate and reconcile divisions within a capitalist class that is seldom, if ever, fully united as a class: In Marxist categories, the state helps to "organize the unity of the bourgeoisie." In the case of Alberta's Conservation Board, this unifying function has now been extended beyond the familiar confines of the petroleum industry. The agency was reconstituted as the Energy Resources Conservation Board in 1971 and given broad authority over the province's energy industries, including coal, electrical generation and transmission, and non-conventional petroleum resources. In 1974 the Lougheed administration empowered the ERCB to issue industrial permits for the local use of feedstocks, and thereby to regulate and promote the growth of the province's nascent petrochemical industry. Traditionally tied to the interests and outlook of oil and gas producers, Alberta's Conservation Board is thus playing a more complex role in steering the development of the province.

Alberta Gas Trunk Line—now Nova, an Alberta Corporation—had its origins in the tangled and controversial politics of natural gas exports in the 1950s. Gas export had long been a recurring and volatile issue in Alberta before exploding into the national arena in 1956 at the time of the Trans-Canada Pipe-Lines affair. That episode, which was so revealing of the inner workings of the federal political economy and of the complex demands placed upon the state at both the national and provincial levels by the rapid postwar development of Alberta's oil and gas, is far too tortuous a tale to justify another discussion here. What is worth noting, however, is that the prospect of large-scale sales of surplus gas set in motion a sweeping expansion of provincial powers over Alberta's gas reserves between 1949 and 1954, of which the formation of AGTL was but one important step. It is in part because of this strongly interventionist legacy that the Lougheed government is in the position today to use natural gas as the cornerstone of its industrial development strategy.

No issue was so contentious, so loaded with potential friction in post-Leduc Alberta as the question of exporting gas from the province. On no other policy matter did Ernest Manning's Social Credit government move with such extreme caution and trepidation. And with reason:

...gas kept the street lights on and the barn warm and the house cheerful. The vast caverns of natural gas beneath the farm or the thousands of cubic feet running by in a pipe was part of the everyday life and folklore of Alberta. God had put it there for the enjoyment of His people. Woe betide the politician who sold such a birthright.[10]

Natural gas was now widely understood to be both a cheap, clean fuel and an important industrial feedstock, and there was virtually unanimous opposition within the province to any further wastage of the resource, and much popular resistance as well to the various pipeline promoters who planned to ship it out in large quantities to eastern Canada and the United States. Both of the small but vocal opposition parties, the Liberals and CCF, opposed gas exports and the Alberta legislature saw several fierce shouting matches and melées over the issue between 1949 and 1954 (it was the main issue of the 1952 election campaign). But it cut more deeply than this. The president of the University of Alberta was speaking for an important segment of the community when he privately informed one pipeline promoter that "I may have a bit of prejudice against the proposal to export natural gas because I have always felt that this resource represented for Alberta what hydro-electric power represented to the St. Lawrence Valley. On this view it would seem unwise to sacrifice for immediate gain our long-range potentialities for industrial development."[11]

During hearings by the Dinning Commission, appointed by the province in November 1948 to investigate Alberta's gas reserves and requirements, the cities of Edmonton, Calgary, Medicine Hat, and Lethbridge, the Union of Alberta Municipalities, the provincial utility companies, the Edmonton Chamber of Commerce, the Coal Operators' Association of Western Canada, the Alberta Federation of Agriculture, the Alberta Research Council, the Alberta branch of the Canadian Manufacturers' Association, and a variety of manufacturers and small businesses all expressed varying degrees of opposition and outright hostility to the plans of the American pipeline promoters, and most insisted that Alberta's requirements be assured for at least 50 years before exports were approved (the government eventually settled for 30 years' protection). Business spokesmen wanted cheap gas protected as a catalyst for industrial growth; the Research

Council anticipated major petrochemical developments; consumers in the cities and municipalities already dependent on gas wanted their supplies assured and worried that exports would increase prices; more remote communities insisted that they be supplied before outside markets were served—in vain did the government plead that this would be wildly uneconomic; while the coal industry was fearful of the effects that gas exports could have on its already dwindling markets. Much of the opposition was expressed in strong nationalist language and the *Lethbridge Herald* was voicing popular sentiments when it argued in July 1949 that if exports were approved they "should be permitted only under strict control and not for the enrichment of absentee capitalists who have no real interest in this country."[12]

Given this protectionist opinion, a good portion of it emanating from the local business community, it is not surprising that the Manning government moved warily in dealing with the interests lobbying for early approval of gas exports. Unsure of its constitutional position and fearful that federally-incorporated pipeline companies would attempt to make individual arrangements with the major producers, in July 1949, at a stormy special session of the legislature, the government greatly strengthened its wellhead control over gas by enacting legislation protecting Alberta's requirements, prohibiting waste, and empowering the Conservation Board to control export permits.[13] The Board itself moved very cautiously and only recommended exports when established gas reserves were conservatively estimated at 6.8 trillion cubic feet, substantially in excess of the province's 30-year needs. Nevertheless, the opposition parties bitterly attacked the cabinet's decision to approve gas exports to the Pacific north-west via the Westcoast Transmission project in early 1952, and Manning evidently felt free to support the much larger Trans-Canada scheme only when he had fought and won an election on the question in that same year. Interestingly, whereas the Liberals and CCF argued that gas sales would have a negative effect on Alberta's prospects for industrialization, Social Credit argued that such industrialization would be impossible *without* gas exports: Alberta's best opportunity, Manning argued, lay in petrochemicals, an industry that would utilize the by-products extracted from natural gas before export. Failure to approve exports was "restricting an important phase of potential industrial growth," he charged, adding that with completion of Trans-Canada "we may anticipate a program of gas exploration, development, processing and industrialization that may equal or exceed the development of our vast oil resources."[14] The debate about Alberta's industrial development is thus an old one.

Impending approval of the Trans-Canada project in early 1954 necessitated a further controversial intervention by Alberta into the natural gas business. A precondition of new gas exports was the creation of a corporate instrument to defend the province from encroachments into its resource base by the federal government—to appropriate a well known concept of Aitken's,[15] what was required was a new round of "defensive expansion" by Social Credit. On constitutional grounds, the Manning government had long worried that federally incorporated and regulated pipeline companies, by extending their gathering lines into Alberta's major gas fields, could thereby also extend Ottawa's jurisdiction into Alberta and give the Dominion authorities wellhead control over the province's reserves; this, in turn, could undermine Alberta's emphasis on local priority in regard to supply and price. Fear of a marketplace under federal regulatory authority was partly behind some of the earlier interventionist legislation discussed above, and it was clearly the dominant consideration underlying the idea (first mooted in the 1949 report of the provincial Natural Gas Commission) to create a provincial monopoly over gas gathering within the province. A single grid or integrated gathering system would act as a common carrier inside Alberta, distributing pooled gas to export companies at the provincial border. This would keep gas pipelines within Alberta under exclusive provincial jurisdiction, and such a grid or trunk line could also serve the secondary community-building objective of supplying gas to outlying areas of the province.

The nature of the vehicle created by Social Credit was highly revealing of the specific ideological boundaries of post-war public enterprise in Alberta. On the one hand, the government rejected an application by the two major provincial utilities and their parent, International Utilities of New York, to build such a grid, apparently because of the concern that it would be reluctant to perform the relatively uneconomic function of supplying gas to small communities.[16] On the other hand, the cabinet also rejected legal advice that it create a Crown corporation to shield Albertan interests: "public ownership is bad in principle, worse in practice," Manning told the legislature, adding that a Crown corporation would infringe on industry rights and disturb the province's business climate.[17]

As a half-way measure, the cabinet had formulated the ingenious structure of Alberta Gas Trunk Line Company. Incorporated by an act of the legislature in April 1954, the company was confined exclusively to the business of gathering and transmitting gas and was expressly forbidden to enter into arrangements with gas exporters that could give the latter indirect control of the company. Two types of common stock, Classes A and B, were authorized: non-voting Class A shares numbering 8 million; and voting Class B shares totalling 2,002 and divided among four groups—producers, gas exporters, Alberta utilities, and the Alberta government (holding 2 shares). The Class B shares were divided and appointments to the board of directors defined so as to give an overwhelming preponderance to the producers, utilities, and government-appointed directors and to make it virtually impossible for the privately-owned company to pass into the hands of external interests such as Trans-Canada.[18] A large block of non-voting Class A shares were sold in 1957: restricted to bona fide residents of Alberta, the issue was so heavily over-subscribed that brokers and bankers had to ration sales. The emphasis on 'people's capitalism,' which was of course central to the ideology of Social Credit, quickly proved out, as the market value of the shares increased markedly.[19] And, as Trans-Canada's historian noted:

> By forming this organization Premier Manning avoided the distasteful prospect of using a government department or crown corporation to control the direction and price of Alberta gas, while at the same time he effectively achieved the same thing by keeping jurisdiction over gas-gathering pipelines within Alberta.[20]

Manning's refusal to make Trunk Line a crown corporation was, in retrospect, a crucial decision. He thereby made possible the eventual emergence of one of contemporary western Canada's largest and fastest-growing empires of indigenous private capital. Reflecting the new development priorities of Alberta under the Lougheed Conservatives in the 1970s, the company has, under a management dominated by Robert Blair and a board comprised of representatives of oil, gas, agribusiness, and the service industries as well as central Canadian banking interests, evolved well beyond its original defensive role and is engaged in a major programme of corporate expansion and diversification. With the blessing of the provincial government, Blair's Trunk Line has engaged its ancient adversary, TransCanada (now controlled by another Calgary based empire, Dome Petroleum), in a struggle for control of the Canadian gas industry and for the disposition of Alberta's large surplus of natural gas. Trunk Line's affiliate, Foothills, triumphed in 1977 over the Arctic Gas consortium of US and central Canadian companies for the right to transport Arctic gas south, and in the summer of 1978 Blair defeated both Occidental Petroleum Company and PetroCan, the national oil company, in an epic takeover fight over Husky Oil. Diversifying backward into steel, pipe production, and valve manufacturing, forward into petrochemicals, and horizontally into oil, Trunk Line has become a major force within a new *arriviste* bourgeoisie in Alberta which has broken with the constrained role in life marked out for local capital by Social Credit. But it would not have been so as a Crown company because the driving force— private accumulation—would have been missing. In creating Alberta Gas Trunk Line in response to the threat of federal encroachment, Ernest Manning himself helped set the process of regional capital accumulation in motion—an interesting instance of the unintended consequences of government intervention.

The origins of Alberta's oil conservation system and of its gas trunk line monopoly nicely illustrates some of the determinants, and also the limits, of state intervention in the oil and gas industries in post-war Alberta. The rule of capture, market failures, and the need to cartelize an unstable industry and to prevent waste led the state to intervene in order to regulate oil production in the name of conservation, while the fear of federal encroachments and pressures to give priority to local interests were the most important variables influencing the growth of government management of the natural gas industry. Unquestionably, this process contributed to the expansion of the executive arm of government—placing enormous powers in the hands of administrative agencies—and weakened the system of ministerial responsibility and accountability in Alberta. Yet it is also true that the pressures to intervene were balanced by a strong determination on the part of Social Credit to protect property rights and to ensure the kind of business stability necessary to attract outside capital. 'Businesslike management' of resources was the hallmark of the Manning era. Crown corporations were carefully avoided and so too was the sort of draconian intervention that, at least from the standpoint of rational resource management, might well have improved the efficiency of Alberta's development policies (for example, as an alternative to market demand prorationing, Alberta could have enforced compulsory utilization of oil pools, but this would have involved a large degree of interference with property rights). The fear of disturbing Alberta's 'stable business climate'—a factor that Premier Manning considered to be the province's strongest suit in competing with other oil-producing areas for new capital[21]—and the unwillingness of the cabinet to dispute the property rights of producers weakened the position of the Crown *vis-à-vis* private interests who used the powers of the state to invest business preferences with the authority of the law. Consequently, when the province finally emerged from the Social Credit era in 1971, its oil and gas industries were operating in an environment that was at once highly protective of the interests of private enterprise but also characterized by extensive government regulation of all phases of development.

3. The Lougheed Era: The Genesis of Alberta's Development Strategy
Alberta's large and growing urban middle class, nurtured by 25 years of oil and natural gas development, acceded to political power in the provincial election of August 1971. In retrospect that election, which saw Peter Lougheed's revived Progressive Conservative party take 49 seats and thereby write *finis* to the 36-year dynasty of Social Credit, represented an inevitable, though much delayed, response of the electoral system (delayed, in part, by Social credit's careful gerrymandering and the deliberate underrepresentation of the cities in the legislature) to post-war population growth, urbanization, and secularization—demographic and social trends that were underway before Leduc and accelerated by the dramatic effects of rapid oil and gas development on the provincial economy and labour force. Ironically, Social Credit's resource management policies and its discretionary spending of oil and gas rents in such areas as secondary and post-secondary education and the growth of urban municipalities helped to undermine the party's own social and political base: the rural, small-town *petite bourgeoisie* described in Macpherson's *Democracy in Alberta* at the opening of the oil boom.[22]

By 1971 Macpherson's view of Alberta as a socially homogeneous province of independent commodity producers was an anachronism. Rapid population growth and the steady migration of Albertans and other Canadians to the province's major urban centres in search of jobs commenced during World War II and has continued to the present. In 1941 approximately half the people of Alberta lived on farms and fewer than a quarter in Edmonton and Calgary; by 1971 less than 20 percent of the population was still on farms while better than 50 percent was concentrated in the two major urban centres.[23] By the opening of the seventies, a major part of Alberta's population worked in white collar occupations for large private or public institutions and rejected Social Credit's blend of agrarian populism and fundamentalism in favour of the secular values of the 'new middle class.' The failure of the Social Credit party to adapt itself to these changing social circumstances following Manning's retirement in 1968 sealed the party's fate.[24]

Under the impact of the heavy capital expenditures of the oil and gas industries, Alberta's economic base shifted in the 1950s and 1960s from its traditional dependence on agriculture to a new dependence on mineral extraction (accounting for about 35 percent of annual productivity) and oil-related construction and manufacturing. The striking impact of the new staples on the work force can be gleaned from a recent study which estimates that oil accounted for *half* the jobs created in Alberta during the 1960s, and that of the 87,000 oil created jobs more than half were in the services and trade. By contrast, relatively few jobs were created in manufacturing and these have been concentrated in satellite industries of the foreign-controlled petroleum industry. The activity of the oil and gas industries did not provide a spur for the creation of large-scale manufacturing or for Alberta's industrialization.[25] The province's generation of prosperity has been dependent, in large part, on the extraction and sale of non-renewable natural resources—as have the fortunes of its business community.

The predominant position of a few very large international companies in the development of Alberta's oil industry is well known and requires no further emphasis here. Eight companies, all of them foreign-owned, have fully integrated operations in Canada, involving exploration, production, transportation, refining, and marketing. What is less well known, however, is that by the late 1960s these major companies had shifted their exploratory operations away from Alberta to frontier regions of Canada in the search for new "elephant" pools, while the 200-plus minor operators (or independents), which tend to be involved only in exploration and production, had begun to account for up to 75-80 percent of new exploratory work in the province.[26] This was not due to any change in Alberta's policies or business climate; rather, it represented a collective decision by the majors that the limits of Alberta's oil-producing potential had been reached and that new exploratory work would bring diminishing returns. The upshot of this was that by the early 1970s it had become apparent that the majors' interest in Alberta was falling off and that the small independent companies would have to take up much of the slack if the province's prosperity was to be maintained. This fact must be constantly borne in mind when assessing Alberta's resource policy.

The dominant status of the majors notwithstanding, the many smaller operators are by no means an insignificant part of Alberta's business community. The capital spending of the majors on exploration, development, production, and pipeline equipment stimulated the growth of many oil-related businesses in the province, including drilling companies, oil service and supply companies, small manufacturers, transportation firms, and so on. Unlike the majors, such companies earn virtually all their income in Alberta and their own future is directly tied to the province's economic prospects. In addition, the expenditures of the petroleum industry spawned the development in Alberta's urban centres of a large body of educated professionals—corporate lawyers, geologists, engineers, landmen, consultants, accountants, and others—providing services of a technical and specialized nature to the oil industry and government. Another important segment of this urban elite occupies administrative positions within the public sector, particularly in government departments and regulatory agencies, such as the ERCB, charged with the job of supervising and managing the development of Alberta's resources. Confident of its administrative competence to manage the huge revenue surpluses of the 1970s and committed to provincial economic planning, this state-bureaucratic elite sees the province as the logical arena for the advancement of its career opportunities and, like its counterparts in the private sector, it is fiercely loyal to the province as a semi-sovereign economic and political unit and deeply engaged in the process of province-building. Much of the pressure to use Alberta's remaining energy resources as a catalyst for diversification appears to originate within the public bureaucracy.

It is not an exaggeration to suggest that these business-professional-bureaucratic elites have begun to make arrangements for their own future by preparing for the inevitable day when the international oil industry pulls out of Alberta. Committed to "Alberta first" in virtually all questions, these elites found many of their aspirations and fears being articulated politically for the first time by the provincial Conservative party, revived by Calgary corporate lawyer Peter Lougheed and a small coterie of professionals and businessmen in the mid-1960s. Preaching the need to reduce Alberta's dependence on outside forces, to modernize and diversify the province's oil-dependent economic base, and to enhance employment and investment opportunities for Albertans Peter Lougheed was the embodiment of the values and aspirations of a rising urban middle class impatient for change. Lougheed's cabinets have been dominated by corporate lawyers and successful small businessmen, most of the senior portfolios going to representatives of Calgary and Edmonton constituencies. More important than the location of state personnel, however, has been the direction of the government's development policies.

Since taking power in 1971, the Lougheed administration has proven itself to be markedly activist and interventionist in its economic policies. To cite but a few examples, oil and natural gas royalties have been increased dramatically; the government has increased its controls over the pricing, marketing, and utilization of energy resources; Alberta has acquired its own regional airline, Pacific Western Airlines; the Lougheed cabinet has created the Alberta Energy Company and invested equity in the giant Syncrude oil sands project; the government is diverting a portion of its huge surplus revenues into the Alberta Heritage Trust Fund for economic diversification; and the province is attempting to foster its own world-scale petrochemical industry, a venture that led the Lougheed government into unsuccessful negotiations for special tariff arrangements with the United States. More significant than any of these, however, is the emergence in Edmonton of a province-building administration committed to long-range economic planning, policy coordination, and a consistent strategy of economic development.

The essentials of Alberta's development strategy were evolved by Peter Lougheed and his closest political associates while in opposition in the late 1960s. Perceiving that the province was near maturity as an oil-producing region and that its position as a land-locked, thinly populated hinterland far from distant markets was impeding industrial growth, the Conservatives accepted the need for an activist government to steer the province's development. Rejecting the 'industrialitis' syndrome that has plagued so many of the poorer provinces such as in the maritimes, Lougheed argued the necessity of fostering 'natural' industries—such as petrochemicals and agriculture processing—out of the province's strong resource base. An internal government memorandum on this subject, dated 1974, commented that the province is at the point of transition "from a primarily extractive economy, where our resources are exported for processing to other parts of Canada and the rest of the world, to an industrialized economy which will see further processing of our raw materials, increased manufacturing and...satisfying employment opportunities for Albertans." But, the document cautions, unless the government manages growth and steers the economy in desired directions, this transition might not occur and the province could become even more dependent on its natural resources.[27] Alberta's industrial strategy seems to be rooted partly in the implicit assumption that regional economic growth typically occurs in a unilinear sequence of "stages of growth," the region evolving from a subsistence economy through the exploitation of its resources to the early and advanced states of industrialization. A failure to make the transition to a modern industrial economy, according to this viewpoint, dooms the region to stagnation and decay as emigration results and living standards fall.[28]

Where should one seek the determinants of Alberta's push for diversification in the 1970s? A major source appears to lie in the status and occupational drives of dissatisfied elites who would transform the province from a peripheral into an industrial core area where power, wealth, and attractive careers are located.

These elites view the West as an exploited dependency of central Canada: confederation and its political and economic arrangements are perceived to be the instruments of Ontario and Quebec interests, the heritage of Macdonald's National Policy. Discontent with such issues as the lack of secondary industry on the prairies, the practices of Canada's financial institutions, national freight rates, tariffs, and federal taxation of the resource industries, comments one observer, "can be seen as a mixture of dissatisfaction with the inevitable fate of a small region in a market economy, and unhappiness with distortions in such a system initiated or a least tolerated by the federal government."[29] Prairie economic alienation is essentially the quarrel of hinterland elites with a market economy, but, probably inevitably, regional protest tends to focus on federal policies that are believed to buttress distortions and on demands for various kinds of remedial state intervention. A familiar western grievance, for example, is that national tariffs, federal purchasing policies, freight rates, and so on conspire to obstruct the normal evolution of economic development on the prairies.

Underlying the quarrel of Lougheed's Alberta with the market economy and with Ottawa is an assumption, verified by historical experience, that the West's narrow economic base, its vast distance from the major population centres of North American, and its dependence on outside capital, communications, transportation, and volatile commodity markets have produced a society whose well-being and security are precarious, always at the mercy of decisions taken by outsiders. This is compounded by an acute awareness of Alberta's reliance on the oil and gas industries. "Since entering public life over nine years ago," Lougheed told the Calgary Chamber of Commerce in 1974, "my theme has been that this province's economy is too *vulnerable*, it is too dependent upon the sale of depleting resources, particularly oil and natural gas for its continued prosperity." Alberta had a decade to diversify, Lougheed argued, adding that the government's development strategy was rooted in three fundamental objectives:

The first one is to strengthen the control by Albertans over our own future and to reduce the dependency for our continued quality of life on governments, institutions or corporations directed from outside the province. Secondly, to do this as much as possible through the private sector and only to move through the public sector if the private sector is not in a position to move in essential new directions and then only in exceptional and very specific circumstances. And thirdly, to strengthen competitive free enterprise by Albertans which to us means giving priority to our locally-owned businesses. Our basic guidepost [is] to maximize the number of our citizens controlling their own destiny.[30]

This 'economic provincialism' has great political appeal among local businessmen and professionals and, taken to its extreme, manifests itself in the activities and studies of the neo-separatist Independent Alberta Association. Lougheed's declared intentions to shift economic power to the West from central Canada should be interpreted, in part, as an expression of the desire of the Alberta business community to be liberated from its traditional dependence on eastern financial interests. "Half the businessmen you meet," comments one journalist of Alberta, "from Carl Nickle, whose father was a Calgary shoe salesmen who became enormously rich during the first oil strikes of the 1940s, to Don Getty (Minister of Energy and Natural Resources in Lougheed's second cabinet), who was born in the East but made his millions in oil during the 1960s before turning to politics—talk bitterly of how they were treated by officials in banks and investment houses on Bay or St. James Streets when they went there seeking development money."[31] This hostility has been strongly reinforced by new federal resource taxation policies (such as the oil export tax, 1973) and by decisions of the Supreme Court of Canada which have been generally interpreted in Alberta (and Saskatchewan) as thinly-disguised attempts by Ottawa to undermine the oil-producing provinces' jurisdiction and to gain indirect control of their energy resources. Business anxiety over further federal encroachments and interventions into the oil and gas industries provides the Alberta government and its regulatory arms with a powerful base of support for market interventions undertaken in defence of provincial rights. The Alberta business elite supports a positive, strong state at the provincial level as a buffer against a predatory national government.

Fear of economic stagnation provides a second crucial support for state intervention. Alberta's elites are well aware that the booming economic conditions of the 1970s have been essentially a function of rising demand for non-renewable oil and gas reserves; and the fact that production from most of the province's major conventional oil fields has begun to decline has created some anxiety among businessmen and professionals—many of whose families, certainly Peter Lougheed's, were hard-hit by the Great Depression. Uncertainty about the future gave Alberta business an incentive in the early 1970s to overcome its conservative dislike of bureaucracy and 'big government' and to support a regime dedicated to the planning and promotion of an economy less dependent on resource extraction and less under the control of outside institutions and, on the condition that the province resists the temptation to set up Crown corporations to compete with private enterprise (the purchase of Pacific Western Airlines and the creation of the Alberta Energy Company each produced some uneasy stirrings in local business circles), the Alberta business community still perceives that it has much to gain by supporting an activist government that is willing to use its powers in support of such objectives as: restricting the power and bargaining rights of labour; ensuring "fair market value" for oil and gas producers; diverting a share of rising resource revenues into capital funds for economic diversification; processing of more resources in Alberta; securing local control over western transportation routes; offsetting the costs of geography by holding down provincial gas prices; establishing a tax incentive system favorable to small businesses; and maintaining a business climate favorable to new foreign investment while insisting on various forms of 'participation' by Alberta businesses and investors in the ownership and control of major projects.

Closely resembling turn-of-the-century Ontario's "manufacturing conditions,"[32] the strategy of development being pursued in Alberta puts great emphasis on the processing and upgrading of resources at the source. By increasing its control over the pricing, supply, and utilization of feedstocks (particularly natural gas), the state can reduce the export of raw materials—and jobs—to markets in eastern Canada and the United States and promote forward linkages in the Alberta economy. A viable manufacturing sector, based on the processing of resources at the source, will, it is argued, attract new advanced technologies to the province, assist the development of a skilled industrial labour force, and stimulate the growth of related industries. Alberta's leaders believe that the world energy crisis, and the shift in bargaining power from consumers to producers, gives the province the leverage it requires to make the transition to a modern industrial economy. Using Alberta's large but depleting conventional reserves of oil and natural gas as bargaining tools, in a situation of energy scarcity with consumers increasingly concerned about the availability and security of future supplies, an aggressive government can negotiate a transfer of industry, high income jobs, and power from the central Canadian heartland to the West. This is what lay behind Alberta's lengthy struggle with Ottawa and Ontario over the future of the petrochemical industry in Canada. Lougheed argued that here Alberta has "a natural economic advantage over other areas since the importance of assured feedstocks under current energy conditions is becoming as significant as proximity to markets," and that the chemical industry offers the province the promise of high income jobs and important opportunities for small businessmen.[33] However, Ottawa's support for a rival Sarnia based project (Petrosar) jeopardized Alberta's petrochemical plans and constituted in the eyes of Premier Lougheed and his supporters yet another sorry episode in the historical exploitation of the West.

4. "Alberta First": The Uses of the State
Within the context of these economic development plans, the Lougheed government has exploited its constitutional powers to the fullest possible extent since about 1972-73 in an effort to impede aggrandizing moves by Ottawa and to protect its control over its natural resource base. Fear of federal encroachments and distrust of a market economy under outside control have manifested themselves in a series of interventions, virtually all of which have been justified in the name of Alberta private enterprise. The objectives of state intervention are best understood through a brief exegesis of several related policy themes.

First, "Alberta First" is the key to understanding the province's highly protective natural gas policies. Albertans tend to view natural gas as a special birthright or natural endowment and since 1949 the province has strictly controlled the production, sale and utilization of gas through such legislation as The Gas Resources Preservation Act. The strong opposition in Alberta to the wastage or export of the resource after World War II was a logical precursor to the policies of the present administration. These policies begin from the premise that Albertans have hitherto been denied a just return for the depletion of their gas reserves, including the opportunity to utilize the resource as a catalyst for industrial development, and that outsiders have earned a disproportionate share of the benefits from the exploitation of the province's gas.

Following a comprehensive study of the field pricing of Alberta natural gas, the Energy Resources Conservation Board concluded in 1972 that the prevailing prices were substantially below commodity value (that is, the value of equivalent energy in competing forms, such as oil, in the same market), and argued that a lack of competition among gas purchasers was the vital cause of underpricing.[34] Acting on the Board's recommendations, the Lougheed cabinet quickly intervened on the side of gas producers to challenge Trans Canada Pipelines' monopsonistic (buyer's monopoly) position. Approval was withheld from new applications to remove gas from the province until prices increased substantially, and the province amended its arbitration legislation governing the redetermination of gas prices paid by pipelines to producers: such prices are now to be redetermined every two years on the basis of full commodity value.[35] These steps, which were vigorously opposed and protested by Ontario—the target of Alberta's interventions—have had an enormous impact on gas pricing in Canada, but the Lougheed government has thus far sheltered Alberta consumers from the full effects of the increases through its two-price policy of natural gas rebates.[36]

Natural gas is regarded as the basis of Alberta's future industrialization, and this has shaped the province's attitude to the use of feedstocks. Alberta's world-scale petrochemical complex, involving Alberta Gas Trunk Line, Dome Petroleum, and Dow Chemicals in a complicated joint venture, is to be based on ethylene manufactured from ethane, a natural gas by-product. Under legislation enacted in 1974 the ERCB now has the power to issue industrial development permits, subject to cabinet approval, and thus can control the utilization of gas within Alberta. The Board also retains the authority, again subject to cabinet approval, to issue permits for the removal of gas judged to be surplus to the province's own 30-year needs, and there is every reason to think that these powers will be exploited to the full as Alberta bargains for concessions and tradeoffs in the area of industrial development in return for its approval for new sales of natural gas.

Second, Alberta has sought to increase its share of the revenues from its depleting stock of natural resources in the interest of diversification. The province's dependence on outside capital can be mitigated by a more aggressive acquisition of resource rents. One of the earliest initiatives of the Lougheed government—its 1972 "Natural Resource Revenue Plan"—sought to raise petroleum royalties fixed at a maximum of 16 2/3 percent in longterm leases. Concerned over rising government expenditures, the shifts of the majors into the frontier regions, and a declining life-index of reserves, the province determined to raise its royalties by imposing a new tax on mineral rights; this was combined with a new system of drilling incentives "designed to benefit those operators who actually undertake exploration for crude oil in Alberta."[37] The incremental revenues would be used "to stimulate substantial diversification of the Alberta economy over the next 10 to 15 years":

The Government is aware that, as the conventional crude oil industry reaches maturity in Alberta, economic growth of the Province may tend to level off unless new and imaginative programs are initiated soon to diversify the Alberta economy along logical courses.

Diversification of a significant nature will be difficult for a number of reasons, not the least of which are our relatively 'thin' consumer markets and transportation hurdles which affect the cost of inbound material and outbound products. It is the position of the Government that, in the Alberta public interest, significant expanded sources of Government revenues must begin to flow into the provincial treasury now in order to provide part of the funds for new programs specifically designed for such diversification...to help finance industry for Albertans. Clearly, revenues from a depleting natural resource are an appropriate source of such funds.[38]

However, the prospect of increased federal taxation of Alberta's resources—first through the oil export tax; later in the elimination of provisions allowing resource companies to deduct provincial royalties when calculating their federal income tax—jeopardized these development plans. Predictably, federal encroachments resulted in a vigorous, albeit defensive, expansion of the province's own powers. In a decision that startled the oil industry, in the fall of 1973 the Lougheed cabinet suddenly scrapped its new royalty plan—the subject of months of careful negotiation with industry—and announced that royalties would henceforth rise with international oil prices.[39] The province's objective was evidently to force Ottawa to withdraw its oil export levy by squeezing the oil industry; damage done to the industry could be repaired by Alberta later on. In a striking departure from the long established practice of prior consultation, this decision was taken with no advance discussion with representatives of the oil industry.[40] In December 1973 the province also created the Alberta Petroleum Marketing Commission, a Crown corporation with broad powers relating to oil pricing. To date, the Commission has had little influence on prices, which are presently set through federal-provincial agreement, but its powers could be called upon in the future.[41]

Not surprisingly, Alberta's aggressive defence of its jurisdiction and its development plans set the province on a collision course with the international oil industry. Between September 1973 and September 1975 the average well head price of Alberta crude oil increased from $3.80 a barrel to $8.00 a barrel. Alberta's percentage take on an average barrel (royalties plus provincial income tax) increased from 24 percent to 39 percent, while the private producer's share of revenue declined from 51 percent to 34 percent. That many companies increased their net income in these two years does not alter the fact that the lion's share of the incremental revenues from rising prices went to Alberta—a point that the consuming provinces have oft noted in opposing new price increases.

Following Ottawa's 1974 decision to eliminate the deductibility of provincial royalties in the calculation of taxable income, the major petroleum companies (after consultations with the federal government) confronted the western producing provinces with a well coordinated capital 'strike'—withdrawing drilling rigs, cancelling new investments, laying off employees and, in the case of Saskatchewan, launching legal proceedings designed to test the constitutionality of provincial legislation. In Alberta this campaign took on the air of staged melodrama, culminating in February 1975 with the salvaging of the giant Syncrude oil sands project (rescued with vast federal subsidies to Alberta and the private members of the consortium), but it nonetheless threatened many of the province's small oil-dependent businesses with sudden recession.⁴² The Lougheed government came under severe pressure from the province's business community and the media, and was forced in December 1974 to reduce its royalties through a new exploration incentives scheme. Ottawa thereby demonstrated its ability to drive a wedge between Alberta and the oil industry. While this episode certainly confirmed the vulnerability of the province to pressures from the oil industry (while simultaneously confirming Lougheed's own presentiments about Alberta's extended dependence on oil), perhaps the most revealing fact about this conflict was that the majors had found it necessary to use such coercive methods in order to prevail.

Relations between the Lougheed government and the integrated oil companies have improved markedly in the booming years since 1975, thanks in part to new discoveries and to the province's royalty rebate and drilling incentives programmes. But it would be quite mistaken to conclude from this that the Conservative regime is merely the 'instrument' of foreign/monopoly capital. These changes at the political level have forced the dominant foreign-controlled resource industries to reassess their relations with the western provincial regimes that took power in Edmonton and Regina at the start of the 1970s. Traditional provincial-corporate alliances, used so successfully at the close of the 1960s to defeat federal tax reform, were weakened during the 1973-74 crisis. The opportunity costs of inertia were deemed to be so high, and the jurisdictional threat of federal actions so great, that the provinces threw caution to the winds and unilaterally abrogated their regulatory regimes. Since capital, like perfidious Albion, has neither permanent allies not permanent enemies, only permanent interests, it was natural that the multinational companies turned to Ottawa for support.

Third, there are direct links between Alberta's development strategy and its highly defensive position on constitutional questions. The constitutional issues are by no means academic, even if the arguments used by the proponents of provincial and federal rights often border on the metaphysical. Given the constitutional limitations on their legislative powers, the ability of the provinces to advance their separate paths of development is not open-ended, despite Crown ownership of resources. The Crown *as owner* can do little more than the private owner of a resource can and, since 1973, the western provinces have sought, through legislation and administrative orders, to strengthen their positions as proprietors. In doing so, they have come into conflict with both corporate interests and the federal government; and Saskatchewan has lost two very important Supreme Court of Canada judgments, on the grounds that it had invaded federal powers over taxation (*CIGOL*) or trade and commerce (*CENTRAL CANADA POTASH*). In both these cases, Ottawa intervened directly on the side of the corporate interests, while Alberta and a number of other provinces backed Saskatchewan. Lougheed's administration has shared the fears of Saskatchewan that the Supreme Court is pursuing, to use Premier Allan Blakeney's words, "a more activist, centralist role than its predecessors in creating policy through judicial decisions." Blakeney's charge that Ottawa has been engaged since the mid-seventies in a campaign through the courts "to limit and abridge the clear constitutional rights of the provinces in dealing with resources" reflects Alberta's position as well. There are sound reasons, it turns out, for Alberta's anxiety.

Several critical pieces of Alberta's regulatory legislation for oil and gas appear to rest upon dubious constitutional foundations. Consider, for instance, the Alberta Petroleum Marketing Act of 1973, passed as part of the province's campaign against the federal oil export tax. This act set up the Alberta Petroleum Marketing Commission, a provincial Crown corporation with broad powers relating to the sale of oil produced from Alberta Crown-owned leases. Traditionally, Alberta's leases transferred ownership of oil at the wellhead from the province to the producing firm. Once this occurred, the province lost its proprietary rights over these resources, including its power to influence the pricing, processing, and marketing of Crown-owned oil. An objective of the marketing act was to assert the province's control of oil *after* production at the wellhead by requiring all producers to sell their oil through the Commission and by providing that the royalty share of oil produced on Crown leases remains the property of the province. These powers have not yet been used, but the Commission reportedly intends to adopt a more activist role in marketing to ensure that new petrochemical industries locating in Alberta can be given priority in the provision of feedstocks. The oil industry frowns on any movement by government to interfere with its traditional control over the marketing of oil in

Canada, and any attempt to implement an "Alberta first" policy that discriminated against industrial consumers in, say, Ontario, could well provoke a constitutional challenge. Such a challenge would almost certainly succeed. Since the CIGOL and CENTRAL CANADA POTASH decisions there are new ambiguities concerning the legal status of Alberta's post-1974 royalties and its oil prorationing scheme—ambiguities that have driven the Lougheed government into the constitutional fray in the quest for far more stringent guarantees over provincial resource ownership and jurisdiction.

Finally, the cornerstone of Alberta's economic diversification strategy and the area in which a great deal of its available entrepreneurship, public and private, is being committed is the petrochemical industry. The strategy is based on classic development economics. First, use the powers of the state to retard the export of valuable raw materials and their by-products, then upgrade the feedstocks locally through an integrated complex of processing and derivative plants, thereby fostering a forward-linked manufacturing industry out of the province's resource base—attracting new technologies, building a highly skilled labour force, and creating additional spinoff benefits through the growth of related "downstream" industrial activities. In common with other oil exporters, Alberta holds the view of petrochemicals as a logical step forward from an export-dependent petroleum economy. And, like other producers, Alberta has argued that the emergence of scarcity conditions in world energy markets since the early 1970s fully justified the effort to force a transfer of this industry from its traditional location in central Canada to the resource-exporting area.

Alberta's world-scale petrochemical complex began to come on stream in 1980, and expansion has continued through the first two years of the present decade, despite the appearance of the worst international recession since World War II. Nova Corporation, which initiated the push into petrochemicals, has emerged, typically in partnership with multinationals such as Shell and Dow Chemicals, as the dominant corporate actor in Alberta's chemical industry; and this, combined with Nova's control of Husky Oil, has protected Nova from a serious downturn in the provincial gas industry. Ironically, Nova's strategy of corporate diversification was originally intended to move the company away from its heavy dependence on revenues from a depleting reserve base; but, as things have turned out, the gas industry has slumped because of a glut of newly discovered reserves and a decline in demand for Alberta gas in the US market.

Whether Alberta's newly established petrochemical industry will prove to be economically viable in the face of recession and competition from abroad, or whether it will suffer a serious contraction (not unlike the crisis that overtook the Saskatchewan potash industry in the late 1960s) requiring extensive subsidies from the state, is still impossible to say. There is some evidence that the province has already provided considerable subsidy to chemical producers via the sale of gas feedstocks priced below the regulated price prevailing in the Canadian market (which in turn is substantially beneath the export price for gas). In the event of a major crisis, the industry would either have to be permitted to contract or the province would have to step in with extensive financial subsidies. The burden of either choice would, of course, fall on the workers, communities, and taxpayers of the province. The plants themselves appear to achieve full pay-out in a matter of two or three years, a remarkably short period, and the risk to the private partners of a severe contraction is thus minimal.

As to the larger issue of whether the Lougheed government would attain its goal of diversifying the Alberta economy, by the early 1980s it was becoming clear that the strategy was not—chemicals notwithstanding—likely to succeed, and that the Conservatives themselves had begun to disown the entire idea. Most of the available economic indicators suggest that the Albertan economy has become more, not less, dependent on the primary extractive industries, especially crude oil and natural gas, since the early 1970s; and it is also evident that the dependence of the provincial government itself on revenues from the oil and gas industries has grown. Probably this was in part the inevitable outcome of provincial and federal policies that have encouraged the search for new petroleum and gas reserves (rich incentives can bid capital and labour away from other activities); but to a greater extent the failure of diversification simply reflects the impact of larger economic forces over which no Canadian government has had much control. The shift in the terms of trade towards energy producers in the early 1970s, driven by the rising short-term demand for oil in all advanced capitalist countries, has increased specialization: in the short run at least, the staple sector grows by attracting capital and labour away from other sectors. Norrie and Percy have shown, in a study prepared for the Economic Council of Canada,[43] that while the West as a whole, and Alberta in particular, have experienced a relative economic gain since about 1973, the changes in their share of economic activity have really been surprisingly small. They found no evidence to suggest that the four western provinces are in the midst of diversifying beyond areas of traditional comparative advantage (staples) into ones more directly competitive with those of central Canada. There has been little if any "structural shift," and any growth in manufacturing and services that is evident appears to be directly tied to the expansion of the primary sector, especially the energy industries. They also conclude, it is worth noting, that the slower growth rates and economic problems that have plagued central Canada in recent years have not been caused by the energy boom in the West. If anything, the East has done better than it would otherwise have done because it has had access to western oil supplies at prices substantially below those prevailing in the world market.

In any event, it seems clear that Alberta's strategy of economic diversification has not succeeded, and this perhaps explains why Premier Lougheed has stopped talking about the issue. Although the Heritage Fund was originally established in 1976 with a dual focus—to act as a savings fund and thus to hold down personal taxes, and to be available as a tool for diversification—Mr.

Lougheed has more recently argued that the latter objective was never the real purpose of the Fund. This may in fact be true, for there is nothing in the existing portfolio of the Fund that seems to promote the cause of industrial diversification. The provincial New Democratic Party has argued that the Heritage Fund should now be scrapped altogether and replaced with an "Alberta Development Fund" whose primary purpose would be that of diversification. Whether the NDP would be able to overcome the many barriers to diversification of the prairie economy seems doubtful; there are certainly some good prospects, but the Saskatchewan CCF failed miserably in its efforts to diversify that province's economy in the late 1940s, precisely because they insisted on ignoring the area's real natural strengths and attempted to engage in import substitution.

Apart from its difficulties in reshaping the economic base of the province, the Alberta government has also had to contend with the growth of federal intervention in the energy sector, and especially with the 1980 National Energy Program of the federal Liberals. Although, as we have seen, Alberta has encountered and resisted federal interventions after 1973, these had been of a mostly *ad hoc* nature. By contrast, the NEP was comprehensive and coordinated, and it thus reflected the growing assertiveness of the federal authorities in the energy sector.

5. Alberta and the National Energy Program

The complete origins of the NEP lie well outside the scope of this chapter, but the motivations of the Trudeau government were reasonably straightforward.[44] Through a new package of pricing, taxation, and 'Canadianization' measures, the federal Liberals hoped to accomplish three related goals: (1) to expand their political control over the oil and gas industries and to improve the federal fiscal position; (2) to lower the costs of entry by Canadian capital into the profitable and dynamic oil and gas sector, and to encourage the formation of large Canadian-controlled oil companies, and; (3) to stimulate the development of the "Canada Lands"—the federally-owned lands in the North and the offshore areas. To these ends, the Liberals proposed a radical restructuring of the oil and gas industries and a major shift in oil and gas investments away from the conventional producing areas of western Canada. The NEP established a new "blended pricing" regime for conventional oil, a mechanism for shifting the costs of oil import subsidies to oil consumers from the federal treasury, new federal taxes on oil and gas production, expanded federal public ownership and state participation in the oil and gas industries, and a radically different system of incentives for petroleum exploration and development. The NEP was interventionist, centralist, and nationalistic, and it challenged virtually all of the political and economic assumptions underlying Alberta's strategy of development. In effect, the Trudeau Liberals intended to establish federal primacy in the entire energy field and to replace Alberta as the oil and gas industry's principal 'patron.'

Whether the Alberta government could have avoided the unilateral imposition of these measures by negotiating more flexibly with the Trudeau government or its predecessor, the short-lived Conservative administration of Joe Clark, is a matter on which opinions will differ. The view of this writer, discussed in detail elsewhere,[45] is that Premier Lougheed virtually invited drastic federal intervention by staking his entire negotiating position on the principle of provincial resource ownership. As owner of the resource, Alberta appeared to argue throughout the long and difficult prelude to the NEP in 1979 and 1980, the *province* would determine what 'share,' if any, the federal government would receive from the development of Alberta's oil and gas. The fiscal position of the national government, which had come under enormous pressure from the cost of subsidizing oil imports and oil-related equalization payments after 1979, was not even to be matter for discussion in the energy talks. Alberta's only published offer to the federal government, dated July 1980, called for moving Canadian oil prices to 75 percent of the world or Chicago price by 1985 with no change in existing royalty arrangements, and went on to require "that the federal government respect the ownership rights of the province by not imposing: (a) a tax on natural gas exports, (b) a wellhead tax on either oil or natural gas." Ottawa, the province argued, must obtain its revenues via taxes on oil industry profits, and not through any form of direct federal taxation on the province's resources. To the federal government, which seems to have been more interested in revenues than in the constituional debate over provincial property, Alberta's position was unacceptable, and after July 1980 a crisis was probably unavoidable. Alberta shared a good measure of the responsibility for this.

Alberta responded to the NEP by reducing conventional oil production by 15 percent (in three, phased cutbacks), by withholding approval for the big Alsands and Cold Lake non-conventional oil projects, and by launching court action against the federal tax on natural gas. The provincial government, backed by the governments of Saskatchewan and British Columbia, also sought to isolate the federal Liberals by finding allies among several of the non-producing provinces and influential sections of Canadian (and foreign) capital. By refusing to approve the new oil sands projects, for example, Alberta gained some leverage over the Canadian steel industry and over central Canadian manufacturers eager to win new contracts for the construction of the Alsands and Cold Lake plants. Thus, the Canadian Manufacturers Association criticized the NEP on the grounds that lower-than-world oil prices would damage the prospects for self-sufficiency in oil. The major chartered banks, anticipating a massive capital investment boom in new energy projects, were particularly outspoken in their attacks on the NEP. And Alberta itself came under enormous political pressure to compromise from small oil and gas producers, the oil service sector (drilling companies, suppliers, etc.), and those businesses and municipalities expecting to benefit from oil sands development.

Whether by deliberate design or not, the NEP also opened up a breach between the Lougheed government and several of the rising stars of the Canadian oil industry, notably Dome Petroleum and Nova Corporation. Unlike many of the smaller Alberta based oil and gas producers, the larger Canadian firms had extensive investments and commitments beyond Alberta's borders, and they also stood to benefit from the NEP in a number of important ways: Canadian-controlled oil companies investing on federal lands can get the state to bear virtually all of the exploration costs and a significant amount of the costs of development as well. The NEP expands Petro-Canada's presence in the oil and gas industries, but it also encourages the growth of large privately-owned Canadian oil corporations as well. While many of the smaller independent Canadian companies (who lack the finances and asset base to participate in the frontier plays) voted against the federal energy programme by shifting their exploration programme to the United States, the larger Canadian firms (Dome, Nova, Pan-Canadian, Norcen, Petro-Canada, CDC Oil and Gas, etc.) responded by acquiring foreign-owned companies and by reallocating their investments from the West to the Canada Lands in the North and eastern offshore.[46] The Lougheed government was visibly angered by the defection of Alberta-grown companies such as Nova (in fact, Nova only gave qualified support to the NEP and balanced this with proposals to "assure permanently" provincial ownership of resources), and some observers suggested that it may have been deliberate Liberal strategy to detach the larger regional oil companies from Alberta's Conservative government and support for provincial rights. In any event, the new western bourgeoisie has few permanent political loyalties—a characteristic it shares with capital everywhere.

In September 1981 Alberta and the federal government signed a five-year energy pricing agreement (EPA), under whose terms Canadian oil prices are scheduled to rise much more rapidly towards world levels than under the NEP. Whereas the NEP gave the lion's share of the available rents from conventional oil and gas to consumers (via low prices) the complicated EPA appeared mainly to benefit producers and the federal government; both Alberta and the federal government were able to improve their revenue positions at the expense of consumers, and the industry appeared (despite its usual disclaimers) to improve its position slightly. The agreement seemed likely to promote a somewhat more efficient pattern of energy development (unlike the NEP, it did not favour high-cost over low-cost resources), and both sides won some political points. The producing provinces were able to argue that they had successfully beaten off a federal invasion of their jurisdiction, and Ottawa had won the Lougheed government's grudging endorsement of its Canadianization programme.

In the aftermath of the National Energy Program, one thing is certain. Alberta will now have to live with a greatly expanded presence in the Canadian oil and gas industries; Ottawa has by its own design become the 'senior' level of government so far as the petroleum industry is concerned, and there is little a provincial government can do about it. Politically, this has left Alberta's Conservatives in a rather vulnerable position. On the right wing of Alberta's political spectrum, Lougheed has been castigated as a 'sell-out' for having signed *any* energy agreement with the Liberals, and there have even been signs of political unrest within the ruling Conservative party over the terms of the pact with Ottawa. The surprising victory of a western separatist candidate in the Olds-Didsbury by-election in February 1982 was widely interpreted as a strong protest vote directed as much against the provincial government as against Ottawa. Whether the separatists could mount an effective grass-roots challenge to Lougheed's political hegemony on the basis of this single victory seems doubtful—Alberta in 1982 is not the Alberta of 1935—but the electoral history of the province has been such that one cannot rule out a sudden shift in voter affiliations, especially in the rural parts of southern and central Alberta. As this article has stressed, however, Alberta is now overwhelmingly an urbanized white collar society, and the appeals of separatism may be somewhat limited beyond Olds-Didsbury and a handful of other constituencies. The immediate prospect is that the Lougheed government will make a sharp turn to the right in order to contain the separatist sentiment within and without his own party.

6. Conclusion

Alberta's economic provincialism, with its stress on the use of the state to foster an indigenous industrial-technological core, must be interpreted as the frustrated reaction of elites in a hinterland region to the uneven diffusions of growth that are characteristics of a market economy. In a capitalist setting, where the regional distribution of industry is a question resolved essentially according to profit-maximizing principles, the normal tendency is for industry, economic activity, and wealth to concentrate around growth centres, and for the rate of growth of wealth and economic activity at these centres to be faster than the diffusion of growth to peripheral regions. According to one student of economic location, this uneven development "will normally be accompanied by a series of dis-placements, from the periphery to the center of the principal factors of produc-tion: labour, capital, entrepreneurship, foreign exchange, and raw materials in unprocessed form."[47]

Such unevenness and its accompanying displacements often have important political implications as well, producing a frustrated sense of dependency and subordination among elites in the periphery which aspire to the top but feel blocked. This frustration typically vents itself in some variant of economic nationalism, which, as Karl Polanyi pointed out, emerges historically as a protective response to market forces.[48] Economic nationalism reflects the desire of a peripheral political, cultural, or ethnic group to possess and enjoy an industrial core of its own where wealth, attractive careers, and power are located. "Its objective is to transform this division of labour through industrialization and to transform its territorial base into a relatively independent industrial core."[49]

Viewed from this perspective, the industrial underdevelopment of western Canada is the normal fate of a small and thinly populated region in a market economy. And Alberta's interventionist development strategy is a predictable rejection of market forces that have created a division of labour between an industrialized core and the "hewers of wood and drawers of water" of the periphery. Its present policies reflect the anxieties and aspirations of a dependent business community and an ascendent urban middle class, neither of which seek the elimination of the market economy—merely promotion within it. It is the relentless pressure of these dissatisfied groups, combined with the impact of the international energy crisis on the Canadian political economy, that makes Alberta a "province pas comme les autres."

Notes

1 On the theme of 'province-building,' of E.R. Black and A.C. Cairns, "A Different Perspective on Canadian Federalism," *Canadian Public Administration*, IX, no. 1 (March 1966), 27-45.

2 M. Crommelin, "Government Management of Oil and Gas in Alberta," *Alberta Law Review*, XIII, no. 2 (1975), 146.

3 E.J. Hanson, *Dynamic Decade* (Toronto, 1958), 47.

4 The rule of capture and related theories of ownership of oil and gas are discussed in the large body of writings on petroleum law, property rights, etc. A useful analysis is in D.F. Lewis and A.R. Thompson, *Canadian Oil and Gas*, vol. 1 (Toronto, 1971); also E.J. Hanson and E.H. Shaffer, Economics of Oil and Gas," in John Chant, ed., *Canadian Perspectives in Economics* (Toronto, 1972).

5 *Alberta's Oil Industry:* The Report of a Royal Commission appointed by the Government of the Province of Alberta under The Public Inquiries Act to inquire into matters connected with Petroleum and Petroleum Products, Chairman Hon. A.A. McGillivray (April 1940).

6 The Oil and Gas Resources Conservation Act (1938): *Alberta Statutes (1938).*

7 *Alberta's Oil Industry.*

8 American influence on Alberta's thinking about petroleum conservation can be seen in the McGillivray Commission's *Report* of 1940. On the US history, see R. Engler, *The Politics of Oil* (Chicago, 1967), especially chapter 6; H.F. Williamson et al., *The American Petroleum Industry: The Age of Energy 1899-1959* (Evanston, Ill., 1963), chapters 9 and 15; H.M. Larson et al., *New Horizons: History of Standard Oil Co. (New Jersey) 1927-1950* (New York, 1971), 80-93; and L.M. Logan, Jr., *Stabilization of the Petroleum Industry* (Normal, Okla., 1930).

9 The board was given the power to proration to market demand in amendments to conservation law passed by the legislature in July 1949. The Board instituted it in 1950. Alberta's conservation policies are discussed in *Alberta Law Review: Petroleum Law Supplement*, VII, no. 3 (1969); and in M. Crommelin et al., *Management of Oil and Gas Resources in Alberta: An Economic Evaluation of Public Policy*, University of British Columbia, Department of Economics Discussion paper no. 76-19. See also J. Richards and L. Pratt, *Prairie Capitalism: Power and Influence in the New West* (Toronto, 1979),

on the influence of US precedents on Albertan and Saskatchewan resource conservation policies.

10 W. Kilbourn, *Pipeline* (Toronto, 1970), 18-19.

11 R. Newton to J. Walker (Northwest Natural Gas Co.), 31 January 1949. University of Alberta Government Publications. *Report of the Province of Alberta Natural Gas Commission*, Chairman R.J. Dinning (1949).

12 *Lethbridge Herald*, 11 July 1949. The same day the *Medicine Hat News* argued that "consent to export might well open industrial development elsewhere which could set back similar progress within the province for 50 to 100 years…Let American export be held as a last resort, because once the flurry of field exploitation is over…all the increment that will be left within our borders will be watchmen's wages to supervise the 'liquidation of our empire.'"

13 For accounts of this debate, much of which centered on the growth of cabinet powers and the accountability of the regulatory agencies, see *Calgary Herald*, 5, 6, 7, 9 July 1949; *Edmonton Bulletin*, 5 and 7 July 1949; *Edmonton Journal*, 7 July 1949. The controversial legislation, The Gas Resources Preservation Act (1949) is in *Alberta Statutes* (1949).

14 *Edmonton Journal*, 6 March 1954.

15 H.G.J. Aitken, "Defensive Expansionism: The State and Economic Growth In Canada," reprinted in W.T. Easterbrook and M. Watkins, ed., *Approaches to Canadian Economic History* (Toronto, 1967), 183-221. Aitken, of course, used his concept to explain the behaviour of Canadian governments faced with external threats, especially from the USA. Alberta's obsession with federal encroachments in the post-war era must be seen in the context of the disallowance of most of its Social Credit legislation in the late 1930s. See J.R. Mallory, *Social Credit and the Federal Power in Canada* (Toronto, 1954).

16 *Edmonton Journal*, 1 and 8 April 1954.

17 Ibid.; and information obtained from interviews and correspondence.

18 The Alberta Gas Trunk Line Company Act (1954), *Alberta Statutes* (1954).

19 Hanson, *Dynamic Decade*, 247.

20 Kilbourn, *Pipeline*, 56.

21 On-the-record interview with Senator E.C. Manning, 28 July 1976.

22 C.B. Macpherson, *Democracy in Alberta: Social Credit and the Party System* (Toronto, 1953).

23 Cited in T.E. Flanagan, "Electoral Cleavages in Alberta During the Social Credit Regime 1935-1971," mimeo, Department of Political Science, University of Calgary (1971). Also, T.E. Flanagan, "Stability and Change in Alberta Provincial Elections," *Alberta Historical Review*, 21, no. 4 (Autumn 1973), 1-8.

24 See J. Barr, *The Dynasty* (Toronto, 1974), for some details of Social Credit's declining years.

25 E.H. Shaffer, "The Employment Impact of Oil and Natural Gas on Alberta 1961-1970," mimeo, University of Alberta Faculty of Business Administration (1976); and his essay "The Political Economy of Oil in Alberta," in this book.

222 Essays on the Political Economy of Alberta

26 Alberta, *Tentative "Nature Resources Revenue Plan,"* (April 1972), 14-15.

27 Alberta Department of Industry and Commerce, "Management of Growth," mimeo (29 May 1974).

28 This view of growth is discussed and criticized in D.C. North, "Location Theory and Regional Economic Growth," *Journal of Political Economy* (June 1955), 243-58; see also J.C. Stabler, "Exports and Evolution: the Process of Regional Change," *Land Economics* (February 1968).

29 K.H. Norrie, "Some Comments on Prairie Economic Alienation," *Canadian Public Policy*, II, no. 2 (Spring 1976), 212.

30 Premier Peter Lougheed, "Alberta's Industrial Strategy," Speech to the Calgary Chamber of Commerce, 6 September 1974 (Edmonton, Office of the Premier).

31 C. Newman, "The New Power in the New West," *Saturday Night* (September 1976).

32 See H.V. Nelles, *The Politics of Development* (Toronto, 1974), chapter 2. There are also close parallels with the industrial development policies of the Levesque government in Quebec. See the *Globe and Mail*, Report on Business, 10 February 1979.

33 Statement by Premier Lougheed re Petrochemicals, 16 May 1974.

34 ERCB, "Field Pricing of Gas in Alberta," ERCB report 72-E-OG (August 1972).

35 Crommelin, "Government Management of Oil and Gas in Alberta," 194-200.

36 R.C. Muir, "Utilization of Alberta Gas," *Alberta Law Review: Petroleum Law Supplement*, XIII, no. 1 (1975), 67.

37 *Tentative "Natural Resource Revenue Plan."*

38 Ibid.

39 *Oilweek*, 10 October 1973.

40 Based on interviews with petroleum industry and government officials.

41 H.R. Ward, "Marketing and Pricing Legislation," *Alberta Law Review: Petroleum Law Supplement*, XIII, no. 1 (1975).

42 L. Pratt, *The Tar Sands: Syncrude and the Politics of Oil* (Edmonton, 1976).

43 K. Norrie and M. Percy, *Westward Shift and Interregional Adjustment: A Preliminary Assessment,* Economic Council of Canada discussion paper no. 201 (May 1981).

44 For a general interpretation of the NEP, see L. Pratt, "Energy: The Roots of National Policy," *Studies in Political Economy*, no. 7 (Spring 1982).

45 See "Whose Oil is It?" in L. Pratt and G. Stevenson, eds., *Western Separation* (Edmonton, 1981).

46 For preliminary data see Petroleum Monitoring Agency, *Canadian Petroleum Industry Monitoring Survey 1981* (first half) (Ottawa, 1982).

47 J. Friedmann, *Regional Development Policy—A Case Study of Venezuela* (Cambridge, Mass., 1966), 12-13.

48 K. Polanyi, *The Great Transformation* (Boston, 1968; 1st ed., 1944), chapters 17-18. See also A. Breton, "The Economics of Nationalism," *Journal of Political Economy*, 72, no. 2 (1964), 376-86.

49 R. Gilpin, "Integration and Disintegration on the North American Continent," *International Organization*, 38, no. 4 (Autumn 1974), 857.